Tradition and Politics

Volume 9

*The Modern Middle East Series, The Middle East Institute,
Columbia University, New York*

*A complete listing of publications of The Middle East
Institute appears at the end of this book.*

Tradition and Politics

The Religious Parties of Israel

Gary S. Schiff, 1947–

Wayne State University Press   Detroit   1977

Library of Congress Cataloging in Publication Data

Schiff, Gary S   1947–
    Tradition and politics.

    (The Modern Middle East series ; v. 9)
    Bibliography: p.
    Includes index.
    1.   Political parties—Israel—History.
2.   Israel—Politics and government.   3.   Religion
and state—Israel—History.   4.   Religious Zionism
—History.   I.   Title.   II.   Series.
JQ1825.P37S34   329.9'5694   77-5723
ISBN 0-8143-1580-1

To Shellie

Contents

Foreword

Tradition and Politics is the first analysis of religion and politics in Israel that does not get lost in theological wrangle. The religious parties are the self-appointed custodians of religion in the Jewish state. However, they espouse divergent ideologies, so that, apart from their opposition to the secularization of the society and the state, they also diverge in their politics. In a word, the mode of analysis that Gary S. Schiff has chosen is well calculated to reveal how the prevalence of religious ideologies has reinforced the divisions within Israel's multiple-party system.

The value of the book inheres in its broad perspective. The author traces the religious parties from their origins in Europe early in the twentieth century, in response and in reaction to the rise of Zionism, and their transplantation to Palestine, their adaptation to the new realities, their participation in the quasi-government of the Jewish community under the British Mandate, and their unfolding roles after independence. He characterizes Mafdal's operational ideology as "the nationalization of religion" and that of Agudat Yisrael and its labor offshoot as one of institutionalized separatism. In his judgment, this helps explain why, after the creation of the Jewish state, those religious parties which had integrated Zionism into their ideologies merged into a single party and became full participants in the new society, and why those which persisted in their rejection of Zionism in the main preserved their original divisions and, after some initial limited attempts at affecting social policy, largely reverted to sectarian pursuits.

Because Mafdal, and its antecedent parties, have taken part in every coalition government in sovereign Israel, the book provides a fresh perspective on the functioning of the political system.

It also illuminates the impact of the religious parties on educational development, and incidentally proves true the assumption that the religious parties are basically discrete entities. But, above all, the work is valuable for the light that it sheds on the varying responses of the religious parties, which by definition uphold tradition, to the profound pressures of change that inescapably have accompanied the building of a modern society.

In a word, *Tradition and Politics* furnishes the reader a mode of understanding the most profound ideological controversy in Israel over the final structure of its polity and its society.

J. C. Hurewitz
Director
Middle East Institute
Columbia University

Acknowledgments

Only when sitting down to write the acknowledgments of a book of this scope, involving years of research and writing, can one begin to appreciate the number of people who in one way or another contributed to its ultimate publication.

Firstly, I owe a debt of gratitude to Professor J. C. Hurewitz of Columbia University, whose guidance and assistance at every stage of this book, from germination of the original idea to final publication, is reflected in his excellent Foreword. As Director of Columbia's Middle East Institute, Professor Hurewitz was also instrumental in having the book accepted into its well-respected Modern Middle East Series, and in having an earlier manuscript edited by the Institute's own masterful editor, the late Wayland Schmitt. Professor Hurewitz's predecessors as director, Professors Charles Issawi and John Badeau, were also helpful at various points, as were Professors Douglas Chalmers, Amitai Etzioni, and Arthur Hertzberg, who read earlier drafts, as did Mr. Zvi Yaron of Jerusalem. Numerous students and various colleagues of mine at City College of the City University of New York and at Yeshiva University also provided inspiration and encouragement.

In a more practical sense, the Foreign Area Fellowship Program of the Social Science Research Council, the American Council of Learned Societies, and the Ford Foundation made possible the year and a half of field research and subsequent preliminary write up of the findings. The Danforth Foundation, and particularly Miss Lillie Mae Rose, were also helpful in overcoming some of the fiscal hurdles, as was the Woodrow Wilson Foundation.

In the course of my research in Israel, the cooperation of the staffs of the Hebrew University-Jewish National Library, the Central Zionist Archives, and the Religious Zionist Archives (especially Rabbi Tzvi Reich) was much appreciated. In New York the staffs of the Zionist Archives and the Columbia University libraries were of assistance.

My gratitude must also be expressed to the personnel of the religious parties themselves: to their ministers and members of Kneset who consented to be interviewed at length; to their staffs at the Kneset (particularly to Mr. Yaakov Eliav of Mafdal); and to the staffs of the parties' world and national headquarters and branches (especially to Mr. Moshe Gewirtz of the Agudat Yisrael world headquarters and to Mr. Yitzhak Goldschlag of the world center of Mizrahi-ha-Po'el ha-Mizrahi).

My thanks also go to my Wayne State University Press editor, Mrs. Jean Owen, who doggedly persisted through my undecipherable hieroglyphics, interminable teeth-breaking transliterations, and sundry linguistic idiosyncracies to produce such a clear and readable text. Thanks also to Mrs. Saundra Blais for assistance with the index.

Finally, I am pleased and proud to express my thanks to my family for all their help: to Jeremy, who was literally born into this book, and to Rina, who came in at the tail end, for being so patient and cooperative while their parents were working on the book; and mostly to my dear wife Shellie, who served devotedly as sole typist, meticulous research assistant, chief editor, objective critic, and constant inspiration. While I willingly shoulder the full responsibility for this book, this statement can only be understood in light of her enormous and unique contribution.

Tradition and Politics

Chapter 1
Introduction

The Crisis of Religion and Modernity

The presence within Israel, a small but ostensibly modern state, of four component religious political parties is a phenomenon which is both intrinsically interesting to students of Israeli politics and potentially instructive for the comparative study of the relationship between tradition and politics in general. While the question of religion and politics in Israel has been examined before,[1] the religious parties themselves have not been rigorously studied. As a result, the discussion of religion and politics in Israel has largely been issue-oriented, concerning itself with particular manifestations of this most basic of Israeli political problems and with vague generalizations on the broader implications of the question, rather than with its fundamental causes and its chief vehicles, the religious parties. Because of the lack of historical or analytical focus, the latter are usually lumped together indiscriminately, distinguished largely by the degree of "extremism" they are supposed to represent. The inability to identify the parties as discrete political entities is symptomatic of the essentially hostile ideological approach which most writers on Israeli politics bring to bear on the subject. More generally, it is characteristic of the tendency of many Western political scientists to view all aspects of tradition as obstacles to the modern state. Where such traditional vestiges exist, they are to be grudgingly tolerated or carefully manipulated at best, or systematically uprooted at worst.

It is the aim of this study to examine the case of each of the religious political parties of Israel historically and analytically, be-

fore proceeding to evaluate their present and future roles in the
Israeli political system and to derive whatever comparative insights
they may afford. We assume no prescriptive, normative stance
toward the parties. We begin only with the assumption that the
several religious parties of Israel constitute different and ongoing
responses of tradition to the challenges of modernization, particularly to modern Jewish political nationalism, or Zionism.

Our analysis of the parties begins with an investigation of the
particular historical circumstances under which they arose. As
Maurice Duverger has cautioned, "parties are profoundly influenced by their origins."[2] What were the challenges presented by
Zionism, modern Jewish political nationalism, to traditional religious life in Europe, where the two forces first confronted each
other? What were the responses to it by different groups of orthodox Jews? How were the demands of modern life accommodated,
if they were? What ideological positions were formulated? What
patterns of behavior predicated on these ideological assumptions
were initiated? Specifically, how did the different religious groups
view the idea of cooperation with secular Zionists?

Although the initial reactions to these challenges and their for-
mulations in ideological and behavioral terms have been of cardinal
importance for later developments in the parties, no deterministic
"inevitability" is implied. On the contrary, the founders of the religious parties had great freedom in their early actions—perhaps
greater freedom than their descendants today—even while they took
account of the various forces and interests in operation at the time.
But however voluntary the decisions of any "founding fathers" may
have been, they seem to take on an aura of inviolable sanctity as
time passes. This attitude tends to limit the options and choices of
later generations. Thus, the legacy of Israel's founding era remained
strong, even into the state period and even on specific issues.

Once the state had been established, these ideological positions and behavioral patterns had to be accommodated to the reality of a sovereign polity. They operated as institutions within the
system. An examination of specific issues and institutions is necessary here to evaluate the different reactions of the religious parties
and their effect on the political system in general. These ideological
values and behavioral patterns are transmitted to the next generation through the process of socialization, which is a key to under-

standing why this "vestigial" traditionalism has not yet disappeared and what its future prospects are.

In order to determine how effective the political socialization is, we must ascertain who the voters for the religious parties are, how many there are, and where they live. Whatever regular voting patterns can be discerned may in turn reflect the more fundamental sociological and ideological bases of the different parties. But one must ascertain how many of these voters are actually party members and whether the concept of membership is applicable in the same way to each of the parties.

This analysis engenders a consideration of the organization of the parties in general. Are they characterized by mass individual membership, labor organization bases, elaborate bureaucracies, far-flung branches, and professional leadership cadres? Or by intermittent or ascriptive membership with no mass organizational base, bureaucracies which rise and fall with electoral needs, part-time branches, employees, and a more amateurish leadership outside the top elite? The elite itself may be marked by certain social, educational, religious, professional, and other characteristics. From what sources are its members recruited? How do they compare with the membership they represent?

All these characteristics—historical, ideological, sociological, organizational, and political-behavioral—will provide the basis for a comparative evaluation of the parties *qua* parties. The central question here is whether the religious parties fit any of the models for parties in the modernization scenario posited by many political scientists. If they do not lend credence to the unidirectional model of modernization, they may be, as Giovanni Sartori suggests,[3] a unique case. However, they may also suggest a necessary modification of the prevailing theory.

Some contemporary political theorists would dismiss Israel's religious parties as a curiosity, a quirk destined to be ironed out by the inexorable modernization process. Such writers as Gabriel Almond, James Coleman,[4] G. B. Powell,[5] and Daniel Lerner[6] tend to view the passage from the "traditional" through the "transitional" to the "modern" (i.e., Western) forms of society and polity as inevitable and desirable. This unidirectional view, based on an exaggerated secular interpretation of the Western experience, discounts the possibility—much less the desirability—of continued, if modified, traditional influence on the politics of the developing countries. Where such traditional structures continue to exist, they are viewed as vestigial at best.

The case of Israel and its religious parties casts strong doubt on this model. There is neither a native landed, aristocratic, traditional elite nor an indigenous traditional peasant mass, both of which are essential to the modernization scenario, for Israel is a highly urban and industrial state. In short, it is already a modern political system, yet one in which traditional Judaism exerts a strong influence. Indeed, the question of the degree to which religion ought to penetrate the society and polity constitutes the chief social cleavage in contemporary Israel. This issue reaches the very *raison d'être* of a state which claims religious legitimacy.

No internal issue can divide and arouse the Israeli public more than questions of religion and state. Regional disputes hardly ever arise, and the fundamental legitimacy of the state is almost never questioned, at least among the dominant Jewish majority. Indeed, on basic security matters the government enjoys broader support than in most other states. The conflicts between socialism and capitalism have been handled pragmatically, resulting in a mixed, though socialist-dominated, economy. In any case, economic issues bear no direct relationship to the more fundamental religious question, since the religious parties themselves are split on economic policy.

The only issue in the system which is as deep-seated and politically explosive as that of religion is the ethnic question. The conflict between Ashkenazim (Western Jews) and Sephardim (Eastern Jews) has many economic, social, and political implications. While this issue cannot be minimized, the fact remains that ethnic parties per se have failed to take hold in Israel, despite its multi-party system. Ethnic interests must be channeled through the parties if they are to be dealt with at all, and they lack the easily definable institutional form that religious interests have in the religious parties. Furthermore, as we shall see, the ethnic issue in Israel overlaps with the religious one in many ways.

Before examining the religious parties as responses to modern Jewish political nationalism, or Zionism, it is necessary to examine that wider phenomenon itself, as the context in which the parties developed.

The Return to Zion

Ever since the loss of Jewish sovereignty over Palestine, symbolized by the Roman destruction of the Second Temple in 70 C.E., the return to Zion (literally, a hill in Jerusalem) has been a preoccupation of Jewish thinkers, a pervasive theme of Jewish literature, and the leitmotif of Jewish liturgy and ritual in the many lands of the Jewish Diaspora.

While the eschatological religious view of the ultimate return to and restoration of Eretz Yisrael (the Land of Israel) by divine intervention prevailed throughout most of this two-thousand-year period,[7] occasional practical attempts were made to force the divine hand to redeem "His Chosen People." Particularly in times of severe persecution of Jews and general social upheaval in Europe and the Middle East, self-proclaimed prophets and messiahs, patrons and princes, undertook grand schemes to fulfill the dream, with little success. On a more humble plane, an unsteady trickle of scholars and other Jews flowed into Palestine, there to replenish the numbers of the small, traditional Jewish community, the Old Yishuv, a community preoccupied with pietistic, other-worldly pursuits.

It was not until the nineteenth century, however, that the confluence of certain social and political forces began to transform the long-held religious-nationalist dream into a political reality. The eighteenth-century rationalist movement, culminating in the French Revolution, had promised equal rights for all citizens, including Jews, and in most western European countries that promise was realized. With the removal of legal, political, and economic (though not necessarily social) restrictions, many western European Jews were rapidly assimilated. Many of them converted to Christianity and married non-Jews.

This eighteenth-century style of liberalism, however, was rapidly being overtaken in Europe by a more powerful social and political force, nationalism. In its more extreme form, local nationalism excluded Jews from the national consensus, no matter how much a part of the society they may have seemed. To explain this exclusion, extreme nationalists turned to traditional religious, nativist, and other sources of anti-Semitic sentiments, and combined them with their own chauvinistic ones to produce a new phenom-

enon, modern political anti-Semitism. (The qualitative differences
in the level of organization and sophistication, as well as the quantitative differences in intensity, between this phenomenon and its
predecessors were to be made clear in the Nazi period, with its
display of the ramifications of modern political anti-Semitism.) In
the late nineteenth century, the newly assimilated western Jews
were deprived of their illusions of assimilation by the infamous
Dreyfus Case, in which a French military officer who was Jewish
was falsely accused and convicted of treason, releasing a torrent of
nationalistic anti-Semitism in that supposedly enlightened land.

The implications of the Dreyfus episode for the future of Jews
in the Diaspora were understood by a young Viennese journalist,
born in Budapest, who covered the story. His name was Theodor
Herzl. He concluded that anti-Semitism was an endemic condition
and that the only secure future for Jews lay in a state of their own.
Borrowing from the idiom of the nationalisms of his era, Herzl
proposed just such an entity in his pamplet *The Jewish State,* published in 1896.[8]

Herzl then proceeded to give political form and substance to
his idea. In 1897 he convened the first and founding congress of the
World Zionist Organization in Basel, Switzerland. The congress
adopted a declaration, the keystone of political Zionism, which
asserted that "the aim of Zionism is to create for the Jewish people
a home in Palestine secured by public law." It recommended a
series of practical steps to this end: colonization of Palestine by
Jewish agricultural and industrial workers; the establishing of an
international Jewish organization to promote Zionism; the strengthening of Jewish national consciousness; and the obtaining of the
assent of the relevant governments to these steps.[9] The WZO was
to build the necessary political, financial, propaganda, and other
institutions to achieve these goals.

Herzl was not the only Jew who was pressing for a nationalist
solution to the "Jewish problem." A number of individual rabbis,
such as Yehudah Alkalai (1798–1878) of Serbia and Zvi Hirsh Kal-
isher (1795–1874) and Shmuel Mohilever (1824–1898) of Poland
took their cues from indigenous nationalist movements they witnessed and began to urge self-help in securing the long-awaited
redemption of the Jewish people.[10] While these religious thinkers
were in a decided minority, attracted no following to speak of, and

established no organizational framework, they laid the ideological foundations for religious Zionism, from which the Mizrahi movement later sprang.

By far the largest groundswell of Jewish nationalist feeling arose among the masses of East European Jews in the Russian Empire. Here only a relatively small number of Jews were allowed access to higher education and other avenues of possible acculturation, where they absorbed the various ideologies current in late Tsarist Russia. When rejected by the very movements which embodied nationalist ideas, however, they began to turn to Jewish nationalist solutions—whether Bundism (Jewish socialism), Jewish autonomism, or Zionism. Meanwhile, the masses of Russian Jews continued to suffer under the repressive and anti-Semitic Tsarist regime. A series of pogroms in the early 1880s motivated one of the educated minority of Russian Jews, a physician named Dr. Leo Pinsker, to write a book called *Auto-Emancipation,* in which he made much the same diagnosis and prognosis that Herzl would make later. Indeed, like Herzl, Pinsker created an organization, called Hovevei Tziyyon ("Lovers of Zion"). Under its auspices the first new Jewish settlements in Palestine were founded, funded largely by Jewish philanthropists in western Europe, including some members of the Rothschild banking family. Despite these practical undertakings, the Hovevei Tziyyon movement, a loose federation of groups ranging from some early orthodox nationalists to Zionist socialists of various types, lacked the organizational vigor necessary to establish a nationalist movement. With the establishment of the WZO, much of its constituency was absorbed into the new body.

What they lacked in political skills the Russian Zionists, whether religious or not, compensated for in their closeness to the classic religious nationalist ethic of traditional Judaism, which viewed Palestine as the only possible site for a reconstituted Jewish political entity. The grass-roots affinity to folk Zionism was lacking in the Westernized elite of the early WZO, which tended to view Zionism almost exclusively as a solution for anti-Semitism, and hence considered the ultimate locale of the homeland of only minor significance. The two viewpoints collided in 1903, when the WZO was offered an area in East Africa by the British government. In rejecting the offer in 1905, over the protests of some of Herzl's followers (Herzl himself died in 1904), who saw it as an expedient haven, the majority of the WZO reaffirmed the link between that manifestation of modern political Jewish nationalism and the chain of Jewish tradition.

Both the practical and political efforts of the WZO now focused on Palestine,[11] then a somnolent province of a decaying Ottoman Empire. Although direct attempts were made to obtain a charter from the Ottoman government, the WZO concentrated its political efforts in this period on the Great Powers, most notably Britain and Germany, who were themselves awaiting the demise of the Ottoman state and the distribution of its imperial legacy. Little in the way of political concessions was achieved in this early period.

The Zionist Organization's ambitions in Palestine were stimulated by World War I, when Ottoman suzerainty over Palestine was removed by the presence of the British army of occupation. The arrival of Britain in Palestine was particularly significant for Zionist aspirations. Britain had committed herself to "viewing with favour the establishment of a Jewish national home in Palestine" in the Balfour Declaration of November 2, 1917, for some combination of self-serving imperialistic and genuinely humanitarian motives.[12] With the incorporation of this declaration into the League of Nations mandate to Britain regarding Palestine in 1922,[13] the Zionists achieved their aim of at least partial recognition of their claims in public international law. The mandate also authorized the establishment of a Jewish Agency to represent world Jewish interests in the development of the national home, and recognized the WZO as such an agency.

In Palestine, however, the British were careful not to offend the newly awakened Arab national consciousness by any recognition of Jewish sovereignty. The local Jewish community was permitted to develop only within the existing framework of religious communal autonomy inherited from the Ottomans, called the *millet* system, that the local Muslim and Christian communities enjoyed. Under an expanded version of the system, approved by the mandatory government in the Religious Communities Ordinance of 1927, the Zionist-oriented Jewish population in Palestine, the New Yishuv, proceeded to organize an ostensibly religious-ethnic organization called Kneset Yisrael. It was actually a proto-state, with its own parliament (Asefat Nivharim), cabinet (Va'ad Leumi), and other organs, including a chief rabbinate and rabbinical court system, necessary to preserve the *millet* character of the body.

Participation in Kneset Yisrael, much as in the WZO, was by proportional representation of parties. These ranged from various brands of socialists organized in the Histadrut labor federation, most of which ultimately coalesced into Mapai and then the Labor party of today, to several middle-class factions whose right wing, the Revisionists (today's Herut half of Likud) broke with the WZO in the 1930s over its alleged softness toward the British and the Arabs, to the orthodox Zionists organized in Mizrahi and ha-Po'el ha-Mizrahi, today's Mafdal. Unrepresented by choice were many of the Old Yishuv who, opposed to Zionism on religious and ideological grounds, formed Agudat Yisrael.

With the rapid political and economic development of the Jewish community, fueled by successive waves of immigration (*'aliyot*), Arab opposition grew, at times taking violent form, as in 1920, 1921, 1929, and particularly in 1936–39. The British responded to each of these outbreaks by dispatching investigative commissions to Palestine, the reports and recommendations of which reflected increasing hostility to Jewish national aspirations there. After the 1936 disturbances, the Peel Commission recommended a more fundamental solution to the conflict of nationalisms in Palestine: its partition into separate Jewish and Arab states. In the face of Arab rejection and rather half-hearted Jewish acceptance of this plan, the British took another tack and called a conference of world Jewish and Arab leaders. It took place in February and March of 1939, and the talks were soon deadlocked: the Arabs insisted on the cessation of Jewish immigration and the establishment of an independent (Arab) Palestine; the Jews urged the opening of the gates to the national home promised them at this time, when millions of Jews were imperiled by the rise of Nazism. With World War II almost a certainty, the British chose to cement their ties with the Arabs and issued a White Paper in May which severely limited Jewish immigration and land purchase and spoke of a unitary independent (and Arab-dominated) Palestine within ten years.

The Zionists viewed the White Paper as a betrayal of the letter and spirit of the Balfour Declaration and of the Mandate. In 1942, in New York, they adopted the Biltmore Program, which

called for the establishment of a Jewish state in all of Palestine at
the end of the war and unrestricted immigration immediately. Nevertheless, official Zionist policy was to support Britain's war effort
against its far more anti-Jewish enemy, Germany, though a number
of groups not affiliated with the Zionists began to take military
action against British installations in Palestine.

With the close of the war, in which six million European Jews
were killed, the momentum for the establishment of a Jewish state
grew, and with it Arab opposition. Despairing of its ability to de-
vise a satisfactory unilateral solution, Britain turned the Palestine
problem over to the General Assembly of the newly established
United Nations, which appointed an investigating commission. It
recommended partition. On November 29, 1947, the General Assembly voted for partition, to take effect after the British withdrawal scheduled for May 14, 1948.

On that day the Va'ad Leumi of Kneset Yisrael proclaimed
the establishment of the State of Israel. At the same time, the
armies of five neighboring Arab states invaded Palestine, hoping to
abort the birth of the Jewish state. After months of desultory
fighting, in which the Israeli forces pushed back the invaders and
expanded the territory of the state, separate armistice agreements
were signed. The state of Israel had survived its birth pangs.

The Dynamics of the Political System

The new state's difficulties had just begun. Years of war, civil
disturbances, and neglect left the country, which had few natural
resources to begin with, in a perilous economic condition. At the
same time hundreds of thousands of immigrants, many of them
destitute survivors of the holocaust in Europe or dispossessed refugees from the Arab Middle East, poured into the new state. They
needed every type of social service, from medical treatment and
housing to schooling in Hebrew and employment. Furthermore, the
unremitting hostility of the surrounding Arab states made constant
military preparedness a necessity. Under such burdens the new
government vastly and rapidly expanded the scope of its authority.
These challenges would have strained the most efficient and experienced of bureaucracies and imperiled the most stable and demo-

cratic of political systems. How much more so was the difficulty for a government which had almost overnight transformed itself from an ostensibly religious-ethnic community based on voluntary adherence and fragmented by an ideological multiparty tradition of jealously guarded "neo-feudal" party fiefs.[14]

The multiparty tradition of the state stems from Kneset Yisrael and, ultimately, from the World Zionist Organization. As a voluntary organization composed of Jews from different countries with widely divergent ideologies and social systems—ranging from classical nineteenth-century liberalism to Marxian socialism—the WZO had to develop a system of proportional representation and coalitional leadership to avoid being deflected from its ultimate goal, the re-establishment of a Jewish state in Palestine. When these factions were transplanted to Palestine and included in Kneset Yisrael, each began to rebuild Zion according to its own ideological blueprint: for doctrinaire socialists, *kibbutzim* (agricultural collectives); for more moderate socialists, *moshavim* (agricultural cooperatives); for middle-class parties, urban and private agricultural developments; for religious groups, various types of religious and educational institutions, and so on. Each party zealously guarded its preserves, which generally encompassed a wide range of services and institutions, usually including newspapers and publishing houses, youth and women's auxiliaries, banks and insurance companies, urban and rural housing developments, and cultural, recreational, and educational activities.

In attempting to overcome this divisiveness and to avoid the immobility characteristic of some other multiparty systems, the dominant (though not majority) party, Mapai, a pragmatic and moderate socialist faction led by David Ben-Gurion, embarked on a course of what it called *mamlakhtiyut* (literally, statism).[15] It sought to nationalize, insofar as possible, the numerous autonomous spheres of power that the several parties had built up, placing them under the more neutral state bureaucracy (and, indirectly, under its own control). But as the bureaucracy itself was subject to the "party key," a device whereby patronage is divided up on the basis of proportionate party strength, the legislative effect of *mamlakhtiyut* was somewhat blunted. Furthermore, as Mapai itself had large "colonial" holdings, particularly through its domination of the Histadrut or labor federation, the nationalization was applied unevenly. Mapai also met with strong resistance from the other parties whose cooperation was necessary by virtue of the coalitional nature of the system.

Nevertheless, *mamlakhtiyut* was applied with varying degrees of success to a number of major areas of authority in the new state. For example, the private military forces of both right- and left-wing groups were decisively quashed and absorbed into the Israel Defense Forces. The autonomous educational systems known as "trends," sponsored by parties or groups of parties (see Chapter 7 below) were partially nationalized—thereby enabling Mapai to socialize the bulk of the immigrants—though provisions were made for the autonomy of the religious educational systems. The Histadrut's vast Qupat Holim, or medical insurance plan, however, was kept under the auspices of the labor federation (and Mapai), as Mapai feared the loss of this key attraction to new members and voters. Thus the national government's political power was sufficiently expanded to meet the pressing economic, social, and military needs of the state, while at the same time other parties were allowed enough independence of action to make them amenable to coalition participation. Mapai, the kingpin of coalitions, managed to avoid immobility at a time of great stress through the deft use of the political mechanisms available.

In order to understand how paralysis of the political organs in times of crisis was avoided, it is necessary to know what those organs are and how they operate in relatively normal times. The formal structure of the Israeli political system reflects the dynamic balance between ideological multipartism compounded by pure proportional representation and stable coalitional government based on a dominant party.[16] Theoretically sovereign and omnipotent, the unicameral 120-seat legislature, the Kneset,[17] is elected by a pure proportional representation system for a four-year term, unless dissolved earlier. Any list of candidates which receives at least 1 percent of the vote in the single country-wide election district is entitled to share in the distribution of seats; slightly over 12,000 votes were needed for a seat in the election of 1973. The party lists which one votes for and the order of candidates on these lists are drawn up by small party elites, thus giving them great control over their members in the Kneset, if they are not themselves members.

Given the relative ease with which representation in the

Kneset can be obtained, it is not surprising that two dozen or more lists have competed in some elections. However, in the 1969 Seventh Kneset elections, for example, only half that number earned Kneset seats, while in the 1973 Eighth Kneset vote the number of lists declined to nine. The winners were the Labor Alignment (46.2 percent and 56 seats in 1969;[18] only 39.6 percent and 51 seats in the 1973 elections), a loose amalgam of socialist parties formed in 1968 which included Mapai, two formerly independent parties, Mapam and Ahdut 'Avodah, which are further to the socialist left, and Rafi, a party to the right, which broke away from Mapai under the leadership of David Ben-Gurion. A smaller group of dissidents led by the one-time prime minister refused to return to the fold of Labor and the coalitions it headed, and formed instead the State List (3.1 percent and 4 seats in 1969; merged with Likud in 1973). On the left, outside of the Israeli political consensus, were the two tiny Communist parties, the largely Jewish Maqi (1.1 percent and 1 seat in 1969; renamed Moked in 1973, it received 1.4 percent and 1 seat), and the mostly Arab Raqah (2.8 percent and 3 seats in 1969; 3.4 percent and 4 seats in 1973). Two Arab lists affiliated with Mapai together received 3.5 percent and 4 seats in 1969 and 3.3 percent and 3 seats in 1973. The radical secularist group ha-'Olam ha-Zeh ("This World") earned 1.2 percent and 2 Kneset seats. Though it failed to gain any seats in the 1973 election, its secularist constituency found a home in the new Citizens' Rights party, which won 3 seats, or 2.2 percent of the vote.

The core of the right-wing opposition in the Seventh Kneset (1969–73) was the Gahal party, with 26 Kneset seats and 21.7 percent of the vote. It was composed of the Herut movement, which was heir to the militant Revisionists who left the WZO in the 1930s because of its alleged excessive moderation vis-à-vis the British and the Arabs, and of the right wing of the Liberal party (formerly called the General Zionists, who were the dominant group in the Zionist Organization abroad before the state was founded). The left wing of the old General Zionists, once called the Progressives, is now the Independent Liberal Party; it received 3.2 percent and 4 seats in the 1969 elections and 3.6 percent and 4 seats in those of 1973, and it generally participates in coalitions with Labor. A Herut splinter faction, the Free Center, picked up 1.2 percent and 2 seats in 1969. In the 1973 Eighth Kneset elections

Gahal joined with the State List, the Free Center, and the new Greater Israel Movement to form Likud, which won 30.2 percent of the vote and 39 Kneset seats in the wake of the war.

Finally, there are the religious parties: Mafdal (ha-Miflagah ha-Datit-Leumit, or "National Religious Party"), composed of the former Mizrahi and ha-Po'el ha-Mizrahi parties, which received 9.7 percent of the vote and 12 Kneset seats in 1969 (only 10 seats and 8.3 percent after the 1973 war); Agudat Yisrael, with 3.2 percent and 4 seats; and Po'alei Agudat Yisrael (PAY), its erstwhile labor offshoot, with 1.8 percent and 2 seats. The last two joined forces in 1973 and won only 3.8 percent of the vote and 5 seats.

Given this profusion of parties, one would expect that Israel would be as paralyzed politically as other multiparty political systems, notably those of the French Third and Fourth Republics, Weimar Germany, and Italy. The fact that it is not is largely the result of the way governments are formed. The president asks the member of Kneset who is the leader of the largest party (thus far invariably Mapai/Labor) to form a government. When the government formed receives a vote of confidence from the members for the program it presents, the new government has been established.

As no party commands a majority, governments are always coalitional. The programs they present, therefore, are of necessity compromises worked out in advance. They are highly detailed documents which set out the legislative program of the government and the rights and duties of each party. Governments also try to anticipate and avert potential crises which may upset the coalition. Once the agreement is concluded and ratified by the Kneset, all decisions taken in the government are by majority vote, and as Mapai (now Labor) has always held a majority of cabinet portfolios, it is then in a position to control government policy.

The coalition member parties are duty bound (first only by precedent, later by law) to vote for any bill the government for which they share collective responsibility proposes, thus assuring an almost automatic majority in the Kneset for government-sponsored legislation, though certain reservations and rights of abstention may be included in the agreement. Apart from these few exceptions, the failure of a coalition party to support the government, whether passively, in refusing to vote for its legislation, or actively, by voting with the opposition, brings on a government crisis which usually brings down the government. In cases where negotiated solutions are not possible, it brings down the Kneset too, as in December of 1976, when this book was going to press.

Israel has had more than its share of governments in its brief history—some seventeen in the first twenty-five years, but because of the dominant position of Mapai (now Labor) in the political system, the same (Labor) individuals regularly return to the new cabinets, there being no viable alternative to Labor government. Thus the Israeli cabinet system of government seems to bear a closer resemblance to the stable British model than to the unstable continental multiparty systems mentioned above.

Labor's domination is based not only on its sheer size—ranging from 32 to 46 percent of the vote and from 40 to 56 Kneset seats—but also on the centrism of its ideological positions, which facilitates its accommodation with both socialist and non-socialist parties. Mapai's pragmatic socialism has been flexible enough to incorporate non-collectivist groups and interests.[19] In the past this flexibility facilitated occasional cooperation with the non-socialist moderate right, particularly the General Zionists, who harbored a nineteenth-century liberal economic philosophy. The rigid Marxian socialism of Mapam and Ahdut 'Avodah, on the other hand, often prevented them from joining a government formed by Mapai and the General Zionists, who likewise eschewed coalitions with parties at the opposite end of the ideological spectrum. Only Mafdal could be counted upon to form a coalition with either combination.

In the field of foreign policy, Mapai's pragmatic pro-Western policy (and policy of rapprochement with West Germany and acceptance of reparations) stood midway between the pro-Soviet (and vehemently anti-German) Mapam on the left and the violently anti-Soviet (and equally implacably anti-German) Herut on the right. With Herut, Mapai had such long-standing political, ideological, and personal differences as to preclude sharing in any coalition with it (except for a brief honeymoon in the National Unity Government of the Six Day War). Mafdal's moderately nationalist foreign policy rendered it a desirable coalition partner until, as immediately after the 1973 war, it reverted for a time to a militantly nationalist stance, which precluded its initial participation in the government.

In the realm of religion and state, Mapai was midpoint on the scale between the militantly anti-clericalist Mapam and Ahdut 'Avodah and the avowedly clericalist Agudat Yisrael. The relatively small importance of religious issues for Mapai—preoccupied as it was in the early years with political, military, and economic issues—combined with a lingering sentimentalism toward religion among many of its older leaders predisposed the party to overcome its basically secularist beliefs and to reach compromises on matters of religion (this pattern has been changing recently, however). These compromises on religious questions were generally concluded with Mafdal, for whose members they were of paramount concern. The coincidence of the general interests and ideology of Mafdal with those of Mapai on issues other than religion was remarkably close, and as a result Mafdal participated in every government formed by Mapai-Labor in the first twenty-five years of Israel's history. In return, Mafdal was given control of the religious establishment, a control which was exerted so firmly as to make Mapai's later attempts to penetrate it difficult. It was only in the twenty-sixth year of nationhood that this relationship was temporarily suspended, when a religious-ideological issue, the definition of who is a Jew, whose resolution would ultimately affect Mafdal's control of the religious establishment as well, was pressed beyond the compromise point.

Practical politics propelled Mapai toward perennial partnership with Mafdal in its coalitions. The range of alternatives had always been limited at best. It became more so when both left and right formed blocs in the 1969 Kneset elections. It has become even more constricted since 1973, when several of the remaining splinter parties were absorbed into the blocs. In the pre-bloc period Mapai could turn to the left (Mapam or Ahdut 'Avodah) or the right (the General Zionists and Progressives) in addition to Mafdal for enough votes to provide a comfortable 70-seat majority in the Kneset. This flexibility no longer exists. Mapam and Ahdut 'Avodah, after steady declines, were incorporated into the Mapai-based Labor Alignment in 1968 (though Mapam maintains a measure of independence), along with a Mapai breakaway faction, Rafi. Despite the amalgamation, the new Labor list earned only 56 Kneset seats in 1969, far short of a safe majority. The decline of Labor to 51 seats in the 1973 elections only underscores its vulnerability and its need for reliable allies.

On the right, the General Zionists (or Liberals) entered into the Gahal alliance with Herut for the 1965 elections, thereby rendering them as undesirable and unthinkable a partner for Labor as Herut itself. The brief experience of the 1967–70 National Unity Government, in which Gahal participated, only reinforced this long-standing antipathy. The expansion of Gahal and three other parties into Likud in 1973, which removed those smaller parties from contention as possible coalition partners for Labor, and the large Likud vote (39 Kneset seats) further narrowed the field.

When parties which, for reasons of anti-system ideology or miniscule size or both, Labor could not consider (the Communists, Ha-'Olam ha-Zeh, Agudat Yisrael, PAY, among others) were excluded, Labor was left in 1969 with only the small Independent Liberal (or Progressive) party, with 4 Kneset members, its affiliated Arab lists, and the substantial 12-man delegation of Mafdal to compose a government with a comfortable majority. As a result of Labor's decline in the 1973 elections and the clustering of some of the former independent factions into larger groupings, mostly Likud, Mafdal's position as the only party of sufficient size to guarantee a stable and long-lived coalition has been enhanced. Hence, as a result of the crystallization of the Israeli right and left and their increasing equalization of strength, the relative political weight of Mafdal has increased, not only for Labor but for any future right-religious coalition that might emerge. The formation of several new centrist, secularist, reformist parties in anticipation of the 1977 elections—such as Amnon Rubinstein's Shinui, Yigal Yadin's Democratic Movement, and Ariel Sharon's Shlomzion— are likely to draw votes away from the large Labor and Likud blocs, thereby weakening them and making Labor even more reliant on the relatively stable Mafdal vote.

Thus, while the often remarked relative stability of the Israeli political system, despite its rampant multipartism, is due primarily to Mapai-Labor, it is attributable secondarily to Mafdal. Its long-standing willingness and ability to join in coalition with Mapai have provided an element of stability and continuity lacking in some other multiparty systems. The two parties constitute the core of the dominant party system that has kept Israel a smoothly functioning democracy.

Given the pivotal position of Mafdal, then, it is little wonder that it has been inordinately successful in terms of its operational ideology, the nationalization of religion. And given its importance as a coalition partner, on those occasions when issues arise which fundamentally threaten or thwart the application of its ideology, the stability of government in Israel will be challenged.

A classic example of the continuing crisis of religion and modernity as embodied in the religious parties took place in December of 1976 (as this book was going to press). At that time Rabbi Kalman Kahana of the PAY faction of the united PAY-Agudah list presented to the Kneset a motion of no confidence in the Rabin government. The immediate reason for this opposition religious party move was the official welcoming ceremony for the first three new F-15 aircraft from the United States, held on a Friday afternoon and allegedly overlapping into and violating the Sabbath.

Nine of the ten Mafdal Kneset members abstained on the crucial vote, violating their coalition obligations and thereby becoming liable under law for possible expulsion from the government. While the government managed to survive the test by a bare majority, and initial indications were that Prime Minister Rabin would not press the issue, he subsequently reversed himself and, invoking the law of collective responsibility, expelled the two Mafdal ministers who had abstained from the cabinet (the third, Yosef Burg, resigned), thereby ousting the party from the coalition, which now no longer enjoyed a parliamentary majority. Rather than face another certain no confidence motion and the possibility of the fall of his government, Rabin tendered his own resignation, which automatically ended the tenure of his cabinet. This was followed by the dissolution of the Eighth Kneset and the scheduling of new elections for May 17, 1977.

Speculation as to Rabin's motives varied. Some attributed his actions to the exigencies of domestic politics. In terms of internal party competition, this was seen by many as an attempt by Rabin to maintain the leadership of the Labor party against the challenge of Defense Minister Shimon Peres by precipitating an early and unexpected election. Similarly, some explained Rabin's decision to hold Kneset elections promptly as an attempt to catch the newly formed reformist centrist parties such as that of Yigal Yadin off guard, before they had a chance to organize a viable party machine and a credible political alternative. As indicated above, these parties are likely to draw their strength largely from Labor itself as well as from Likud, and probably the only result will be to render Labor more dependent on Mafdal than before.

Others interpreted Rabin's actions largely in the context of foreign policy. Some saw it as a maneuver to delay any peace negotiations, recently given impetus by an Arab peace offensive and a new American administration anxious for movement in the Middle East impasse, by involving Israel in an election campaign. Once such negotiations were imminent, the theory went, Rabin would use them to enhance his position in the electoral contest by portraying himself as the most experienced leader and negotiator. Furthermore, the argument ran, Rabin would be able to strengthen his hand in any preliminary negotiations by eliminating the rather hawkish Mafdal from the transitional government in order to present a more flexible image to the United States. Early elections would have the additional advantage, for Rabin, of taking place before he had to make any hard concessions as a result of such negotiations, and would also come before the full impact of the foreign economic slump would be felt in Israel (and blamed on Rabin).

Whatever the motivations, the likely outcome of the Ninth Kneset elections of 1977, given the traditionally stable and sizeable vote of the religious parties, Mafdal in particular, and the splintered and contested constituencies of the two largest parties, Labor in particular, is the restoration of the traditional Labor/Mafdal alliance (barring the unlikely eventuality of a Likud/Mafdal coalition). This most recent episode highlights the pivotal position of the religious parties in general, and of Mafdal in particular, in the political system of Israel, and underscores the urgency and significance of understanding their unique nature.

Part I
The Development of the Religious Parties

Chapter 2
Parties of Participation

By far the largest of Israel's religious political parties, Mafdal is, as noted earlier, the product of the 1956 union (or more precisely, reunion) of the Mizrahi party and its labor offshoot, ha-Po'el ha-Mizrahi. While it has waged an incessant battle for religious causes both inside the government and out, Mafdal has generally participated in government coalitions since the establishment of the state. This propensity to participate cannot be viewed merely as a tactical preference or as an ideological weakness, however, for its methods of participation and the very nature of the issues involved are deeply rooted in the historical circumstances and social milieu in which the party arose and developed. The ideological choices made during its formative years in Europe relate to the central question of the accommodation to modernity, as embodied in modern Jewish political nationalism or Zionism.

Mizrahi

The formal enunciation of Zionism as a political movement at the First Zionist Congress in Basel in 1897 touched a chord in the hearts of the masses of East European Jews, at whose core "remained the tradition, with its uniformity of religious practice and its elastic community organization, its historic and eschatological myth of Exile and Redemption, and its well established channels of communication to all Jewry throughout the ages and in all parts of the globe, the Hebrew language and system of traditional Jewish education."[1] Although the movement was dominated by non-observant Jews, a small group of East Europe's religious Jews and their leaders participated in it, actively if warily, because of their common concern with the redemption of Israel—a goal long since abandoned by most Western Jews—and, in a general, as yet undefined way, with Hebrew and Jewish education. The questions of education and culture acted as catalysts in the development of religious factions in the World Zionist Organization, factions which were the forerunners of the religious political parties of Israel.

As early as the Second Congress (in Basel in 1898), religious Zionists demanded a clarification of the organization's attitude and relationship to Jewish tradition. They sought a positive affirmation of it, or at least a total exclusion of cultural questions from the Zionist program, fearing that any other type of cultural activity would be inimical to religion. The official response was that the Zionist movement regarded religion as a purely personal matter and took no formal position on it.[2] While this was clearly not the ideal answer to the religious Zionists, it was calculated to pacify both religious and secular elements and would have sufficed had the Zionist Organization remained a purely political-diplomatic body. However, in 1901 the Fifth Zionist Congress passed a resolution making educational work (defined in purely secular nationalist terms) compulsory for Zionists,[3] and this decision evoked deep-seated fears of secularism among religious Zionists. They organized the first formally separate faction within the Zionist Organization, called Mizrahi, an acronym for Merkaz Ruhani, or "Spiritual Center." The religious forces were joined by some nonreligious leaders who also advocated a "purely political Zionism" in order to preserve the young movement's strength.[4]

As reflected in the founding proclamation (*Kol Koreh*) and the party program[5] issued at the founding conference of Mizrahi, held in Vilna, Lithuania, in 1902, the period between that conference and the first Mizrahi world convention, held in Pressburg, Hungary (now Bratislava, Czechoslovakia), in 1904, was marked by conflict between the religious and the secular "pure political" groups in Mizrahi. The political faction insisted that Mizrahi's purpose was negative and supervisory—to exclude cultural, educational, and all nonpolitical activities from the Zionist Organization—whereas the religious group opted for a more positive program, now that the Pandora's box of "culture" had been opened, and urged that extensive religious educational-cultural work be undertaken in Palestine and in the Diaspora.[6]

By the time the first Mizrahi world convention met, the influence of the politicals had all but disappeared. Although it still officially opposed cultural work by the World Zionist Organization, Mizrahi committed itself to such work in its own orthodox circles. The election as president of Rabbi Yitzhak Ya'akov Reines, who introduced such educational innovations as secular studies into the traditional yeshivah curriculum,[7] indicated the path Mizrahi would take once the politicals were eliminated. As a transitional figure in the accommodation of orthodox Jewry to modernity, Reines laid both the theoretical and the practical groundwork for Mizrahi, and later Mafdal.

In reiterating its acceptance of the basic tenets of political Zionism, the Pressburg convention's resolutions gave them a specifically religious coloration:

> 1. The Mizrahi is an organization of Zionists standing on the basis of the Basel program aiming for the survival of the Jewish people. The Mizrahi sees the possibility for the survival of the Jewish people in the observance of the Torah and Commandments and in the return to the land of our fathers.
> 2. The Mizrahi stays within the Zionist Organization, fighting for its views within the organization, but it is creating a separate organization to attend to its religious and educational work.
> 3. The aim of the Mizrahi is: to realize these aims by the employment of all legal means, to popularize its ideology among the thinking orthodox by the creation of a religio-national literature, and by the rearing of the young in that spirit.[8]

In 1905 Mizrahi headquarters were transferred from Russia to Frankfurt, Germany. Unlike East European orthodoxy, the smaller West European orthodoxy, and that of Germany in particular, had turned to the device of communal separatism "to defend against the domination of the community by adherents of more liberal religious views internally"[9] and against the combined onslaughts of religious reformism and modern political anti-Semitism externally, pressures which led large numbers of German Jews to convert to Christianity.[10]

The atomization of German orthodoxy into small, self-sufficient *kehilot,* or communities, and its alienation from the rest of Jewry caused the majority of German orthodox Jews to oppose any pan-Jewish undertaking, particularly the Zionist movement. Its intellectual leaders, like Rabbi Samson Raphael Hirsch, devised a philosophy of strict adherence to tradition internally and accultura- tion externally, known as *Torah 'im Derekh Eretz* ("Torah and the way of the world"), a Jewish confessionalism, as opposed to the traditional Jewish nationalism, which displayed vehemently anti- Zionist, hence also anti-Mizrahi, sentiments.[11] The tendency to separatism, coupled with a somewhat lesser devotion to the Zionist aspects of the program, characterized the German Mizrahi leader- ship. When the Tenth Zionist Congress (1911) voted to make cul- tural work compulsory for all Zionists, most of the German Mizrahi delegates, true to their separatist ideals, withdrew from both the Mizrahi and the WZO and helped found Agudat Yisrael the follow- ing year.

In 1908 the world Mizrahi sent Rabbi Yehudah Leib Fishman to Palestine to open an office to further its educational goals there. Soon the world Mizrahi's headquarters were transferred to Jerusa- lem, where the organization's new president, Rabbi Meir Berlin (Bar-Ilan), settled in 1922.

Although rudimentary Mizrahi branches had been established in Jaffa and Jerusalem in response to the world movement's first proclamation in 1902,[12] no concrete grass-roots manifestation of Mizrahi organizational activity appeared among the veteran, in- digenous religious Jewish population (the Old Yishuv, as distin- guished from the New Yishuv of Zionist-inspired immigrants) until the closing days of World War I. There was a marked lack of political consciousness among the traditional Jewish community— adhering, as it did, to the purely religious eschatological view of redemption—until some of their leaders were jarred by the suffer- ings of the civilian, particularly Jewish, population under the out- going Ottomans; the Balfour Declaration, which lent credence to the Zionists' aspirations; and the British occupation, which facili- tated the rise of representative Jewish political institutions. They turned, via Mizrahi, to the new political community being formed to protect and promote their primarily religious interests, which they felt were being discriminated against by the nascent Jewish political institutions. Leading rabbis of the Old Yishuv, both Ash- kenazi (western) and Sephardi (eastern), as well as lay leaders were included in the founding meeting of the Mizrahi organization in Palestine held in Jaffa in 1918.[13]

The rise of a national Mizrahi organization parallel to the world headquarters located in Jerusalem was to prove a continual source of friction and conflicts, severely hampering the development of a strong, independent, national Mizrahi party. Like its parent body, the party hoped to influence the course of Jewish public life in Palestine in the direction of religion through comprehensive participation in all phases of the Yishuv's endeavors. Its goals were expressed in the resolutions of the first convention:

> 1. The Mizrahi organization demands of the Constituent Assembly and of the other institutions of the Yishuv that Mizrahi participate in the actual work of and on the committees relating to all [general] Yishuv and cultural matters.
> 2. The Constituent Assembly must provide the necessary material means to support the religious educational institutions in the land, and must set them up under the separate administration of a religious board of education.
> 3. The Yishuv, with the aid of the Constituent Assembly, must establish in the land, and in the cities and central settlements, an organized rabbinate, composed of the various Jewish [sub-]communities.[14]

The national Mizrahi made its first public appearance as an organized political force at the Second Constituent Assembly of the Jewish community in Palestine, held in the summer of 1918. The demand for financial support of religious education, now directed to the WZO itself, was in no way to interfere with the operation of an independent religious board of education.[15] Two years later the WZO decided to accept this financial responsibility only if there was to be one board of education. The religious educational network was granted autonomy, however, and Mizrahi accepted the compromise.

Mizrahi also made a formal demand for a chief rabbinate to the Second Constituent Assembly. In fundamental and portentous legal debate, its representatives staunchly opposed the postwar reestablishment of the Jewish civil courts, which had adjudicated civil cases between consenting Jews according to non-Jewish jurisprudence. They regarded "this creation as a foreign growth in our lives, coming as a substitute for rabbinical justice."[16]

The question of women's suffrage—a key indicator of ac-

comodation to modernity—also made its debut at this assembly.
On this issue, as on many others, the world organization and the
national organization of Mizrahi differed sharply. The Palestine
Mizrahi caucus at the assembly, in the spirit of its Old Yishuv
orientation, opposed the granting of the franchise to women, as it
was "not in the spirit of religion"[17] (though the national Mizrahi
did establish a women's auxiliary in the same year). The world
Mizrahi, which had a far broader, more sophisticated constituency
of religious Jews in Europe (and even America) to contend with
and had far more experience in political dealings with the non-religious in the Zionist Organization and elsewhere, took the stand
that the question of the female franchise in the embryonic Jewish
state was not a religious one. Pointing to Mizrahi's acquiescence in
the participation of women in the Zionist Organization from the
very outset, it argued that this was a purely political question and
therefore warranted an appropriately political solution, the con-
ducting of a referendum on the issue.[18] Eventually, in the face of
vehement opposition from other political parties and religious
groups to such a vote, the national Mizrahi reluctantly agreed to
participate in the General Assembly (Asefat Nivharim) of Kneset
Yisrael, women and all.[19]

At the same time, the roots of Mizrahi's youth wing were
being planted. In 1919 a group of younger people from the Old
Yishuv formed an organizaion called ha-Tza'ir ha-Eretz Yisraeli
("The Land of Israel Youth") to undertake suburban agricultural
settlement and to organize religious youth.[20] No sooner had it
affiliated itself with the national Mizrahi, whose social origins and
ideological outlook it shared,[21] than another, more powerful organization, ha-Po'el ha-Mizrahi, arose to challenge and eventually
eliminate it. Indeed, the new group grew to such proportions that it
overshadowed the national Mizrahi and ultimately became the
chief component of today's Mafdal.

Ha-Po'el ha-Mizrahi

After World War I the WZO, interested in building up the
Yishuv rapidly, encouraged the immigration of young workers
rather than of the middle classes from whose ranks Mizrahi had

traditionally drawn most of its membership.[22] Nevertheless, this wave of immigration, known as the Third 'Aliyah, brought many young religious people, mostly from Poland and Lithuania, as well. Some of these young people had been members of the Mizrahi youth movement, Tze'irei Mizrahi ("Mizrahi Youth"),[23] which, under the influence of socialist thinkers and parties in eastern Europe, had begun to develop a synthetic ideology of religion, nationalism, and socialism known as Torah va-'Avodah ("Torah and Labor").[24]

The immigrants received little moral or material support from the national Mizrahi, which did not put a high value on manual labor. Even its youth organization, though it had undertaken some manual projects, took a dim view of the new workers' organization. By the spring of 1922 ha-Po'el ha-Mizrahi ("The Mizrahi Worker") had formally established itself, and the older youth organization had been renamed ha-Mizrahi ha-Tza'ir ("The Young Mizrahi") to distinguish it from its competitor. Objecting to the "unnecessary" establishment of another Mizrahi youth movement, its members sensed a deep psychological and ideological gap between themselves and those of ha-Po'el ha-Mizrahi, who emphasized manual labor.[25]

The Torah va-'Avodah ideology was compounded of religion, nationalism, and socialism. The last element distinguished it from Mizrahi, whose slogan was "The Land of Israel for the People of Israel according to the Torah of Israel," but ha-Po'el ha-Mizrahi was not a typical "socialistic" organization. Both its theory and its practice consistently emphasized the religious and, more particularly, the nationalist aspects of the credo rather than any new socialist faith. Although it was intimately concerned with labor issues and often cooperated with and adopted many of the forms of the socialists in Palestine (such as the *kibbutz*), it is most aptly described as a party of religious-nationalist workers.[26] Indeed, it defined itself at its founding convention in Jerusalem in 1922 as "a religious Zionist labor pioneer movement which aims to serve Judaism and all its internal values through the establishment in Eretz Yisrael of a . . . religious labor Commonwealth in Eretz Yisrael. . . . [based] upon productive pursuits in agriculture and industry."[27]

Its chief ideologue, Shmuel Hayyim Landau, subordinated even the concept of Torah to the nationalist ideal:

All other national values are significant only to the degree that they
serve as instruments of the absolute—the nation. Even the rebuilding of the land is secondary, for the land was created for the nation
and not the nation for the land. . . . Even the idea of *Torah va-
'Avodah* (Torah and Labor), which we have made our fundamental
blueprint for the regeneration of Eretz Yisrael, must be measured by
this yardstick.[28]

Landau distinguished between the personal obligations of the individual Jew commanded in the Torah, which have no bearing on the
national renaissance, and the national aspects of the Torah, which
constitute its prime motivation. Similarly, 'Avodah (Labor) was
significant not because of any contribution it might make to the
improvement of the economy, nor even because of any positive
effect it might have in the direction of "social morality and righ-
teousness (lofty as these values may be)" but only insofar as it
contributed to the "national renaissance." In short, ha-Po'el ha-
Mizrahi believed that "the national rebirth is the ultimate value of
both Torah and Labor."[29]

Socialistic elements were subordinated to nationalist goals in
the positions taken by the majority (though not the small leftist
minority[30]) of ha-Po'el ha-Mizrahi on some of the basic questions
hotly debated among the Jewish left in Palestine. It rejected the
Marxian socialist notion of class war for Palestine being advocated
by some in the Histadrut (General Federation of Jewish Workers)
and disclaimed any common interest with the "international prole-
tariat," declaring that the Jewish people's primary interest as a
whole lay in the establishment of an independent state and society.
Likewise, it spurned the idea of joining the Socialist International.[31] Thus, whatever influence socialistic ideas may have had
on the mainstream of ha-Po'el ha-Mizrahi's "Jewish Socialism,"
they were at best derived from the democratic, Utopian, non-vio-
lent, non-dialectic, and non-dogmatic strand of socialism, and were
invariably subject, in the final analysis, to prior religious and national considerations.

The overriding nationalist considerations of ha-Po'el ha-
Mizrahi created marked Revisionist tendencies in the 1930s and
1940s,[32] when the party supported that most right-wing political
group on general political questions (such as opposition to Weiz-
mann's leadership in the WZO and the demand for a stronger

stance against both the British and the Arabs) and on "proletarian" issues (such as the substitution of arbitration for strikes in settling labor disputes).[33] Traces of this strident nationalism are evident in some elements of Mafdal today, particularly on questions of Israel's policy vis-à-vis the Arab states and the occupied territories. Nevertheless, ha-Po'el ha-Mizrahi did cooperate with the Histadrut in areas of mutual practical concern. For this purpose, it made distinctions between the Torah and Labor sides of its ideology. For example, it joined the Histadrut's medical insurance plan, Qupat Holim, but not without first exacting, in good Mizrahi style, concessions on the maintenance of *kashrut* (Jewish dietary laws) and the observance of the Sabbath in all Qupat Holim hospitals and clinics.[34]

One Israeli analyst views such cooperation as a fundamental misunderstanding by ha-Po'el ha-Mizrahi of the depth and nature of the "enemy"'s motivations and beliefs. The problem, he argues, originated earlier with Mizrahi and continues to characterize the politics of the religious parties in Israel today.[35] But the ability to participate on behalf of the common weal in spite of clearly perceived ideological differences may also be viewed as a positive sign of the political maturity and acumen necessary for the proper functioning of a multiparty, coalitional system. It is precisely the inability of small ideological parties to overcome ideological inhibitions and cooperate with others that has elsewhere caused the paralysis considered characteristic of "multipolar" multiparty systems.[36]

Ha-Po'el ha-Mizrahi did not initially aspire to become a political party. But it grew increasingly dissatisfied with Mizrahi's representation of its interests in Yishuv and in Zionist political bodies, and as its ranks swelled through continued immigration, it concluded that it needed its own political organs to promote its distinct interests. Thus it began to run independent lists for Yishuv elections. The transfer of the leadership from ideologues such as Landau to politicians such as Moshe Shapira symbolized the change. The new political leadership was able to withstand the protestations of the small but influential minority of committed socialists who advocated separation from the Mizrahi and union with the Histadrut (which in fact occurred briefly, from 1924 to 1928, during the severe economic slump in Palestine).[37]

Factionalism and Compromise

Some fundamental differences between Mizrahi and ha-Po'el ha-Mizrahi were crystallized at the Mizrahi world convention in 1926. Over the strong objections of Mizrahi and ha-Mizrahi ha-Tza'ir, ha-Po'el ha-Mizrahi's exclusive jurisdiction in a broad range of fields was recognized.[38] Thus three separate Mizrahi organizations were now operating in Palestine simultaneously, apart from the world executive of the movement, nominally superior to all three, which was located in Jerusalem.

As early as 1920, the Amsterdam convention had called for unity of the three Palestine groups, but with no success. In 1926 the Antwerp convention gave explicit recognition in the constitution it drew up to the existence of factions but clearly subordinated them to the world and national organizations. Thus, paragraph 4 of the constitution (which was to remain in effect, if in amended form, until the establishment of the Mafdal in the 1950s) gave Mizrahi members with distinct outlooks on economic and settlement questions the right to found separate national and international bodies (which ha-Po'el ha'Mizrahi had already done the year before). It was understood, however, that in general political matters all such factions were subject to the regular world and national Mizrahi organizations.[39]

Despite the dissipation of the movement's strength by factionalism, it proceeded to implement its plan of ordering public life in the Yishuv along religious lines. It played a major role in the establishment of the chief rabbinate in 1921, in the face of continued opposition from both the secular elements in the Yishuv, who sought to limit the jurisdiction and influence thereof, and from Agudat Yisrael and other non-Mizrahi religious elements, which opposed its establishment altogether.[40] Mizrahi's partner in this endeavor was the British Mandatory Government, which, as administrator of Palestine, sought a more rationalized and representative form of the *millet* system of religious communalism inherited from the Ottomans.[41] An additional, unstated motive may well have been the government's desire to keep a damper on Jewish (or, for that matter, Arab) nationalism by placing each group under the more docile authority of its traditional religious leaders. In any case, Mizrahi saw an excellent opportunity to create a means by which the public life of the Yishuv might be stamped in a religious mold.

The founding conference, arranged and financed by Mizrahi, was composed of one-third practicing community rabbis, one-third religious representatives—i.e., rabbis of the various Jewish sub-communities—a total of 66 rabbis, and one-third lay secular communal and municipality representatives. Originally the government preferred equal lay and rabbinical representation in order to be "more representative" of the Yishuv, but it settled for this ratio when it met stiff opposition from the leading Ashkenazi rabbinical personality of the day, Rabbi Kook, who was then elected Ashkenazi chief rabbi.[42]

This ad hoc arrangement was given more definite form in 1936, at the time of the second election to the chief rabbinate. A regulation was issued maintaining the rough two-thirds–one-third ratio but paring the number of electors down to 42 rabbis and 28 laymen. The composition of the rabbinical delegation was given to an electoral committee of eight, half of whose members were representatives of the chief rabbinate itself, while the other represented Va'ad Leumi, the executive body of Kneset Yisrael.[43]

The conference elected a (chief) rabbinical council, consisting of four Ashkenazi and four Sephardi rabbis, including one chief rabbi for each. The council doubled as the chief rabbinical court, capping the network of lower rabbinical courts. This judicial system retained "the exclusive jurisdiction in matters of marriage and divorce, alimony and confirmation of wills of members of their community" that they had had under Ottoman rule.[44] Mizrahi immediately pointed out that this jurisdiction was significantly less inclusive than that of the *shari'ah* (Muslim religious) courts and tirelessly demanded parity for the Jewish courts.[45] But the authority of the (chief) rabbinical council was specifically confirmed in the Religious Communities (Organization) Ordinance of February 1926, which formally recognized the setting up of Kneset Yisrael, the organized Jewish community in Palestine.[46]

Mizrahi also argued that similar organs should be set up on the local level to maintain the local rabbinate, ritual slaughter (*shehitah*), ritual baths (*mikva'ot*), and the synagogue. These services would be paid for by fees supplemented by the local council. The local organs, which were ultimately to become known as religious

councils, were dominated by Mizrahi. Among other demands regarding the public religious character of the state-to-be, Mizrahi
advocated public observance of the Sabbath, support for and autonomy of its religious school system, the institution of Jewish
jurisprudence, the establishment of a nation-wide organization of
rabbis, retraction of the female franchise from the four "holy"
cities (Jerusalem, Hebron, Tiberias, and Safed), and raising the
male voting age from eighteen to twenty-one.[47]

Although some demands for the public observance of religion
were, at least formally, recognized by and incorporated into the
institutions of the Yishuv, many more were ignored. Mizrahi and
ha-Po'el ha-Mizrahi grew increasingly dissatisfied with the WZO
and Kneset Yisrael. Their general disenchantment with the Zionist
Organization's politics of appeasement toward the ever less sympa-
thetic British in the 1930s led to further splits. When the Eighteenth
Zionist Congress rejected Mizrahi's demands for Sabbath observance in settlements located on Jewish National Fund lands, for
dietary law observance in public kitchens, for excusing workers of
the Mandatory government on the Sabbath, and for the government's validation of the Sabbath laws already passed by Jewish
municipalities, Mizrahi withdrew into opposition in the WZO, declaring its non-confidence in and non-responsibility for the actions
of the Zionist executive elected at that congress.[48] This move,
uncharacteristic of Mizrahi, represented a victory for those who
favored a more militant stance against the non-religious.[49]

At the national Mizrahi convention in the spring of 1934 the
majority ordered Mizrahi's representative on the executive committee of the Va'ad Leumi to resign. He refused to do so and
formed a new faction, ha-Mizrahi ha-Vatik ("the Veteran Mizrahi").[50] Alarmed by this breach of party discipline and by the
appearance of still another faction, in addition to the increasing
restlessness of ha-Po'el ha-Mizrahi, the central committee of the
World Mizrahi Organization decided in 1934 to send a mission to
Palestine to negotiate with ha-Mizrahi ha-Vatik and ha-Po'el ha-
Mizrahi. The agreements reached provided representation for these
factions in the world body on a coalitional basis.[51] Thus the existence of factions in Mizrahi, a condition from which it still suffers
today, was made permanent.

Disappointment with the development of the religious character of the Yishuv led some Mizrahists toward greater unity with Agudat Yisrael. This rightist trend, which skirted perilously close to the abandonment of Mizrahi's Zionist ties, found its ideological exponent in Rabbi Moshe Avigdor Amiel, a prominent Mizrahi leader in Poland and later chief rabbi of Antwerp and of Tel Aviv. Amiel's argument, expressed as early as the Antwerp convention, was that Mizrahi's primary loyalty was to other orthodox Jews. Its mission was to arouse their dormant nationalist feelings, and its attachments to non-religious Zionists were of a decidedly secondary, expediential nature. In fact, the secularism of the other Zionists stood in direct contradiction to all that was basic in Mizrahi's religious ideology. Because it formed such a small minority in the WZO, Mizrahi had failed to influence the larger body in a religious direction; if anything, it itself had been influenced by the secularists. Amiel concluded that only by drawing closer to Agudat Yisrael could Mizrahi hope to promote religion in the Yishuv.[52]

Although the mainstream of Mizrahi, led by Rabbi Fishman, objected in principle to Amiel's dichotomy between religious and nationalist aspects and in practice to any alliance with its old gadfly, Agudah,[53] the organization swallowed its pride and agreed at its Krakow convention (1935) and then at its Zurich convention (1937) to seek closer ties with the latter.

After extensive correspondence and negotiation, the Mizrahi and Agudah delegations reached an agreement in Paris in 1938. This accord provided for joint work in the fields of religious education, labor, and immigrant settlement, and for the establishment of a joint committee on the constitution of the now-anticipated Jewish state. Although this far-reaching, historic pact between two old and bitter rivals was ultimately vetoed by the "right wing" of Agudah, it nevertheless set an important precedent for actions taken later, in the first years of the state of Israel.[54]

The New State

Mizrahi's views on the emerging state appear in the report of the world executive to the last Mizrahi world conference before the war and the establishment of the state, its Geneva conference of 1939, which took the form of a memorandum originally submitted in 1938 to the Royal Commission sitting in London, at the latter's request. Rabbi Meir Berlin, president of the World Mizrahi Organization, prefaced the Mizrahi program by stating that "according to our Torah and our traditional way of life we have no separate notions of nation and religious body (state and church)." This explained the first point of the program, which stated that "the Constitution of the Jewish state will be based on the law of the Torah." In order to apply this law in a modern state, the program suggested the establishment of a council of religious experts on Jewish law. Point 2 dealt with the establishment (or rather, the continuation) of the chief and local rabbinates, to be supported by the state and to have jurisdiction in *all* religious and personal questions, specifically marriage and divorce (point 3). All public institutions funded by the state were, according to point 4, to observe *kashrut* (Jewish dietary laws).[55]

In those provisions which touched on the rights of the non-Jewish minorities, Mizrahi's pronounced nationalism was in evidence. Non-Jews were guaranteed "absolute freedom" to organize their religious lives according to their own religious laws, but only with government approval. The Hebrew language was to be the sole official language of the state, and the Jewish Sabbath and holidays were to be the official days of rest in the state, with complicated exceptions in certain localities. Finally, *all* Jewish education in the state was to be "in the spirit of the Torah of Israel and its traditions," though there the document noted that various types of Jewish schools could be encompassed within that definition. In conclusion, Berlin stated it was to achieve these essential points that Mizrahi had formed itself into a separate faction in the WZO. It would continue to battle for them in the upcoming Jewish state.[56]

Once Israel had been transformed from a voluntary political community to a sovereign state, the various political bodies had the opportunity to become full-fledged parties in an independent political system. They would bear the heavy responsibility of maintaining that system, whether in the government or in the opposition. The pressures to readjust their political thinking were particularly intense as a result of Mapai's drive toward *mamlakhtiyut* ("statism"), by which it set about nationalizing the parties' formerly autonomous spheres of operation. The religious parties, which had held that these were inviolate, altered their behavior somewhat, but their basic orientations reasserted themselves after only four years. Each party, consistent with its distinctive ideology and history, viewed the rise of the state of Israel through its own particular lens.

Mizrahi and ha-Po'el ha-Mizrahi saw the reestablishment of an independent Jewish political entity as an historic moment fraught with great religious significance. It retroactively justified their adherence to the Zionist organization, despite its secularist inclinations. But the secular spirit was now ensconced in the body politic of the state, and both groups realized that, barring a religious majority, the implementation of their ultimate goal—the establishment of a state run by Torah law, as well as the preservation of past achievements in the institutionalization of religion—would be difficult and gradual at best. They were heirs to the tradition of participation, bargaining, and compromise with non-religious Zionist parties, particularly Mapai, however, and their pattern of political behavior was well suited to continued coalitional life in the new state.

The Decline of Mizrahi and the Rise of Ha-Po'el ha-Mizrahi

After World War II the decimation of European Jews severely curtailed the pool of potential immigrants which Mizrahi and ha-Po'el ha-Mizrahi traditionally drew upon, and they consequently sought new adherents elsewhere, particularly among the hundreds of thousands of largely traditional Sephardi immigrants who arrived in the early 1950s. The rapid absorption of these newcomers affected the sociological, economic, organizational, and even religious complexion and behavior of the parties. The changes were particularly strong in ha-Po'el ha-Mizrahi, which had long monopolized the movement's absorption mechanism in Israel and therefore embraced the lion's share of the new group via the device of the party key (dividing up the immigrants, or anything else, by the percentage of party strength).

Mizrahi organized its own world union within the joint world movement in 1949, as ha-Po'el ha-Mizrahi had in the mid-1930s,[57] in the hope that its remaining sources of strength, mostly in the United States, with their important financial resources, would counterbalance the disproportionate influence of ha-Po'el ha-Mizrahi in Israel. The device failed because Mizrahi had not understood that, while control of financial and political resources abroad was still important, power in the new state was measured in terms of votes and voters. The era of the party of notables had given way to that of the mass party. Ha-Po'el ha-Mizrahi, by building most of the movement's rural and urban settlements, providing members with the services of a comprehensive labor union, and developing an ideology to acclimate them, had obtained their loyalty and votes.

Mizrahi was also losing hold of its chief asset in Israel, its independent educational system. As the founding educators grew older and their number decreased, the younger teachers, many of whom were members of ha-Po'el ha-Mizrahi, were becoming a majority in the Mizrahi educational system.[58] The Mizrahi political leadership was also aging. Its president, Rabbi Meir Berlin (Bar-Ilan), died in April 1949 at the age of sixty-nine. Its other distinguished elder statesman, Rabbi Yehudah Leib Fishman (Maimon), was in his early seventies at the time of the establishment of the state, and although he served in the cabinet during the First Kneset, he retired from active political life soon thereafter. Mizrahi's chief lay political leader, David Tzvi Pinkus, who served as minister of transportation in the Second Kneset, died on August 14, 1952, at the age of fifty-seven. No new Mizrahi leaders were on the horizon. The Mizrahi youth organization, No'ar ha-Mizrahi, had always been much smaller than the two ha-Po'el ha-Mizrahi youth movements, B'nei 'Akivah, which attracted youth with its pioneering ethic, and ha-No'ar ha-Dati ha-'Oved ("Religious Working Youth"), which offered vocational training. Ha-Po'el ha-Mizrahi itself, of course, had originally been a Mizrahi youth organization and had drained off many of the parent body's potential cadres.

Whereas membership in ha-Po'el ha-Mizrahi meant participation in a comprehensive labor union of the western European socialist type, with all the appurtenances normally associated with such organizations—membership cards, regular dues deducted from salary, frequent meetings, elections of officers, a bureaucracy to handle day-to-day affairs, machinery for the protection of the workers, branches, and so forth—membership in Mizrahi was far less conventionally organized. In Duverger's terms, it was a party of notables.[59] More precisely, it was led by religious notables, largely rabbinical though there were also lay leaders. As typical with such parties, organization was generally weak and sporadic.[60] Membership entailed few of the practical obligations of ha-Po'el ha-Mizrahi members, whose ranks contained both rural agricultural workers and settlers and urban white-collar workers and blue-collar laborers. Mizrahi was largely composed of rabbis, teachers, and other religious functionaries and intellectuals, small businessmen, and some professionals.[61]

The technicalities of formal membership in Mizrahi, particularly the financial ones, were less rigidly observed than in ha-Po'el ha-Mizrahi, which had to provide extensive services to its membership. But such services, which included aid in obtaining employment, were needed by the vast majority of religious immigrants. Because Mizrahi could not provide them, it remained a small ideological political party in the Yishuv. Meanwhile, ha-Po'el ha-Mizrahi grew into a mass political party. Eventually—like Mapai among the secular parties[62] and like many pre-independence movements elsewhere whose roots lay in labor organizations—it became both the largest and the dominant political party of its type in Israel.

Nevertheless, Mizrahi did retain a certain prestige as the parent party headed by the movement's distinguished rabbinical leaders.[63] It had been alloted one-third of the 62.5 percent of the total vote it shared with ha-Po'el ha-Mizrahi for the United Religious Front (URF) formed with Agudah and PAY for elections to the First Kneset. That this allotment to Mizrahi of half the strength of ha-Po'el ha-Mizrahi was unrealistic was made clear in the 1951 Second Kneset elections, when each of the four component religious parties ran on its own ticket. Whereas ha-Po'el ha-Mizrahi earned some 6.8 percent of the total national vote and eight Kneset seats, Mizrahi received a mere 1.5 percent, enough for only two Kneset seats. This was only one-quarter of the ha-Po'el ha-Mizrahi percentage.

With the continued absorption of most of the immigrants by ha-Po'el ha-Mizrahi, the gap between it and Mizrahi could only be expected to grow. Moreover, the break-up of the URF and the later withdrawal of Agudah and PAY from the government left the small Mizrahi party increasingly isolated at a time when the more difficult battles over the role of religion in the public life of the new state necessitated the unity of the orthodox forces. It is no surprise that in the early 1950s the majority of Mizrahi leaders began to agitate for the complete merger of Mizrahi and ha-Po'el ha-Mizrahi into one political party.

Factional Conflict in Ha-Po'el ha-Mizrahi

Although ha-Po'el ha-Mizrahi was, at least in relation to the other religious parties, in an enviable position of strength at the time of the founding of the state, its situation was far from ideal. The establishment of an independent Israel revived all the old factional debates.[64] Because religion, nationalism, and socialism had not been completely synthesized in its ideology, and because it encompassed larger, more diverse social groups than any of its sister religious parties, it was far more open to factionalism. The problem was aggravated by the necessity of making political alliances and policy choices in the new multiparty political system. Was ha-Po'el ha-Mizrahi to prefer political cooperation with the other religious parties, with the other socialist workers' parties, or even with the nationalist right, with which it had long-standing sympathies? While numerous factions and splinter groups appeared over the years, three main trends emerged during the crucial first years of the state. These divergent outlooks threatened the very unity of the party.

On the right, the faction known as el ha-Maqor ("Back to the Source"), formally organized before the Seventh ha-Po'el ha-Mizrahi Convention in 1935 (though its roots went back to the right-wing split following ha-Po'el ha-Mizrahi's ill-fated entry into the Histadrut in 1924), was not only vehemently opposed to close ties with the Histadrut but even urged the severance of all existing ties with the general labor federation. This group, which had agreed with the Revisionists on many political and economic issues,[65] advocated closer relations with Mizrahi and other orthodox groups, including Agudah. In fact, it had distinctly clericalist leanings, not unlike some Mizrahists and like all Agudists. Its alienation from the

ha-Po'el ha-Mizrahi left ran the whole gamut of economic and social questions. For example, it considered the *kibbutz* an alien concept in Jewish life and particularly injurious to the traditional Jewish family.[66]

As the only faction with rabbis as leaders, el ha-Maqor was
closer to Mizrahi in social composition as well. Its membership
consisted largely of ha-Po'el ha-Mizrahi members who were rabbis,
teachers, and other religious functionaries, and its strength was
largely confined to urban areas most heavily populated with the
more traditionally orthodox. Despite its relatively small size—some
7.7 percent of the vote in the Tenth Convention election of
1950[67]—it continued to argue successfully against any alliance
with the Histadrut and its left parties and for any step that meant
greater unity in the orthodox ranks. Ridiculing the idea that class
differences are of consequence, it called for the revision of ha-Po'el
ha-Mizrahi's ideology to include appeals to small businessmen and
shopkeepers. It was the first ha-Po'el ha-Mizrahi group to advocate
merger with Mizrahi in the early 1950s. It also wholeheartedly
supported the establishment of the URF, decried its subsequent
disbandment, and urged its restoration on a permanent basis.[68]

On the left, the ideological roots of the faction called la-Mifneh ("To the Turning Point") lay in those elements which had
prevailed upon ha-Po'el ha-Mizrahi to enter the Histadrut in the
1920s.[69] Sociologically, it was based largely in the rural settlements, particularly in its religious *kibbutz* movement, ha-Kibbutz
ha-Dati, and to a lesser extent among its religious *moshav* movement, Iggud ha-Moshavim, though some urban intellectuals and
workers were members as well. Prominent among the former were
Moshe Unna, a *kibbutz* member of the Kneset from 1949 to 1969
and former deputy minister of education, and *moshavnik* Michael
Hazani, sometime minister of social welfare; among the latter was
Dr. Yosef Burg, who has been a member of the Kneset since the
establishment of the state and who has held a variety of cabinet
posts, including minister of interior, his most recent position. Many
of the non-proletarian members of la-Mifneh came from the large
German immigration in the 1930s. By 1949 the urban groups out-
weighed the rural in size and influence.

La-Mifneh took the socialist and pioneering elements of ha-
Po'el ha-Mizrahi's ideology very seriously and was therefore

drawn strongly to the overall workers' organization in Palestine-Israel, the Histadrut; it was unattracted to Mizrahi, which to it smacked of the petty bourgeoisie, Agudah, or any combination thereof, such as the URF, though it did feel an affinity to PAY.[70] Its leaders believed that entry into the Histadrut would provide economic advantages to ha-Po'el ha-Mizrahi, increase its political influence, reflect ideological unity in the working classes, and even enable it to propagate its message to a broader audience. Hence la-Mifneh was also opposed to any abandonment of the party's ideological fervor and labor character and to appeals to the middle classes for a broader base.[71]

In fact neither faction's program was ultimately carried out in its entirety. During the early state-building years, ha-Po'el ha-Mizrahi, like other Israeli parties, became far less firm in ideology. In order to appeal to the masses of new immigrants, particularly the Sephardim—for whom the old ideology held little significance—its cries for greater adherence to Torah va-'Avodah and for "unity with the workers" (i.e., the Histadrut) became fainter, and it turned increasingly to ethnic rather than class appeals. These developments made for greater unity with Mizrahi. On the other hand, its increasing responsibilities toward its growing membership led it to become an equal participant in all Histadrut labor union activities, though the agreement specifically excluded cultural, religious, educational, and other non-labor areas. The ideologues of la-Mifneh maintained their radical positions during this period, as seen in the highly controversial "Proposal for the Party Program" written by la-Mifneh chairman, Moshe Unna, and by Meir Or.[72] Among the proposals expressed in this document were the revamping of the entire *halakhic* structure to fit contemporary needs by establishing a new body, the Sanhedrin, which would supersede the chief rabbinate.

While most of their views were rejected by the majority, the faction's relatively large size (it received some 39.2 percent of the vote at the tenth convention in 1950[73]) gave it a virtual veto over the party's policies in many situations, such as the question of renewal of the URF for the Second Kneset election: when la-Minfeh threatened to bolt the party, the URF could not be reestablished.

Straddling the broad center of ha-Po'el ha-Mizrahi were two large polyglot factions, the United and the Central. Each of these encompassed a shifting variety of smaller interest groups, ethnic associations, *landsmanschaften,* cliques, personal entourages, and rank-and-file ha-Po'el ha-Mizrahi members who may have owed their loyalty to one of the center factions because of jobs or other services rendered to them.[74] They were typical of both classical machine-type political organizations because of the services they performed and of the modern catch-all mass party because of their broad social base. As in the case of similar Western political parties, ideology was considerably less important than the elite.[75]

As their programs were designed to appeal to the lowest possible denominator in the ha-Po'el ha-Mizrahi membership, with ideological differences being negligible, the two centrist factions revolved mainly around their respective leaders. Moshe Shapira, the head of the Central Faction and the dominant political figure in ha-Po'el ha-Mizrahi, served in every Kneset and cabinet up to his death in 1970 and, at one time or another, held five ministerial portfolios, Religions, Interior, Welfare, Health, and Immigration. Control over the first two or three of these five ministries was especially important to ha-Po'el ha-Mizrahi and Mizrahi during the formative years of the state. The Religions portfolio was vital for its influence over the appointment of religious functionaries (patronage), the composition and budgets of local religious councils, and the election of the chief rabbinate council. The Interior ministry was of significance for its authority over personal status questions and local council affairs (including religious services). Shapira's long, though not uninterrupted, reign over these ministries, which he filled with his appointees, secured them for ha-Po'el ha-Mizrahi, and more particularly for his faction.

The factional spoils system was a dominant characteristic of ha-Po'el ha-Mizrahi politics. Even la-Mifneh experienced a marked decline in ideological fervor after the early 1950s. Much of the controversy between the factions, while cloaked in ideological garb, consisted of haggling over party appointments and the order of candidates on the party's Kneset list. The inter-factional division is roughly based on each faction's percentage in the internal elections for the convention, though these percentages are often only roughly estimated.

The head of the United Faction, Yitzhak Refael, has been in the Kneset since 1954 and is currently chairman of the party executive, yet he had never held ministerial rank until his appointment as minister of religions in the ill-fated Meir government of 1974 because of the relative weakness of his faction. In turn, that faction's operation had been hampered by the lack of patronage controlled by its leader.

The Road to Merger

The first formal call for a union of Mizrahi and ha-Po'el ha-Mizrahi was issued by A. L. Gelman, chairman of the Merkaz 'Olami ("World Center"), the umbrella organization nominally superior to both. In view of the establishment of the state, the destruction of European Jewry in the holocaust, and the organizational fractionalization and weakness of orthodox Jewry in general and of the world Mizrahi movement in particular, Gelman proposed that the two separate world organizations be eliminated. Their functions would be handled by two separate departments of the Merkaz 'Olami, and they would run joint lists for all elections— Kneset, municipal, and Zionist organizational. The Merkaz 'Olami was to be represented in the deliberations of the joint parliamentary delegation on all questions of religion and education, in which it was to have exclusive jurisdiction. The separate party funds were to be combined under the aegis of the Merkaz 'Olami, which also controlled the party daily, *ha-Tzofeh*. Gelman called for a world convention to ratify these plans.[76]

Merkaz 'Olami, representing a worldwide constituency, was composed in roughly equal parts of Mizrahi and ha-Po'el ha-Mizrahi but was dominated and generally headed by a member of the former. And as most Mizrahi members lived abroad, many of them in the United States, an arrangement such as that proposed by Gelman would have given equal, if not disproportionate, influence over the joint party in Israel to non-Israelis, while ha-Po'el ha-Mizrahi, which was the senior partner in Israel, would have had to content itself with parity at best. Nevertheless, Moshe Shapira, the leader of the largest faction of ha-Po'el ha-Mizrahi, grasped the inherent advantages of a merger, both for his party's (and his faction's) dominance and for the religious parties as a whole. He saw little future for the splintered religious parties unless they united and maintained the political balance between the two large left and right blocs he foresaw crystallizing in Israel. Yet, cognizant of the vociferous opposition of other factions in ha-Po'el ha-Mizrahi, particularly la-Mifneh, to the merger, he preferred a more gradual process. He proposed as a first step the establishment of looser federations, rather than joint organizations abroad, fearing that full merger might subordinate ha-Po'el ha-Mizrahi to Mizrahi.

While these internal realignments were being developed, Shapira, a master of pragmatic politics, urged that joint election lists be instituted immediately for the upcoming Third Kneset. He also demanded joint campaign finance committees, hoping to receive generous contributions for the campaign war chest from Mizrahi members abroad, particularly in the United States.[77] Ha-Po'el ha-Mizrahi was in severe financial straits because of the vast expansion of its activities to handle the mass immigration that was taking place.[78]

As the leader of the much smaller centrist faction, Refael's position was dictated primarily by expediency.[79] At first he spoke against merger, fearing that it would only add strength to Shapira's dominant Central Faction or, at best, that Mizrahi itself would constitute still another faction. But he did favor a joint election list, since such an alliance could add votes and money to ha-Po'el ha-Mizrahi without upsetting the delicate balance within the party. El ha-Maqor had long advocated merger, and the reaction to the proposal by la-Mifneh was predictably negative. Although ideological reservations loomed large in la-Mifneh's opposition, the practical political side of the merger must not be overlooked. The addition of Mizrahi on the right would help to counterbalance la-Mifneh's influence on the left, and would thus give the center, particularly Shapira and his Central Faction, a lever over la-Mifneh, which had up to now enjoyed the undisputed second largest spot in ha-Po'el ha-Mizrahi and a virtual veto over some of its policies. In addition, the inclusion of Mizrahi in the party would probably entitle it to some key party positions, and even Kneset seats, most likely at la-Mifneh's expense.

In the summer of 1954, after four internal conferences, the Merkaz 'Olami was urged to convene a small world convention no later than April of 1955 (before the Third Kneset elections) to decide the merger question once and for all. In the interim it was to promote joint concrete efforts at cooperation between the two parties.[80] In the fall of 1954, the central committee of ha-Po'el ha-Mizrahi approved joint lists with Mizrahi for the upcoming Third Kneset. The vote was 110 to 44, with la-Mifneh outvoted in the opposition. Two months later the committee approved the merger in principle, again over la-Mifneh's vociferous protests, with the proviso that ha-Po'el ha-Mizrahi would continue to exist in the joint party as a labor and settlement organization.

The joint list proved to be a qualified success, increasing the number of ha-Po'el ha-Mizrahi Kneset members from eight to eleven. The results influenced the favorable decision of the world ha-Po'el ha-Mizrahi convention held in Tel Aviv the next month on the question of merger,[81] and this in turn augured well for the final approval of the merger by the Nineteenth Mizrahi-ha-Po'el ha-Mizrahi World Convention, which opened the next day in Jerusalem.

In adopting the final merger proposal, the world convention declared: "with the purpose of strengthening and unifying national religious Jewry, the World Convention of Mizrahi-ha-Po'el ha-Mizrahi hereby decides on the merger of the two organizations into one single united party."[82] Official ratification came at a specially convened ceremonial merger convention. The functions assigned to the new Merkaz 'Olami were somewhat narrower than had originally been proposed. They included organization, literature, propaganda, tourism, religious settlement, and Zionist politics. Questions of religion and education were assigned to it only until the next convention. Apparently the party in Israel, particularly ha-Po'el ha-Mizrahi, was reluctant to give the Merkaz 'Olami domination in these two key spheres of operation in the state. The joint organization in Israel was to be responsible for all political questions, both national and local party organization in the state, culture, literature, propaganda, and education (the last area presumably jointly with the Merkaz 'Olami until the next convention).

As a religious labor organization ha-Po'el ha-Mizrahi continued to handle questions of labor (and ultimately, of agricultural settlement), the protection of rights of workers, the development of labor and pioneer values, and the representation of ha-Po'el ha-Mizrahi in the labor community at large. The regulation that members of the joint movement could not belong to any other political party implied that membership in ha-Po'el ha-Mizrahi as a labor organization was tantamount to membership in the party as a whole.

Not only workers but all economic groups were allowed to organize separately within the joint party. The world Mizrahi and ha-Po'el ha-Mizrahi organizations were disbanded, and their worldwide functions were taken over by the joint organization, those in Israel by the joint party. Women and youth ancillaries were also merged. The convention also commissioned the draft of a new constitution and party platform, which the newly reformed eighty-member central committee was authorized to ratify. Despite vociferous opposition from la-Mifneh, the twelfth ha-Po'el ha-Mizrahi convention ratified the merger decision taken at the world convention.[83]

The proposed new ha-Po'el ha-Mizrahi constitution, which was ultimately adopted by the central committee in 1964, provided for ha-Po'el ha-Mizrahi autonomy in labor and settlement questions but specifically excluded from its purview all political activities— national, local, Zionist, and so on. These were to be the exclusive preserve of the new joint party, Mafdal. Nowhere was the organization of this new party spelled out. Apparently the organs of ha-Po'el ha-Mizrahi were to be preserved along the same lines: the national convention, nominally the highest party organ, delegates to which were to be elected by the membership, was to be held every three to four years and was to set out general lines of policy; a central committee was to be elected in which was vested the highest authority between conventions and which could be empowered with the authority of a convention; and an executive was to be chosen by the convention or the central committee acting with the authority of a convention, with the various functional executive departments under it.

These theoretical constitutional proposals on the new structure of the party and ha-Po'el ha-Mizrahi, however, must be viewed against the reality that the internal operations of the party had always been marked by factionalism. Shapira saw as the ultimate purpose of the merger and the proposed reorganization the consolidation of the party's obstreperous factions, preferably under his leadership and that of his Central Faction. This would be the first step toward the long-run goal of uniting all the religious parties. The other factions—la-Mifneh, the nascent Tze'irim, the

Sephardim, Refael's faction, and the *moshavim* bloc—opposed the elimination of factions.

Mafdal

At the thirteenth convention in 1963 factional rule was eliminated. The factions themselves were officially disbanded, and all paragraphs in previous convention decisions or in the constitution giving them recognized status were expunged. Future elections would be held according to a system of personal and local elections, rather than by factional lists.[84]

The convention also remedied some of the organizational anomalies that had resulted from the merger, particularly from the rather artificial autonomy insisted on by ha-Po'el ha-Mizrahi, ostensibly to preserve its labor organization character during the expected influx of non-workers. In fact, the party attracted only five thousand new non-ha-Po'el ha-Mizrahi members, roughly the size of the old Mizrahi membership.[85] Since most veteran Mizrahi members did not join the new party,[86] however, almost its entire membership was still drawn from the labor organization. The maintenance of separate party and ha-Po'el ha-Mizrahi bureaucracies was a fiction that neither could afford any longer. Ha-Po'el ha-Mizrahi and Mafdal still had separate conventions, central committees, executives, and secretariats. Separate local branches were even maintained in many places.[87] The convention thus decided on the merger of most of the higher organs, on a joint budget, and on the complete merger of all branches.[88] The central committee was authorized to approve a new constitution incorporating these changes.

The actual 1964 ha-Po'el ha-Mizrahi constitution brought its organs and the party's into closer coordination. They now have the same convention, central committee, and expanded joint executive, which in turn selects a separate limited executive committee for ha-Po'el ha-Mizrahi and a separate party executive. Similarly, all the economic institutions of ha-Po'el ha-Mizrahi, the party, and the world Mizrahi-ha-Po'el ha-Mizrahi movement were placed under one umbrella organization.[89] Today the world Mizrahi-ha-Po'el ha-Mizrahi movement is decidedly the weakest of the three in determining party policy. At the same time a new party constitution superseded the one adopted at the formal founding convention held in 1956,[90] but this document is primarily an ideological, programmatic restatement of the decisions outlined above.

In the six-and-a-half-year interval between the thirteenth and fourteenth ha-Po'el ha-Mizrahi conventions (the second and third Mafdal conventions), Shapira continued his drive to unify the factions under his aegis. In anticipation of the elections for the upcoming fourteenth convention, he established Gush le-Likud ha-Tenu'ah ("Bloc for the Unity of the Movement"). This was to encompass almost all the diverse factions, including la-Mifneh, to avoid contested elections. Unfortunately, a relatively new faction, the Tze'irim, refused to cooperate.

The Tze'irim arose in the early 1960s out of Mishmeret ha-Tze'irah, a young adult auxiliary. The faction is composed largely of Israeli-born products of the Mafdal socialization system—i.e., religious state education, religious high schools, *yeshivot,* and the party youth movements, particularly B'nei 'Akivah. Most of its members are urban and middle-class people, however, and reject in large measure the *halutzi* ideals and *kibbutz* orientation of B'nei 'Akivah. In fact, no mention of the old Torah va-'Avodah ideology appears among their goals. Rather, they are interested in "the preparation of religious young people to fulfill key positions in the state,"[91] positions which are not limited to the religious sphere but which include the vital areas of security affairs and the economy as well. As a first step to this end, they demanded greater representation in their party, which was dominated by an older, entrenched, East European-born elite with whom they, as native-born Sabras (though largely of Ashkenazi, not Sephardi, extraction), have less in common.

The development of the Tze'irim was accelerated by the Six Day War of June 1967, in whose wake it adopted the maximalist territorial position of the Greater Israel Movement,[92] thus adding an ideological overtone to its position. Later some of the Tze'irim, dissatisfied with the government's and Mafdal's indecisiveness on the question of the retention of the West Bank and other territories and the right of Jewish settlement there, broke with the party to join in the formation of Gush Emunim (the "Bloc of the Faithful"). This group has attempted with some success to force the government's hand by unilaterally establishing settlements on the West Bank.

The rightism of the Tze'irim is reflected not only in its ultra-nationalistic political leanings and removal from the old socialist ideology but also in its preference that the rabbinate have a greater say in the party, as seen in its demand in 1974 that the chief rabbis rule on whether Mafdal could join the coalition without assurances from Labor on defining who is a Jew according to *halakhah*. It has also sought greater cooperation with right-wing parties, particularly Likud, as an alternative to the "historic" partnership with the labor left.

In the 1968 party election, feeling that Shapira's proposed Gush would only freeze a situation in which it was discriminated against, the Tze'irim insisted upon running its own lists of candidates. It ran lists in about half the districts and won some 22 percent of the vote, giving it three of fifteen places on the party executive's nominating committee and placing its leader, Zevulun Hammer, in a safe spot on the party's Kneset ticket for the next year. He was high enough on the party's 1973 Kneset list to succeed to the post of minister of social welfare upon the death of Michael Hazani. Another Tze'irim leader, Dr. Yehudah Ben-Meir, ran a close enough race to succeed to a seat upon the death of Rabbi S. Y. Ben-Meir (Rosenberg), his father, a seat which he retained after the 1973 elections as well.

With the death of Shapira in 1970, his rather precarious Gush disintegrated swiftly. Like so many charismatic leaders, he had failed to institutionalize and depersonalize his authority and prestige and had not groomed an heir-apparent. The internecine conflict over the succession which resulted has yet to be resolved. The party's nemesis, factionalism, quickly reappeared before the elections for the upcoming Fourteenth ha-Po'el ha-Mizrahi and Fourth Mafdal Convention. As no truly contested election had been held since 1952, it was widely felt that one was needed now to determine the relative strength of each faction and thereby to indicate the new party leader.

In fact, the elections, held on November 7, 1972, only served to underscore the divided state of the party. No one faction, and no one leader, received anything like a clear mandate. Indeed, the strengths of each faction changed but little over a twenty-year period. However, as Shapira's bloc splintered into a loyalist group (led by Zerah Warhaftig, with 14 percent), and into *kibbutz* (3 percent), *moshav* (9 percent), and Sephardi (3 percent) factions, it was the la-Mifneh faction, led by Burg and Hazani, with 27 percent of the vote, the Unity faction, headed by Refael, with 24 percent, and the Tze'irim faction, led by Hammer and Ben-Meir, with 20 percent, which were now the dominant forces in Mafdal. This return to outright factionalism necessitated the return to shifting coalitional rule once again.

For a discussion of the implications of such continued factionalism for the party itself as it faces the 1977 elections, and for its positions on such key issues as the administered territories and on who is a Jew, see Chapters 4, 5, and 8 below.

Chapter 3
The Parties of Separatism

Like Mizrahi-ha-Po'el ha-Mizrahi, Agudat Yisrael-Po'alei Agudat Yisrael arose as a response, though a radically different one, to the challenges faced by orthodox Jews in Europe in the late nineteenth and early twentieth centuries. As it confronted the forces of modernity, each movement attracted mass followings of East European Jews, among whom Zionism was especially popular, although both were significantly influenced by West European Jews as well. Within each group, disagreements on fundamental questions caused internal conflicts and factionalism.

It is significant that both movements appeared relatively late in Palestine's Zionist history. Both sponsored networks of religious schools before World War I, but only afterward did they become actual political organizations, in response to the emerging quasi-government of the Yishuv. Thus both drew their initial support from the pre-existing religious community in Palestine, the Old Yishuv, with which later immigrants from Europe came into conflict. Among the immigrants were religious workers, many of them alumni of the Mizrahi and Agudah youth and labor movements of eastern Europe, who founded labor offshoots of the two parties in Palestine. Each labor group ultimately embarked on an independent political course.

In ideology, too, there are parallels and contrasts. On the highest level of eschatological or normative world view, both Mizrahi and Agudah shared a vision of a Jewish state under religious law. On the intermediate level of programmatic ideology, however, they diverged widely. Agudah took the purely instrumentalist stand that Eretz Yisrael was only one of several means to the end of fulfilling the Torah.[1] Mizrahi took the integralist position that Eretz

Yisrael itself constituted an integral part of the Torah's obligations. The differences in operational ideology often led to antithetical positions on specific issues and, consequently, to divergent political behavior on a wide variety of questions. Hence any attempt to examine all of these parties together as a "conservative religious bloc" is simplistic and distorted.

Orthodox Separatism

At the turn of the century orthodox Jews in western and central Europe—Germany, Hungary, and Slovakia—had become a minority, and many, though not all of them, had turned to the device of communal separatism to defend themselves against such powerful social forces as secularism, religious reform, and assimilation. The forces of modernism had also made deep inroads among the millions of East European Jews, most of whom remained orthodox, though the device of communal separatism was not employed there. The differences in communal organization hampered any efforts at establishing an international orthodox organization until the appearance of a new "common enemy," the Zionist movement. With few exceptions, such as Rabbi Reines, the founder of Mizrahi, most orthodox rabbis saw Zionism as the epitome of those forces which had breached the wall of traditional Jewish life: secularism and assimilation. As proof, they pointed to the predominance of secular leaders in the WZO.

Their fears were confirmed when the Second Zionist Congress (1898) declared questions of religion to be outside its purview, a matter for individual decision. This liberal stance, wholly alien to traditional ears, was reconfirmed when the organization undertook "cultural" tasks at its Fifth Congress in 1901. In reaction to these developments, some of the orthodox delegates left the WZO to await the formation of what was ultimately to become Agudah. Those who remained formed the Mizrahi faction.

While Zionism itself was ostensibly opposed to the assimilation of Jews into their cultural surroundings, its program of secular political nationalism was viewed by many of the orthodox as a form of national assimilation. They considered such nationalism a denial of the unique religious quality of the Jewish people and saw the practical program as a presumptuous attempt to force the divine hand into redemption.[2] Yet Zionism's focus on the return to the ancient Jewish homeland, unlike other social movements of the period, which had large numbers of Jewish adherents, had an undeniable appeal to orthodox Jews. Thus any opposition to Zionism had to reconcile its position with these religious ties.

Agudat Yisrael

In the summer of 1909, some of the leading rabbinical figures of the German, Russian-Polish-Lithuanian, and Hungarian communities gathered at Bad Homburg, Germany, under the aegis of Yitzhak Isaac Halevi. Halevi was an East European rabbi and historian whose long residence in and familiarity with the ways of western Europe and its Jews qualified him to act as mediator among the different types of rabbis present. He suggested that the group be called Agudat Yisrael ("Society of Israel").[3] But inherent conflicts were immediately apparent. German orthodox Jews, who had developed a philosophy and a behavior pattern of acculturation in all but matters of religious observance known as *Torah 'im Derekh Eretz,* viewed secular academic education (with a parallel religious one) as both necessary and desirable. Most of the East European and Hungarian rabbis, in contrast, viewed secular academic education as the source of reform, secularism, assimilation, and all the other ills of the modern world and were therefore steadfastly opposed to it.[4]

The question of how communal organization might be applied to the new international orthodox group was also problematic.[5] Underlying these controversies, a more basic question—cooperation with versus separation from non-orthodox Jews—was ultimately to determine Agudah's attitude toward the Jewish quasi-government in the Yishuv and, later, toward the state of Israel. The separatists of Hungary, Slovakia, and Germany insisted that their communal autonomy had to be preserved within the world organization. The rabbis of the Russian Empire, however, while opposing separatism, urged that the new organization not overemphasize Eretz Yisrael in its propaganda and plans. Their fear that Agudat Yisrael might be confused with the Zionist movement was a tacit recognition of the wide appeal of Zionism in their countries.[6] Despite these fundamental differences, the participants agreed in principle upon the establishment of a worldwide organization to spread the spiritual message of orthodoxy, to aid in the economic uplifting of orthodox Jews, and to represent them before various national and international bodies on political questions, such as Zionism. The participants empowered the leaders of the German separatist community to handle the technical details of forming the organization.

When the Tenth Zionist Congress (1911) enacted the "cultural" question into Zionist law, over the strident objections of the orthodox delegates, some of the German leaders in the Mizrahi faction withdrew from it and from the WZO to join the nascent Agudah organization. A convention held in the city of Kattowitz, in Upper Silesia (now Poland), on May 27–29, 1912, formulated some vague guidelines:

> The representatives of observant Jews from all parts of the world, having met here in Kattowitz, and having listened to various proposals, hereby declare the founding of Agudath Israel, and commit themselves to work for the growth of Agudath Israel with all their strength. Agudath Israel will take an active part in all matters relating to Jews and Judaism on the basis of Torah, without any political considerations . . . [attempting] the solution of all problems facing the Jewish people, in the spirit of Torah.[7]

Although it also created the nuclei of some of its principal organs, the conference, sensitive to the fragility of such an organization, stopped short of enunciating a detailed program of action or resolving the basic conflicts.

In addition to the familiar debate about the centrality of Eretz Yisrael, which was favored by a minority,[8] the more basic ideological question of Agudah's attitude to the "scientific and artistic culture of the era," and particularly to secular education, was raised. The autonomy clauses in the conference resolutions provided that each country's rabbinical authorities would determine the religious educational system, as well as the communal organization, appropriate to its indigenous Jewish community.[9]

Perhaps the one concrete accomplishment at Kattowitz was the selection of the core group of Agudah's supreme rabbinical body, Mo'etzet Gedolei ha-Torah ("Council of the Torah Greats," or rabbinical council). The idea that clerical authority was to be paramount distinguished Agudah not only from non-religious Jewish organizations, and certainly from the WZO, but from Mizrahi as well. This concept underlay its fundamental opposition to the secular bases of the quasi-government of the Yishuv and, later, of the state of Israel.

The provisions for autonomy fell short of satisfying the Hungarian delegation and their German separatist allies. Thus the Hungarian separatist *kehilah* did not formally join Agudah until its demands were satisfied at the Second World Convention in Vienna in 1929, though individual communities were allowed to join with the approval of the local rabbi.[10] These early organizational debates reflected the internal controversies within Agudah which helped set a course away from cooperation with the less than strictly orthodox, the non-separatist orthodox, and the Zionist orthodox and toward separatism, thus setting the stage for Agudah politics in Palestine-Israel.

The Kattowitz conference called Agudah's First World Convention (Knesiyah Gedolah) for August 1914 at Frankfurt, but the outbreak of World War I postponed it indefinitely. In Poland, an Agudah delegation came with the German troops of occupation to advise the military government on questions of Jewish communal affairs. With the help of these German advisers, the existing Polish rabbinical leadership soon built up the largest Jewish party among Poland's more than three million Jews. The Polish Agudah created a school system and women's, youth, and labor auxiliaries—the last developing into Po'alei Agudat Yisrael—and gradually became the mass movement its leaders had sought as a counterweight to Zionism.[11]

In Palestine, World War I profoundly shook the Old Yishuv and its institutions, including a handful of Agudah schools. When the occupying British officially recognized Zionist dominance over Jewish communal affairs in Palestine, a situation which many of the Old Yishuv could not or would not accept, some of the orthodox Old Yishuv leaders began to organize politically within the new framework under the Mizrahi banner. But others refused to reconcile themselves to secular Jewish domination and sought different political means to express their opposition. They adopted and adapted the device of communal separatism as developed by

important components in the recently founded Agudah world organization for use in Palestine.

Shortly after the British capture of Jerusalem, a City Council
for the Jews of Jerusalem (Va'ad ha-'Ir li-Yehudei Yerushalayim)
was set up under Zionist leadership. The council embraced most of
the city's Ashkenazi (western) Jews, both religious and non-religious, and virtually all of the Sephardi (eastern) Jews, but the
dissidents of the orthodox Old Yishuv viewed it as an attempt to
place them under the yoke of non-religious Jews. They formed
their own separate orthodox community, or 'Eidah Haredit (literally, "fearful community"), officially named Va'ad ha-'Ir le-'Eidot
ha-Ashkenazim ("City Council for the Ashkenazi Community").[12]
When the British officially recognized only the larger, Zionist-
dominated community in the spring of 1920, the 'Eidah Haredit
revived the dormant Agudah organization in Palestine. The two
bodies became, for the time being, virtually identical, in a manifest
act of political self-defense. The sole motivation behind its establishment, unlike that of the Zionist Kneset Yisrael, then, was the
external political representation of their members vis-à-vis the
Mandatory government and world Jewry.

It was on this dissonant note of opposition and separatism,
rather than on any harmonious one of cooperation, or even of
religious revivalism, that Agudah made its Yishuv debut. Unlike
Mizrahi, it had no practical ambitions in its operational (as opposed
to its ultimate) ideology of imposing religious observance on the
Yishuv as a whole. The device of communal separatism was, how-
ever, to prove increasingly incongruous in the Yishuv. Whereas in
Europe it was possible to limit the effects of separatism to purely
religious affairs because the overall government authority was non-
Jewish, in Palestine, where the Zionist majority in the Yishuv
viewed itself as a quasi-sovereign national body, separatism by
Jews was viewed as treason, a denial of Jewish national unity.
There was antagonism, and occasionally even violence, between
Agudah and the Zionists.

Membership in the small separatist community was limited
exclusively to Ashkenazim, and relations between veteran Ashkenazim and Sephardim in the Old Yishuv were not idyllic. While
both groups were orthodox religiously and traditional sociologically, each maintained its own modes of dress, daily language,

religious rite, and so forth. These differences invariably led to friction in a traditional milieu where such social details carry great weight.

Tension between the groups was aggravated by the fact that under the long Ottoman rule only Sephardim had been appointed to the office of Hakham Bashi (chief rabbi) and other official posts. Indeed, one of the primary motivations in the establishment of the chief rabbinate of the Zionist community (Kneset Yisrael) by the Mandatory government in 1921—which Agudah never recognized—was precisely to give equal representation in the rabbinate to the Ashkenazim. The automatic exclusion of Sephardim from their community sharply curtailed the growth potential of the Agudat Yisrael party in Palestine and, later, in Israel, whose population is now more than half Sephardi and which includes a high percentage of traditionally religious individuals.

The problems between the separatist and Zionist communities were compounded by Agudah's insistence upon the explicit recognition of the sovereignty of Torah law. This condition was rejected outright by every political organism formed in Palestine, though it was not applicable to non-Jewish governmental units such as municipalities, in which Agudah did participate. The fact that the right to vote and to be elected to communal office in the Zionist community was not restricted to adult males only, as Agudah had demanded, constituted another unbridgeable chasm between the separate orthodox community and the broader Zionist one.

Agudah did make some vain initial attempts to obtain representation in the larger bodies in Palestine, but it also sought inclusion in the Jewish Agency set up to represent world Jewish interests in Palestine on the condition that the Agency remain a purely administrative, political, and economic, not a cultural or educational, organ. The WZO, which was recognized by the mandate of 1921 as constituting such an agency, was unwilling to accept such conditions. Agudah's rabbinical council thus ruled that Agudah could not participate in the Jewish Agency. A similar pattern of ultimatum, rejection, and withdrawal was followed by Agudah vis-à-vis the Kneset Yisrael and its executive organ, the Va'ad Leumi. By 1925 it was clear that Kneset Yisrael was about to become the legally recognized Jewish community in Palestine. Agudah mounted an all-out campaign of propaganda and (at times violent) demonstrations against this violation of its religious conscience, sending a stream of protests to the Palestine government, the British government, and the League of Nations.[13]

The most lucid presentation of Agudah's case was made by Dr. Yitzhak Breuer, son of Rabbi Breuer of Frankfurt and a chief Agudah (and later PAY) ideologue and publicist, in his *Jewish National Home*. Breuer distinguished between the Zionists, who considered the nation as the central concept in Jewish life, with the Torah merely a product of the nation's creativity, and the Agudists, who viewed the Torah as central, with both the nation and the land as instruments to fulfill its commandments. He dismissed "the so-called Mizrahi" as "a faction of the Zionist Organization that attempted the impossible in trying to guide the Zionist Reform into the ways of God and His Torah" by maintaining a legitimizing aura of religion about it via such institutions as the chief rabbinate.

Breuer argued that a Jewish state in Palestine should be "constituted from the very beginning in accordance with the commands of God and the Torah." Such a state could be achieved only if there were unanimity among the Jews on the fundamental nature of the state. Lacking consensus, any attempt to establish a Jewish state on either a religious or a secular basis would inevitably result in the oppression of the conscience of the other party—in the present case, the orthodox.

Given the situation, Agudah favored a secular Palestine state, in which Jews were not defined as a nation-state, as they were by the mandate, but were considered ordinary citizens, free to organize communally as they pleased. Breuer envisioned two separate Jewish communities, one "ruled by God and the Torah," the other a Zionist republican community. Thus all Jews, religious and nonreligious (and all Arabs, for that matter), would bear equal rights and responsibilities in secular Palestine, which, like the non-Jewish governments in western and central Europe, would exercise only very general supervisory rights in religious matters.[14]

This proposal was so fundamentally and diametrically opposed to Zionism (in its secular or religious forms), with its basic assumption of the inalienable unity of the Jewish people, that it has constituted the common denominator in the most persistent and radical criticism of Israel's Zionist basis. Similar attacks have come from the Palestine Liberation Organization, from anti-Zionist secularist groups such as the League against Religious Coercion, and from anti-Zionist religious groups such as the Neturei Qarta ("Guardians of the City"). The question of Israeli versus Jewish nationality is the crux of the religion-state question in Israel today. Breuer went on to present his proposal for a constitution for the Torah-bound Jewish community in Palestine.[15] He stressed the voluntary nature of his proposed community, providing for the right of withdrawal, or *yetzi'ah,* as well as the right to establish separate but equal communities in which all units of communal government are subject to rabbinical authority.

Agudah did obtain certain provisions in the Communities Ordinance which enabled its adherents to maintain a modicum of autonomy from Kneset Yisrael, the most important of which was *yetzi'ah,* though no concurrent right to establish separate communities was granted. Some twelve thousand people in Jerusalem and five thousand elsewhere in Palestine exercised the right of *yetzi'ah.* It also gained concessions in practical matters, such as exemption from paying the tax to support Kneset Yisrael[16] and even the right to register marriages on behalf of the separate *kehilah,*[17] though not full-fledged recognition of jurisdiction in matters of personal status.

Agudah objected to the official chief rabbinate of Kneset Yisrael because it had acquiesced in such objectionable *halakhic* (Jewish legal) practices as the female franchise, the end to discrimination between males and females in inheritance, the establishment of a rabbinical appeals court, and the creation of an advisory panel of legal experts.[18] On a personal level, the then Ashkenazi chief rabbi, Avraham Yitzhak Kook, though of impeccable orthodox credentials, was viewed by some Agudists as an ineffectual mystic and a Zionist apologist[19] and by others as an interloper in Jerusalem.[20] After the 1929 Arab disturbances, however, events pushed Agudah into increasing cooperation with the rest of the Yishuv, particularly in matters of self-defense.[21] Some members of the Agudah youth wing, Tze'irei Agudat Yisrael, even joined the underground defense force of Kneset Yisrael, the Haganah.[22] Nevertheless—as often occurs in ideological political parties—it was the young guard that objected most strenuously to the gradual moderation of Agudah policy vis-à-vis the Zionists. After the youth organization broke up in 1934, the majority of its adherents, of Old Yishuv stock and unalterably opposed to any cooperation with Kneset Yisrael, founded the Neturei Qarta, which still accuses Agudah of having abandoned its separatist principles and refuses to recognize the legitimacy of the state of Israel.

Po'alei Agudat Yisrael

In the early 1930s the composition of Agudah's membership was altered by the large wave of immigration into Palestine from Poland known as the Fourth 'Aliyah. This was stimulated in no small part by the Polish government's announced policy of economic discrimination against Jews and by the effective closing of the gates of immigration to the United States after 1923.[23] Among the immigrants were large numbers of orthodox Jews, from both the middle and the working classes, including some members of the Polish Agudah. Upon their arrival in Palestine, they naturally sought out the local Agudah, which, unlike the broad-based political party they had known in Poland,[24] was a small, local, and separatist organization.

The even larger wave of German emigration in the wake of the Nazi rise to power included some Agudah members and leaders. The veteran Old Yishuv leadership relinquished its hold on the Palestinian Agudah in 1934, when a delegation from the world organization arrived in Palestine to grant equal representation in the local Agudah to the new immigrants. As a result, some of the Old Yishuv people broke away and joined in the founding of Neturei Qarta. This change of guard brought about a shift in Agudah's attitude toward Eretz Yisrael, at least insofar as it was a haven, and also resulted in greater cooperation between Agudah and the Yishuv authorities on defense and internal political questions and with the Jewish Agency on immigration and external political questions. Agudah's attitude toward the nationalist effort remained essentially passive and was confined largely to religious education. The few agricultural settlements it attempted to found ended in failure, and it was not making adequate provision for the employment and protection of immigrant workers, many of whom had belonged to the Agudah labor organization, Po'alei Agudat Yisrael (PAY), in Poland.

PAY was founded in 1923 in the textile city of Lodz. Its aims were to protect both the economic and the religious interests of orthodox workers. The organization also undertook to combat the inroads that other labor organizations, Jewish and non-Jewish, had made into the ranks of orthodox workers by providing them with an alternative ideology of social justice based on the principles of the Torah. In matters of religious practice, PAY closely followed the lead of its parent body, Agudat Yisrael.

A branch of PAY was set up in Palestine in 1923, and a rudimentary national convention was held there in 1925.[25] In that same year, PAY's leading political figure, Binyamin Mintz, emigrated to Palestine from Poland. With the flow of hundreds of PAY members from Poland and Germany, the organization expanded, and in 1933 it held its first full-scale national convention in Palestine. As an independent labor organization it engaged, albeit on a much smaller scale (it had some three thousand members in 1936), in the same types of activities (labor exchanges, cooperatives, etc.) as did the secular Histadrut and the religious Zionist ha-Po'el ha-Mizrahi. It also established the first of its *kibbutzim,* Hafetz Hayyim.

Both the veteran Palestine Agudah leadership, with its traditional Old Yishuv mentality, and the newer immigrant leaders, who had condescendingly tolerated PAY in Poland and Germany, viewed such activities—which emphasized manual labor and smacked of the Zionist ethic of *halutziyut* ("pioneerism")—with considerable reserve. Consequently, they were none too responsive to PAY's urgings to purchase further land for such settlements for immigrants.[26] In 1943, PAY accepted land for a settlement from the Jewish National Fund, the official Zionist land purchasing body. This blatant defiance of the ruling of the rabbinical council of Agudah foreshadowed even greater rebelliousness by the independent-minded labor faction.

The New State

PAY found its intellectual and ideological mentor in Dr. Yitzhak Breuer. Since his arrival in Palestine, he had become sharply critical of both the world Agudah organization and the Palestine Agudah, which not only had failed to undertake practical projects in Palestine but also had been unable or unwilling to take a clear stand on the political future of the Yishuv.[27]

When the Peel Commission recommended partition and the establishment of a Jewish state in part of Palestine, Breuer prepared two interrelated constitutional drafts.[28] Although his theocratic views were little changed—indeed, if anything, they were more detailed—he no longer envisioned a separate community under a secular Palestinian government. Instead, he demanded a single, united Jewish state based explicitly on Torah law. Recognizing that such a state would be unacceptable to the current majority of Jews in Palestine, he realistically set out a series of fallback positions—which bear some striking resemblances to those set out by Mizrahi in 1939—as the minimal conditions for Agudah's participation in and de facto recognition of the Jewish state. While the state's civil law should, optimally, be drawn up on the basis of the Torah and the Code of Jewish Law by rabbinical authorities, as an absolute minimum Agudah, like Mizrahi, would accept a state where Torah family and personal status law was maintained. Religious education in the new state would be completely autonomous, under the exclusive supervision of the chief rabbinate and a ministry of Torah, though full government funding would be provided.

Although Breuer still viewed purely religious affairs and institutions as properly placed under a sovereign, tax-collecting chief rabbinate of an autonomous Jewish communal body, from which withdrawal and the establishment of a separate community was always possible, he did provide for the establishment of a ministry of Torah, much like Mizrahi's ministry of religions, as the highest administrative organ in the government of his proposed state. It was to deal with religious affairs jointly with the chief rabbinate and to carry out its decisions. His list of other religious demands raised some of the major questions that still plague Israeli politics: the observance of the Sabbath in public by all governmental agencies and by private individuals; the production and sale of non-kosher food; the legal definition of who is a Jew; the non-recognition of non-orthodox variants of Judaism by the state; and the recurrent furor over autopsies, the performance of which is problematic, to say the least, according to *halakhah*.

Clearly, by 1937 Agudah had shifted from a purely self-defensive separatist stand to an activist one with far-reaching implications. Both the national Agudah and PAY favored, in principle, a partitioned yet independent Jewish state in Palestine, hoping to imprint it with as strong a religious stamp as possible. Important components of the world Agudah organization outside Palestine, including its president, Rabbi Ya'akov Rosenheim, and many Hungarian and Polish leaders, were not willing to accept a truncated Jewish state in Palestine which apparently would not be founded on Torah law. The conflict was referred to Agudah's supreme rabbinical council, which in August of 1937, on religious, national, and political grounds, ruled against Agudah's acceptance of partition. Although the rabbinical decision was confirmed by the Third World Convention of Agudat Yisrael in Marienbad, Czechoslovakia, in September, Agudah was still open to "further negotiations to find a solution to the religious and material needs of the Jewish people and a means of assuring the historic right of the Jewish people to Eretz Yisrael which is based on the Torah."[29]

Though no mention of a Jewish state yet appeared in the world Agudah's lexicon, Agudah reached an agreement with Mizrahi in Paris in 1938 to protect the religious and material aims it sought in Palestine, but the accord was rejected by Agudah's right wing. It negotiated with the British as well: it appeared before the Royal (Woodhead) Commission in Palestine in 1939, a group which was sent there to work out the implementation of the Peel recommendations, and it sent a delegation to the ill-fated Round Table talks in London that year. The political significance of such negotiations was vitiated by the White Paper of May 1939, in which the British government renounced the idea of partition and a Jewish state and severely restricted Jewish immigration at a time when millions of Jews were in dire need of such a haven.

After the outbreak of World War II, the world Agudah organization stepped up its cooperation with the Jewish Agency and the Va'ad Leumi on questions of rescue and immigration.[30] It continued to view Palestine primarily as a haven for the persecuted, rather than as a possible Jewish state, and contemplated the alternative of a Jewish majority in Palestine within a wider federation of Arab states.[31] This long-standing preoccupation with protecting the status of Jews as a minority, as opposed to the Zionists' conception of Jews as a majority in a national political entity, led the world Agudah to object to the Zionists' Biltmore Program of 1942, which urged the establishment of a Jewish commonwealth in Palestine. It also rejected any suggestion of organizing a Jewish army there.[32]

The opinions of the world Agudah were vigorously opposed by the Palestine branch during the war. Breuer not only urged that it be given at least the same autonomy within the world and Palestine Agudah organizations as other national Agudahs had long had, but also insisted on a clear delineation between the powers of the national Agudah and the world organization. He claimed that only Palestine residents could have the necessary first-hand knowledge and experience to guide Agudah policy there.[33]

In anticipation of the 1944 Agudah national convention in Palestine, support for the establishment of a sovereign, independent Jewish government[34] was voiced for the first time in Agudah circles. However, this attitude represented a bow to the "compulsion of reality,"[35] i.e., the war, immigration, and so forth, rather than any abandonment of Agudah's "revolutionary ideology" of a state governed by Torah law.[36] The convention stopped short of endorsing such a declaration of independence but did demand the "establishment of such a political regime as would facilitate the full realization of the mandate for the Jewish people, with the aid of the Mandatory power,"[37] including unlimited Jewish immigration.

Such resolutions were insufficient for PAY, whose central committee had already voted to approve the Biltmore Program and its Jewish commonwealth demand in 1943.[38] At its 1944 national convention, it reaffirmed that decision and called for a "Jewish political regime" in Palestine, refraining from the use of the term "state" only to avoid an open break with Agudah. The convention also urged the Jewish Agency to allow the Agudah movement, PAY included, to join it, and demanded of Agudah that PAY be allowed to take the question of joining the Jewish Agency to the supreme rabbinical council for reconsideration.[39] A minority of delegates at the convention demanded that PAY join the Agency immediately.

The various factions maintained these positions virtually up to the moment that the state was established. PAY clearly advocated an independent Jewish state, hoping to stamp it as strongly as possible in Breuer's religious mold. The Palestine Agudah did

not openly support such a state but favored a reorientation of Agudah priorities toward Palestine; all postwar Jewish immigration
should be directed there, as the only place where an organized life
under Torah could possibly be led.[40] The world Agudah executives, headquartered in New York and London, argued for the
establishment of a "political regime" in Palestine which would
facilitate Jewish immigration and settlement, but they would only
recognize a legal government accepted by the United Nations
there, since then it would be yielding to *force majeure* rather than
voluntarily accepting a secular Jewish state.

Now that PAY's share in the Agudah movement was propor-
tionately far greater in Palestine than it had been in Europe—it had
recently established its own world PAY, to Agudah's dismay—it
demanded commensurately greater representation in the world
movement in general and in bodies dealing with Palestine policy in
particular. An agreement at the Marienbad conference provided for
PAY's representation in the top executive organs of Agudah;
PAY's sole jurisdiction in areas of labor, agricultural settlement,
and immigrant absorption in Palestine was recognized; and the
world Agudah was to be responsible for immigration itself, as well
as for religious, educational, and political questions.[41] These plans
were not carried out, however, and further alienation between
Agudah and PAY culminated in open conflict and the divorce of
the two within the sovereign state of Israel.

Agudah viewed the state with mixed emotions. Like Mizrahi
and ha-Po'el ha-Mizrahi, it desired a reconstituted Jewish state run
by Torah law, and the present reality of a Jewish state headed by
secular Jews was alien and unacceptable to it.[42] Yet events propelled Agudah into its de facto recognition of the state. For one
thing, the holocaust of European Jewry had decimated its membership, and the survivors needed a secure refuge, which Israel afforded. Among the casualties of the war was the old German
leadership of Agudah, which had been particularly cool to Zionism.
The postwar leadership was primarily Polish, and hence more moderate. Furthermore, unlike membership in Kneset Yisrael, a voluntary organization from which withdrawal was possible, citizenship
in the state was automatic and exclusive. It had long been Agudah
policy to recognize and cooperate with any official governmental
authority anyway. Besides, any attempt at separatism from the

state and evasion of the duties of citizenship would not be tolerated, and would only render Agudah a renegade sect of no political
consequence, like the Neturei Qarta.

Thus Agudah chose to organize as a political party within
the Israeli political system. It joined the other religious parties in
the URF during the First Kneset (1949–51) and ran a separate list
for the Second Kneset (1951–55), as did PAY. It also participated
in the government for the first four and a half years; its leader,
Rabbi Yitzhak Meir Levin, served as Israel's first minister of
social welfare.

Agudah's minimal goal was to enable its adherents to pursue
their traditional way of life. To this end it, along with the other
religious parties, obtained assurances in five basic areas prior to
joining the government: the Sabbath and Jewish holidays would be
observed by and in the state; *kashrut* would be maintained in state
facilities; religious education organized in separate "trends" would
remain autonomous; the religious needs of the population would be
provided for by the state; and the laws of personal status for Jews
would conform to the Torah.[43] Its central goal, however, was to
help mold the religious character of the state in these first crucial
years.

When issues were broached that fundamentally threatened
the life style of its adherents, however, Agudah withdrew, not out
of the political system entirely, but to the opposition, where it has
remained ever since. It has returned to a minimalist, defensive
position of its parochial interests, abandoning any attempts to
influence or impose its values on the society at large. Its withdrawal resulted from ideological frustration and practical political
failures. When it found that it could not weaken the grasp over
official religion in Israel of Mizrahi and ha-Po'el ha-Mizrahi, it
reverted to its traditional separatism. This retreat, in turn, precipi-
tated further deterioration in its relations with PAY.

After the state was established in May 1948, the PAY central
committee insisted on separate representation from Agudah in any
government.[44] It also favored the establishment of a URF, as did
Agudah, but again with separate Agudah and PAY representatives.
Once agreement was reached in principle between all four religious
parties on a URF, and the respective percentages of the two blocs
(Mizrahi-ha-Po'el ha-Mizrahi and Agudah-PAY) had been fixed by

an agreed arbitration at 62.5 and 37.5 percent, respectively, there remained the issue of how the Agudah-PAY share was to be divided. PAY preferred parity, while Agudah insisted upon a clear majority in its favor. After the controversy had been submitted to rabbinical arbitration, Agudah was awarded 60 percent, PAY 40 percent. When PAY's breakaway Jerusalem faction, PAGI, decided to present its own list, the shares were readjusted to 55 percent Agudah and 45 percent PAY.[45]

The URF won sufficient votes for sixteen Kneset seats. After some mathematically complicated division of the seats, the eleventh man on the Mizrahi-ha-Po'el ha-Mizrahi list was dropped in favor of a sixth Agudah-PAY member. This decision gave PAY the sixth seat, for a total of three. Thus it achieved the parity with Agudah which it had originally demanded.

When the URF entered the first government of Israel, the Agudah bloc was alloted one cabinet seat. This was promptly filled by the acknowledged political leader of Agudah, Rabbi Levin, leaving PAY with no representatives in the government of which it was a member. PAY leaders announced angrily that they would bear no responsibility for the actions of such a government. When Agudah unilaterally decided to have its educational system become a fourth "trend" recognized by the Ministry of Education,[46] thereby obtaining government funds, PAY, which was contributing money, children, and teachers to the Agudah system, felt that it should have been consulted on the move and should be represented on the new trend's board of supervisors. The trend system was abandoned three years later in favor of two state educational systems, one secular and one religious (i.e., Mizrahi), and Agudah set up its own Hinukh 'Atzmai ("independent education"). While most of the former Agudah schools joined Hinukh 'Atzmai, it is not surprising that many of those under PAY influence, particularly those in PAY rural settlements, joined the state religious system, in defiance of Agudah.[47]

The Crossroads

In February 1951, after the fall of the government over the question of religious education of children in immigrant camps, elections for the Second Kneset were scheduled for July 30, 1951. This time, however, there was no URF: ha-Po'el ha-Mizrahi, the largest of the potential partners, demurred, largely because of strong opposition from the la-Mifneh faction.

Both Agudah and PAY openly favored a renewed URF. A united and strengthened orthodox representation afforded greater possibilities of implementing religious legislation.[48] Furthermore, since these two little parties had also become part of the third largest bloc in the Kneset, they had begun to taste the pleasures of power, including the Ministry of Social Welfare, which Agudah controlled. Yet when ha-Po'el ha-Mizrahi refused to participate, the two Agudah parties were unable to agree on a joint list. The results in the ensuing elections were disappointing, especially for PAY, which received only two Kneset seats, while Agudah maintained its three.

Nevertheless, both Agudah and PAY joined the new coalition. First, however, they demanded assurances from Mapai that no decision would be made for one year on two issues, particularly sensitive to Agudah in light of its traditional attitudes: the conscription of religious girls for National (civil) Service and the abolition of the trends in education. On September 1, 1952, as the moratorium was about to expire, and government action on both these fronts seemed imminent, both Agudah and PAY resigned from the government.

Fundamental changes in the pattern of education and raising of children struck at the heart of Agudah's traditional pattern of socialization and family structure. As Rabbi Levin put it, in speaking of the conscription of women: "Any framework of conscription in any form necessitates discipline which cannot be carried out and enforced except in an army or police situation. The taking of our daughters from the parents' authority into such a framework or to another authority is likely to bring spiritual destruction to them. We cannot let them loose in such an atmosphere."[49] Not only was Agudah's own rabbinical council firmly opposed to National Service in any form but even the official chief rabbinate of Israel, long under Mizrahi domination, issued a proclamation declaring the proposed measure forbidden according to the Torah.[50]

PAY reluctantly followed Agudah out of the government but soon entered into negotiations with Mapai for a new coalition, an act viewed by Agudah as a veritable betrayal. Nevertheless, the rabbinical leadership of PAY succeeded in having the organization bow to the will of Agudah and its "Council of Torah Greats," which specifically forbade rejoining the government.[51] Although PAY stayed out of the coalition and temporarily maintained its ties with Agudah, it boycotted the Fourth Agudah Knesiyah Gedolah ("World Convention") held in Jerusalem in 1954.

Before the Third Kneset elections in 1955, another attempt at establishing a URF was thwarted by ha-Po'el ha-Mizrahi, particularly by its la-Mifneh faction. Mizrahi and ha-Po'el ha-Mizrahi did run a joint list, and Agudah and PAY managed to do the same. The union restored the sixth Agudah-PAY seat (and the third PAY one). Again, Agudah and PAY remained out of the government. But the Agudah-PAY partnership lasted only one full Kneset term. The two Agudah parties ran a joint list for the Fourth Kneset in 1959 with the stipulation that the disputed sixth seat would be held for two years by a PAY representative and for two by an Agudah representative unless PAY agreed to a full merger with Agudah, in which case it would retain the seat.[52] Again, the joint list received six (three and three) seats, with PAY holding the sixth. Some six months later, however, PAY decided to "remove the guardianship of Agudah from itself"[53] once and for all. It entered the government on July 18, 1960, and its leader, Binyamin Mintz, became minister of posts. This declaration of independence led, predictably enough, to the severance of all ties with Agudah and a flood of recriminations rushed forth from all sides.

The government fell over the renewed Lavon affair (a complex controversy between Prime Minister David Ben-Gurion and ex-Defense Minister Pinhas Lavon over the responsibility for an aborted Israeli espionage escapade in Egypt) at the end of January 1961, barely a year after it had been established. As Prime Minister Ben-Gurion was unable to compose a new government after months of deliberations, elections were held in November for the Fifth Kneset. Although Mintz died in June 1961, PAY participated in government coalitions—though it never again received a full cabinet post—until the Seventh Kneset elections in 1969, whereas Agudah consistently stood outside the goverment, including the National Unity Government formed immediately prior to the Six Day War.

There has been an increasing rapprochement between Agudah and PAY since the latter joined the opposition in 1969, and particularly since the death of Rabbi Levin in 1971. It culminated in the establishment of a joint electoral list for the 1973 elections which won only five seats.

Part II
Structure and
Strength of the
Current Parties

Chapter 4
Organization, Membership, and Leadership

The historical and ideological development of the religious parties, especially as reflected in their attitudes toward modernity, has had a profound and lasting impact upon them even in such ostensibly non-ideological areas as party organization, membership composition, and elite characteristics. These developmental factors influence whether a party as presently constituted has an organizational structure based on the largely objective, achievement-oriented value system of a labor union—much like the secular Mapai-Labor party—or based on the generally ascriptive, traditional value system of clerically dominated sects. Similarly, they help determine whether or not the social composition of the party's members is broadly representative of the social classes and ethnic groups in the society. Furthermore, the party's orientation toward modern life clearly affects the educational, age, sex, career, and other characteristics of its leaders.

Mafdal's National Organs

The 1964 constitution made for a clearer division of labor between Mafdal and ha-Po'el ha-Mizrahi. As in Mapai, the trend was toward expansion of the more representative organs and transfer of decisionmaking to higher bodies. However, Mapai has tended to favor informal decision-making bodies, whereas in Mafdal constitutional or other formal bodies retain much authority.

While both parties are based on labor organizations, the intimacy and dependence of Mafdal upon ha-Po'el ha-Mizrahi is far greater than that of Mapai on the Histadrut. Though Mapai is the dominant party in the Histadrut, and the Histadrut sector is an important interest group in Mapai, the party itself maintains its supremacy. It is the party executive, not the Histadrut, that runs internal party organization and administration. Mapai, as the senior party in the government and the state, has other areas of power and interest, such as government corporations, the military, and the foreign service, to offset somewhat the influence of the Histadrut, and thus there is room for, if not a necessity for, informal bodies to reconcile the interests of both.[1]

Mafdal, however, is the only party in ha-Po'el ha'Mizrahi: indeed, the two are almost co-extensive. With few exceptions, membership in Mafdal is contingent upon membership in ha-Po'el ha-Mizrahi.[2] The party's total votership and membership are almost identical with that of ha-Po'el ha-Mizrahi. It is ha-Po'el ha-Mizrahi that manages the internal organization and administrative affairs of the party, down to the local branches, which are identical. Thus the party itself is a much less free agent vis-à-vis its labor organization than Mapai. It is also far smaller than the latter and has fewer alternate sources of strength, if any, and fewer areas of independent policymaking.

Mafdal-ha-Po'el ha-Mizrahi, then, is an exception to the pattern of party-created and party-dominated labor organizations which Medding has discussed in the case of Mapai and the Histadrut.[3] It is perhaps closer to the British pattern, from which Medding distinguishes Mapai, in that the labor organization is the core of the party. This is not to say, however, that the labor organization, as in Britain, created the party. As our analysis of the origins of ha-Po'el ha-Mizrahi shows, it was originally an auxiliary, if always a very independent one, of the Mizrahi party. Thus the formation of informal decision-making bodies along the lines of Mapai's Haveireinu and Sareinu outside the organizational framework imposed by the labor organization nature of the party is unlikely. In addition, the traditional factionalism in Mafdal would pose a challenge to any decision-making body established in violation of each faction's rights, whereas in Mapai formal factionalism has been successfully outlawed, and interests can be reconciled in a less formal fashion.

This is not to say that Mafdal's organs always follow this constitutional scenario; however, the general formal structure is adhered to.

According to the latest ha-Po'el ha-Mizrahi constitution,[4] the convention is the supreme organ of both the party and ha-Po'el ha-Mizrahi. It is chosen by the membership in secret, personal, and local elections—again, in an attempt to eliminate factions—and is held once every four years. As a concession to reality, the constitution allows for the postponement of the convention in a variety of extraordinary circumstances. The convention's chief, if not only, function is the election of a number of key party organs, including the central committee and the joint executive, as well as the administration of the umbrella organization that administers the movement's diverse economic enterprises. The convention may empower the central committee to act with the powers of the convention itself.

In reality, the role of the convention is not a sovereign one. Even if held once every four years, it could at best approve general lines of policy, rather than making specific policy decisions. In fact, the conventions have been held much less frequently, in 1956, 1963, 1969, and 1973. Mapai conventions, held at more frequent intervals, seem to have more influence on general lines of party policy than Mafdal's do.[5]

The new constitution also streamlined the size of the convention by making it one instead of two simultaneous conventions, enabling the number of elected delegates to be reduced from 869 to 536 in the second and third conventions.[6] But the unwieldy size of the body and its brief duration make it unfit for actual decision-making. Compared to Mapai, however, where over two thousand delegates are not unknown,[7] the Mafdal convention is relatively small.

All the conventions except the ha-Po'el ha-Mizrahi one of 1952 and the Mafdal one of 1973 were either completely or in part "agreed" conventions, composed by means of interfactional arrangements. This method casts some doubt on the democratic nature of the convention—though, as in Mapai, the attempt to incorporate diverse social groups is somewhat representative. This is less true for Mafdal than Mapai, however. For example, in 1956 the Mapai Sephardi membership was some 30 percent of its total, while their representation at the Mapai convention that year was 33 percent.[8] The membership of Mafdal in the early 1960s was some 40 percent Sephardi, yet only 20 percent of the delegates to the 1963 convention were Sephardi.[9] The ability of opposition factions to perform their inherent functions effectively under such a system of pre-arranged composition is severely hampered. Only when, as in 1972, real elections are held for the party convention do they serve the additional function of arousing member interest and activity (some 75 percent of those eligible participated in that year). This attitude becomes particularly important when an upcoming Kneset election is anticipated, as was the case in 1973.

The internal organization and procedures of the convention itself also prevent it from serving as a sovereign, decision-making body. Most of the plenary sessions are devoted to ceremonial openings and closings and to long-winded "lectures" by party leaders (which do serve to demonstrate the party's strength, much as in Mapai).[10] What genuine debate there is in the plenum is at best a public articulation of the diverse interests in the party.

The convention's decisions on policy, organization, or appointments are ratified, usually unanimously, as presented to it by the ordering, or standing, committee (also as in Mapai). They are hammered out between the factions in that committee if they are taken to the convention at all. More often the more important political, organizational, and appointment decisions are brought by the standing committee directly to a later meeting of the central committee, convening with the authority of the convention.[11] Furthermore, the existence of a factional "key" which allocates appointments to the party's various organs and departments according to proportional size of the factions makes the convention's, or the central committee's, ultimate selections rather anti-climactic.

In addition, the presidium of the central committee and the executive determine the time, place, and agenda of the convention, thus further narrowing its area of decisionmaking. When the convention itself does in fact take a major decision, such as the merger in 1956, it is merely the culmination and ratification of a longer process of development. Indeed, this function of ex post facto ratification of major changes or, alternatively, of the delegation of the use of its authority to effect such changes—such as the adoption of the 1964 constitution—comprises the chief manifestation of the convention's theoretical supremacy, which can be summed up in the concept of legitimization.

The constitution stipulates that the central committee is the highest party organ between conventions. It must follow the convention's decisions and is in fact elected by the convention, but it is empowered to make decisions on matters of policy and can approve the budget.[12] The central committee's ability to exercise the authority of the convention in terms of appointments and decisions is its most important function. It now regularly takes the place of the convention itself in selecting (or rather ratifying the selections that the joint executive presents to it) the top organs of the party: the separate party executive, the separate ha-Po'el ha-Mizrahi executive, and the joint secretariat, as well as its own presidium.[13] It also issues the convention's decisions, which serve as general guidelines for party policy in the coming years.

Beyond these functions, and that of determining the time and place of the convention and its agenda, the central committee is of limited importance. It shares with the convention the limitations of size (505 members) and infrequent meetings (averaging slightly more than one per year), despite its "supreme" status.

The joint executive is elected under the constitution by the convention itself as its top executive.[14] It in turn appoints, via an appointments committee (much as in Mapai),[15] the ha-Po'el ha-Mizrahi executive and the party executive on the basis of factional strength.[16] It determines the division of labor between the two smaller executives. Once the division has been made, it also establishes the structure and functions of the various departments operating under each smaller executive and appoints their heads. Finally, it appoints the joint secretariat. Given such broad powers of appointment, it is not surprising that the joint executive has become the site of intense interfactional conflict over the division of the party bureaucracy.

The joint executive, like the central committee, has suffered from an inflation of membership, as compared to the smaller separate executives of ha-Po'el ha-Mizrahi and the party it replaced, and therefore from a commensurate decline in its decision-making authority since the merger and the 1964 constitutional reorganization. The separate ha-Po'el ha-Mizrahi executive consisted of 26 members before the reorganization,[17] and the party executive of a smaller number, but the joint executive elected by the 1963 convention consisted of some 137 members, as compared to some 173 in 1969.[18] As in the central committee, almost the entire Mafdal elite, members of the Kneset and ministers, are nominally members of the joint executive; the rest of its membership is composed of lower-echelon party people.

The inflation of its membership and concomitant decline in real decision-making authority are reflected in the frequency of its meetings. The old ha-Po'el ha-Mizrahi executive met some eighty-two times in the seven-year period between the first and second Mafdal conventions.[19] The new joint executive met only twenty-one times in the six-and-a-half-year span between the second and third conventions.[20] It currently meets about once every two months. Furthermore, certain appointive functions are now performed by the new joint body. It is charged with the composition of the various executive departments as well as of the joint secretariat and of the smaller party and ha-Po'el ha-Mizrahi executives, to which real decision-making power has been transferred. Indeed, the joint executive itself has become more like the original central committee, considering general issues of principle such as the political and security position of the state, economic policy, and so forth, but either taking no position on such matters or taking very vague ones at best,[21] unlike the former ha-Po'el ha-Mizrahi and party executives, which dealt with concrete political and economic questions.[22] Even on such specific party questions as coalition talks, the joint executive merely ratifies the agreements worked out by a committee of the party executive.[23]

Decisions on specific matters of policy are now taken by the party executive and the ha-Po'el ha-Mizrahi executive, each body composed of approximately forty members plus five Kneset members.[24] The party executive deals mostly with external or "output" matters, such as the party's policy on foreign and security affairs, the all-important questions of whether and at what price to join (or leave) a coalition government and who should be minister therein, the composition of the Kneset list, and legislation on municipal political affairs. It deals with religious-political matters of national significance, such as legislation regarding the Sabbath, chief rabbinate elections, the state religious educational system, religious court affairs, and so on. It is also the body to which the Mafdal parliamentary delegation is directly responsible.[25]

The ha-Po'el ha-Mizrahi executive deals mainly with those

economic questions which have long been the province of the labor organization, such as wage policy, relations with the Histadrut and its Qupat Holim sick fund, labor relations, and related matters.[26] In addition, it retains control of such important internal or "input" factors for Mafdal as membership, party organization, dues, and so on, once again indicating the centrality of the mass labor organization as Mafdal's base. The functions of the smaller party and ha-Po'el ha-Mizrahi executives are thus also roughly reflected in the division of labor between them.

The two executives have far more explicit tasks than any of the other bodies, they are relatively compact bodies that convene frequently (roughly once every two months over the 1963–69 period), and they are capable of making policy decisions in their respective spheres of authority, but the actual day-to-day conduct of Mafdal politics is handled by two still smaller bodies—the joint secretariat and the party's Kneset delegation—that meet even more frequently.

The joint secretariat is a group of eleven or twelve top bureaucrats, including the heads of key departments and of the various geographic districts into which party branches are grouped. The secretariat is chosen by the joint executive, with clear factional influence, and ratified by the central committee. It meets about two to three times per month.[27] While it is supposed to serve both party and ha-Po'el ha-Mizrahi functions, in fact it largely confines itself to the latter. Indeed, it is composed entirely of bureaucrats rather than politicians. The ha-Po'el ha-Mizrahi bureaucracy handles all matters of internal organization for the party as well. Over the six-year period 1963–69[28] the secretariat dealt with such questions as the religious agricultural settlement organizations, relations with the Histadrut and Qupat Holim and with the PAY labor organizations, the organization of academics in ha-Po'el ha-Mizrahi, religious immigration, and similar technical matters, rather than wider political, religious, and educational issues.

The actual political affairs of the party on the national level, which center around the Kneset and the government, are handled primarily by the parliamentary delegation. This is composed of all the party's Kneset members plus its ministers, if they are not also members—a group of eleven to fifteen people, including the party secretary. As Peter Medding found with Mapai, the Mafdal parliamentary delegation has been granted a marked degree of independence in operation and in taking decisions in accordance with its own view of the parliamentary situation,[29] though more fundamental matters of policy and principle, such as the composition of the Kneset list, the naming of ministers and deputy ministers, decisions on joining or leaving the coalition, etc., are referred to the party executive, if not higher, in case of unresolvable conflict on fundamental principles.

Thus, while coalition agreement talks are conducted by a committee of the party executive, and while the final agreement must be approved by the joint executive, the task of implementing these agreements, whether in the form of legislation, representation, interparty or interministerial agreements, or otherwise, is in the hands of the parliamentary delegation. Insofar as legislation is concerned, Mafdal, as a member of the coalition, must have any of its proposed legislation, even private member bills, approved by the coalition executive, on which three of its members sit.

Mafdal members participate in all Kneset committees as well. Given the size of the Mafdal parliamentary delegation—usually between ten and twelve members—and the fact that the party usually is allotted three ministerial portfolios and one or more deputy ministerial ones, the number of members remaining to conduct the regular Kneset business is limited. This is one of the reasons why ministers Yosef Burg and Zerah Warhaftig agreed to resign their seats so that two additional non-ministerial members could move into the Seventh Kneset. Other reasons include the desire for greater representation and more rapid turnover.

The Mafdal parliamentary delegation, which meets weekly,[30] can in many ways be viewed as the true elite of the party, perhaps much more so than the parallel organ in Mapai. The latter's parliamentary delegation is some four times the size of Mafdal's, necessitating the use of more limited, informal elite groups for efficient decisionmaking.[31] Further, Mapai controls a far broader panoply of institutions and can therefore provide alternative sources of leadership satisfaction. Mafdal must reward the head or heads of each faction with safe Kneset seats. Thus its parliamentary delegation, the site of decisionmaking on national issues, is the highest, most concentrated party organ.

Factional Organization in Agudah and PAY

Internal activity in Agudah in Israel has been based primarily on the same ethnic-geographic origins that characterized the Agudah factions abroad. Rabbi Yitzhak Meir Levin remained the dominant political figure of the Israeli, if not the world, party until his death in August 1971. Despite his Polish origins and his ties to the Hasidic rabbi of Gur (whose son-in-law he was), whose followers comprise the main element in the Central (Polish) Faction of Agudah in Israel, Levin was seen as the overall leader of the party and not merely of his Polish constituency. With his death, however, the factional representation has become more pronounced. Replacing Levin in the Kneset is Rabbi Yehudah Abramowitz, also a member of the Hasidic sect of Gur, who is seen more clearly as a representative of the Central Faction and who lacks Levin's supra-factional standing.

Counterbalancing the Polish Central Faction is the Hungarian-Rumanian faction, based largely on the followers of the Hasidic rabbi of Wishnitz. This faction is represented in the Kneset by S. Y. Gross, who resigned for the last year of his term in the previous Kneset to allow Rabbi Ya'akov Mizrahi, a Yemenite religious leader from Rehovot and head of the Sephardi faction, to have a turn in the Kneset, in the hope that this move would cement its loyalty. Until recently, Agudah had no official faction based on Sephardi supporters as there were comparatively few of these, of course, though the party began to enter the race for Sephardi votes in Israel, particularly among the Yemenites, in the 1950s.

Representing those of the descendants of the Old Yishuv—the original composition of Agudah in Eretz Yisrael, centered largely in Jerusalem—who have not left for the Neturei Qarta and points outside the Israeli political system is Rabbi Menahem Porush. Himself a descendant of an Old Yishuv Jerusalem family, he heads Agudah's Jerusalem faction.

Not based on ethnic-geographic lines but on historical-generational-ideological ones, Tze'irei Agudat Yisrael, nominally Agudah's "youth" branch, is represented by fifty-eight-year-old Rabbi Shlomo Lorincz. Tze'irei Agudat Yisrael has a history of special militancy, and Rabbi Lorincz maintains this stance. He, for example, introduced the controversial bill in the Kneset in July of

1972 calling for the exclusive recognition of orthodox conversions in defining who is a Jew for purposes of immigrant status.

A smaller, and also somewhat young and militant faction, but one for which Agudah has no spare Kneset seat, is the B'nei Torah ("Sons of Torah"), composed largely of yeshivah students.

Each faction is represented in the Israeli section of the World Actions Committee of Agudah, which in turn is headed by the Israeli section of the World Inner Actions Committee executive. The latter, in turn, is topped by the Israeli section of the Agudah world executive, consisting of the parties' Kneset members and a few top political leaders (a total of seven). The current chairman of both the world and Israeli sections of these bodies is Rabbi Pinhas Levin, brother and successor of the late Rabbi Y. M. Levin. It is in the executive, which meets weekly, that the major day-to-day political decisions are made, though ultimately they are subject to the Israeli section of the Council of Torah Greats. Both the Israeli council and the Agudah executive organs in Israel are considered sections of the world Agudah and world Council of Torah Greats executive organs, whose other two branches have headquarters in New York and London.

Indeed, unlike the situation in the Zionist Mizrahi-ha-Po'el ha-Mizrahi world organization, which is more powerful in Israel than abroad, non-Zionist Agudah has never considered Israel its chief locus of activity, either ideologically or practically. It has always been at least as concerned with the status and welfare of orthodox Jews in countries abroad as with that of its adherents in Israel. With the gradual rebuilding of a center of orthodox life in the Diaspora after World War II, particularly in the United States, equal, if not disproportionate, weight in the movement has shifted to circles abroad that are committed to Jewish life in the Diaspora and not in Israel. Reflecting this shift, the majority of members in all Agudah world executive bodies are from outside Israel,[32] though the Israeli delegation is the largest single one. This is a further contributing factor in the change from the early pattern of cooperation with the state.

The international nature of both the Council of Torah Greats and the Agudah executive is given organizational expression not only in terms of their composition but also in substantive decision-making power. Members of these Agudah bodies from abroad regu-

larly participate in the making of key policy, including such questions as whether to join or reject the coalition, the naming of the
parties' Kneset members, and so forth.[33]

The predominance of the international Agudah organization
over politics in Israel does not indicate that there is no Agudah
organization in Israel. Members of the forty or so local branches[34]
elect branch councils, which in turn elect one to three representatives (according to the size of the branch) to a central committee of
approximately eighty, to which the factions send their representatives as well. In theory, the inner executive of this central committee of the Israeli Agudah decides important questions of party policy in Israel in equal partnership with the Israeli section of the
world Agudah Actions Committee and participates in the executive
thereof. In fact, it is the world Agudah executive, with its ties to
the Agudah centers abroad, which is the chief decision-making
body, while the Israeli hierarchy is just another subordinate national Agudah organization.

There is a strong parallel between this relationship and that of
the world Mizrahi movement and the Israel Mizrahi prior to its
merger with ha-Po'el ha-Mizrahi, when the balance shifted to Israel.
Unlike their respective labor offshoots, PAY and ha-Po'el ha-Mizrahi, neither party was based on a labor organization, hence neither
had a very large or easily identified membership. The concept of
membership in each was more one of "followership," or ideological
or socio-cultural adherence, than one of fixed financial commitment.
Since there was little or no need for a regular paid bureaucracy to
provide services, as in the labor parties, the branches were few and
weak, with no full-time employees and no full-time activities of a
political nature other than at election time, and even then the ideologically committed would vote for the party with or without much
electioneering and propaganda. Whatever activities did take place
were largely of a religious-cultural or educational type, both parties
being primarily concerned with their educational systems.

A further indication of its impotence is the fact that the un-
wieldly Agudah national central committee (eighty members) meets
infrequently. Moreover, its composition is of dubious constitution-
ality, as the factional representatives on it were appointed by the
last Knesiyah Gedolah (World Agudah Convention), held in Jerusalem in 1965, according to its estimate of factional strength in Israel,

rather than being elected by a national convention, as they are supposed to be. The fact that no national election or convention of the Agudah party in Israel had been held in twenty-five years, long before the Knesiyah, indicates that decisions of the Agudah party are made largely outside the framework of the Israeli party itself and that, in accordance with its traditional forms, decisions are made and power lies at the top of the party, with little effort made at maintenance of even a facade of democratic voting and other procedures.

A notable step forward in this regard was the holding of internal party elections to select delegates to the national convention in 1976. The main factions fared as follows: Central faction (Abramowicz), 27.7 percent; Jerusalem faction (Porush), 24.9 percent; Youth faction (Lorincz), 21.5 percent; Hungarian-Rumanian faction (Gross), 12.4 percent; Sephardim (Mizrahi), 8.9 percent. The remaining splinter factions followed with negligible totals.

While such an exercise in democratic procedures is relatively novel in Agudah, it does not necessarily represent a democratization of the party. Rather, it reflects a need to adjust the power relations between existing traditional factions, including the determination of the order of candidates on the list (and hence their likelihood of being elected) for the upcoming 1977 Kneset elections. The internal party elections do, however, indicate the increasing importance and autonomy of the Israel Agudah in relation to the world movement.

But the world Agudah organization is no more democratic or less elitest than the national organization. In its over sixty-year history Agudah has held only five world conventions, the last one in 1965, the previous one in 1954, and the one before that back in 1937, despite the fact that such conventions are supposed to be held once every five years and their delegates are supposed to be democratically elected.[35] The party structure in general is undemocratic, traditional, and non-elective; it is in fact controlled by its top executive and rabbinical leadership. While the Mizrahi-ha-Po'el ha-Mizrahi movement has often postponed its world convention in its over seventy-year history and its executive organs often assume the prerogatives of the convention, nevertheless it has held some twenty-two of them, at far more frequent intervals; elections have generally been held for delegates to these conventions.

Above the Knesiyah in the world organizational hierarchy of Agudah is the World Actions Committee. Its three sections—New York, London, and Israel—number approximately 140. Above this body is an Inner Actions Committee of half the size which is similarly divided into three sections, as is the top party organ, the executive, with seven representatives in the Israeli section, four in the European, and four in the American. It is again in the executive that major party decisions are taken on a regular basis.

The "supreme organ of Agudat Yisrael" is the world Mo'etzet Gedolei ha-Torah, or Council of Torah Greats, which again is divided into the three familiar sections, though in fact each national Agudah is supposed to have its own council.[36] The council and its subdivisions (the organization is fluid) convene only as often as necessary to decide matters of Agudah policy and to issue vetoes, orders, and opinions based on the authority of the Torah, or their interpretation thereof, to the Agudah executive organs. Its decisions are not generally made public except on important policy questions such as whether or not to join the coalition. Among other issues dealt with by the Israeli section of the council over the years are the question of National Service for women; the establishment of a URF; the founding of Agudah's independent educational system; reparations from Germany; the entry of PAY into the government and its breakaway from Agudah; missionary activities in Israel; autopsies; etc.[37] The council is composed of rabbinical leaders who are, for the most part, either heads of large *yeshivot* or Hasidic rabbis. Among the latter are, of course, the rabbis of Gur and Wishnitz, whose followers comprise the backbone of two of the largest factions. The council is a traditional, ascriptive, nondemocratic body elected by cooptation.

As in many other areas of comparison, PAY shows some of the organizational characteristics of both Mafdal and Agudah. Based, like Mafdal, on a labor organization, the party must provide the social services expected of a labor party in Israel. It does so via specific agreements with the Histadrut, which enable PAY members to participate fully in the Histadrut's labor unions and Qupat Holim. PAY, unlike Mafdal and Agudah, has many more members (47,000 including working wives[38]) than voters, primarily because many Agudah voters join the PAY labor organization for the social benefits it provides.

Also like Mafdal, the chief focus of PAY—though it remains officially non-Zionist—is Israel. Thus the chief organs of the party are composed of Israelis. These organs include a 155-member central committee, which meets three times yearly and, like the Mafdal central committee, deals only with matters of principle, rather than of specific policy; an executive committee of 29, which meets bimonthly and which does decide broader issues of policy and appointments, such as the composition of the party's Kneset list; a secretariat of 18, headed by Secretary-General Avraham Werdiger, which meets weekly and deals with the day-to-day operation of the party. Given the party's small size and hence its parliamentary delegation of two, matters of party policy or votes in the Kneset and the like cannot be left to the parliamentary delegation alone, as in Mafdal. Thus the party has established a parliamentary committee of nine, including the two Kneset members, for such purposes.

Decisionmaking in PAY is not subject to the ultimate veto of the Mo'etzet Gedolei ha-Torah; in fact, it is in the hands of the party's secular institutions. However, over the years the party has adopted several different leading rabbis as its "rabbinical guides."

Because of the party's miniscule size, it is the most centralized of the three religious parties, as it no longer has even the institution of factions to counteract the consolidating force. What factions there were—pro-Agudah, pro-ha-Po'el ha-Mizrahi, and the dominant pro-independent—were dissolved in the late 1950s as the final break with Agudah loomed imminent and their existence was no longer justified.

Internal party elections to the convention are, as in Agudah, rather infrequent; the last was in 1969, the one before that thirteen years earlier.[39] Like other matters of internal representation, the elections are now divided on the basis of branches and their sizes, rather than factions. There are currently some forty-six branches, with more or less proportionate representation. Thus the secretariat is divided as follows: three representatives from Jerusalem, three from B'nei Braq, three from Tel Aviv, two from Haifa, one from the Negev, one from Petah Tiqva, four from the party's agricultural settlements, and one Sephardi (despite their 30 percent composition in the party). Each of the branches has a paid full-time or part-time secretary, appointed by the central committee. Like Agudah, the branches' activities are in large measure centered about religious-cultural-social activities, but, as in Mafdal, a tax-collecting department handles the regular dues for the labor organization, giving a more permanent character to PAY branches.

The social composition of PAY also resembles the other two religious parties. On the one hand, it was once part of Agudah, so that it shares some of the same sources of strength, particularly Polish and to a lesser extent German orthodoxy. Many of these members are also Hasidim, yeshivah students and graduates, and so forth. On the other hand, PAY as a labor party has a larger labor component, much like ha-Po'el ha-Mizrahi–Mafdal, and, also like Mafdal, a disproportionate percentage of its labor organization members are white-collar office workers, teachers, and so forth, rather than industrial workers. Finally, while it is primarily an urban party, PAY's string of agricultural settlements gives it, like Mafdal, an important rural component completely absent in Agudah.

The Members

While votership rather than membership is the best yardstick for measurement and comparison insofar as the religious parties of Israel are concerned, an analysis of the membership yields certain insights into their nature.

In Agudah, membership drives are held in earnest only before elections to the very rare national conventions, with each faction seeking to inflate its percentage of the vote. Even then membership requires only a one-time nominal dues payment, rather than the regular monthly deductions familiar to ha-Po'el ha-Mizrahi, PAY, or Histadrut members. Hence, following a pattern typical of patron-type parties, its membership figures are as unrealistic as they are unreliable, and those figures are never broken down by categories which would indicate the nature of that membership. The best approximation of the character of Agudah membership may be gleaned indirectly through non-statistical avenues of analysis: the largely ethnic composition of the factions; the more ascriptive, traditional nature of Agudah membership; the highly concentrated pattern of voting strength, confined largely to the religious, traditional, poorer neighborhoods of the older urban settlements; and the nature of its education-socialization system.

PAY, as a labor organization, has a more fixed membership. It is placed at 38,000 (male heads of households; 47,000 if working mothers are counted) by Secretary-General Werdiger. About three-fourths of these are urban workers; one-fourth are members of PAY's rural settlements. Beyond this, there are no statistics to show occupation, educational level, age, or other indices. It is curious that PAY alone among the parties has a far higher membership than votership (some 25,000 in the 1969 Kneset elections), quite the opposite of Agudah. The phenomenon is attributable to the fact that many members of the PAY labor organization maintained their membership even after the split with the Agudah parent party in 1960 for the sake of the social services it provides or has access to, such as the Histadrut's Qupat Holim. When it comes to voting, however, many revert to the Agudah line.

The tendency of many Agudah voters to be formal members of another religious party for the purpose of obtaining health and other benefits has now been extended to Mafdal, with serious repercussions for the delicate factional balance in that party as it faces the 1977 elections. Many younger Agudah voters, particularly students of the large *yeshivot* in Jerusalem and B'nei B'raq who never had ties to PAY, prefer the more comprehensive services available to them via membership in ha-Po'el ha-Mizrahi. As mentioned above, membership in the labor organization automatically confers membership in the parent party, Mafdal. As such a considerable number—estimated at up to twenty-five thousand Agudists—constitute a potential swing vote in any internal elections held in advance of the 1977 Kneset elections to determine, among other things, the relative strengths of the factions, the order of their representatives on the Kneset list, and the dividing up of cabinet posts.

Each of the major factions in Mafdal views this phenomenon from its own perspective. The largest faction, la-Mifneh, headed by Interior Minister Yosef Burg, has the most to lose from this infusion of Agudah votes, given the traditionally more liberal religious and political views of this faction and the fact that it currently controls much of the party machine. The third largest faction, the Tze'irim, headed by Social Welfare Minister Zevulun Hammer, has in fact long propounded the opening up of the party to a broader range of religious voters in Israel. The group they have in mind, however, is not Agudah opportunists but those middle-class, educated graduates of Mafdal's own education-socialization system who, anxious for political power and material success, are no longer attracted to the party by the old ideological appeals or the socialized welfare services of ha-Po'el ha-Mizrahi. The Tze'irim hope to draw in such people by reactivating the constitutional provision allowing individuals to join Mafdal without having to enroll in ha-Po'el ha-Mizrahi.

Both these factions, hitherto in conflict as the party establishment versus the party Young Turks, are nonetheless united in an alliance against the second largest faction, now called Likud u-Temurah, headed by Minister of Religions Yitzhak Refael. The latter, it is alleged, has used his position to allocate government funds to various Agudah-oriented *yeshivot* in the hope of "buying" the loyalties of their students, who are eligible to vote in Mafdal elections. These votes would make Refael's faction the largest and put Refael himself at the top of the Kneset list. Refael's supporters do not deny the fact of the aid but do dispute the motive imputed to it. In any event, the two other major factions have consorted to prevent these Agudah–ha-Po'el ha-Mizrahi voters from exercising their suffrage by inserting into the party's election rules a provision which prohibits any member of another party which held internal elections in the past year (i.e., Agudah) from voting in any Mafdal internal elections held prior to the 1977 general elections. Given this restriction, as well as the fear of other factions that the Tze'irim might make some gains with their ultra-nationalistic appeals, the likelihood is that no new internal elections will be held before the Ninth Kneset elections scheduled for May of 1977.[40]

The only one of the three religious parties for which at least partial detailed data on membership are available is Mafdal, but here, too, there are serious limitations on the quality and quantity of the figures. The only comprehensive membership survey ever conducted was directed in 1966 by the Organization Department of ha-Po'el ha-Mizrahi[41] and therefore automatically excluded some five to six thousand Mafdal members who, for one reason or another, were not also members of the ha-Po'el ha-Mizrahi labor organization. Also excluded were about the same number of members (household heads only) who lived in ha-Po'el ha-Mizrahi agricultural settlements. Both exclusions were probably more technically than politically motivated, since neither group pays the regular monthly dues which cover the social services of ha-Po'el ha-Mizrahi, the former because they do not receive such services, the latter because they pay indirectly through their settlement. Subtracting these 12,000 or so from the 60,000 total party membership that year, the remaining 48,000 members included in the survey do constitute some 80 percent of Mafdal membership. This is an enlightening, if partial, picture of the nature of the party's membership.

From Table 4.1 it is readily apparent that a majority of the ha-Po'el ha-Mizrahi membership remains blue-collar working class. Furthermore, the largest single group is located on the lowest point on the socioeconomic ladder, that of unskilled laborers or hired agricultural workers. In any event, the laborer component of the party is far larger than in the population at large and hence is (or was in 1966) large enough to classify this as a genuine labor party on the Israeli political spectrum. Nevertheless, the 1969 party report notes a decline in the percentage of unskilled laborers in the party ranks,[42] a trend in line with developments in most industrial nations.

At the opposite end of the socioeconomic scale, only a very small percentage of ha-Po'el ha-Mizrahi members were professionals in 1966. This fact caused the party great anxiety and stimulated efforts to recruit young professionals and to rethink its educational priorities, apparently with some success: the 1969 party report points to a gradual takeover of leadership positions from old labor union types by younger professionals, intellectuals, teachers, and the like.[43] Nevertheless, the 1973 party document reports that in the prosperous 1969–72 period the recruitment of professionals for both membership and leadership positions was difficult. Middle-class, well-educated products of Mafdal's own education-socialization system, as well as immigrants from both the affluent West and the Soviet Union, are no longer attracted by the Qupat Holim health services provided through membership in ha-Po'el ha-Mizrahi, preferring private and other health plans.[44] Rising standards of living have also made it difficult to recruit part-time, low-paid branch secretaries, even among teachers who have always been an important component in the Mizrahi–ha-Po'el ha-Mizrahi constituency, manning the Mizrahi school system and propagating the party values. Though much smaller in numbers than teachers, rab-

Table 4.1. Occupational Characteristics of Mafdal Membership

Occupation	Percentage
Workers	
Unskilled laborers and agricultural workers	21.03
Industrial	17.82
Service	3.70
Building	7.86
Unemployed, pensioners, etc.	6.94
Subtotal	57.35
Artisans	6.96
White collar	
Clerks	7.39
Local authority employees	5.41
State employees	5.86
Organizational employees	1.99
Religious council employees	1.94
Subtotal	22.59
Rabbis	0.31
Educators	10.90
Professionals	1.76
Total	99.87
Total taxpaying members	48,460

Source: Ha-Mifkad ha-Irguni. The total of taxpaying members given in the table does not include members of ha-Po'el ha-Mizrahi agricultural settlements because each settlement pays dues for them (see *Report to the Third Mafdal Convention,* p. 10, which lists total membership in 1966 as 53,966, of which 5,506 fall into this category). The total does not include persons who are members of Mafdal only and not of ha-Po'el ha-Mizrahi; there are about 5,500 people in this category. Thus, we have a total of almost 60,000 members in 1966, 48,000 (four-fifths, or 80 percent) of whom are included in *Ha-Mifkad ha-Irguni.* Working wives who are ha-Po'el ha-Mizrahi members are not included in the total; if they were, the figure would rise again to 79,681. Non-working wives and children of members are also excluded from the total; adding them would bring the final figure to 155,172.

bis have traditionally been disproportionately influential in party politics. Other religious-political appointees include the employees of the religious councils, which have long been Mafdal-dominated. Most of the other white-collar workers—employees of local authorities, government ministries, or national organizations like the Jewish Agency—are similarly subject to and dependent upon the amount of political influence their party can bring to bear, for in the Israeli political culture, the device of the interparty coalition and the subsequent use of the party key to divide up patronage is firmly institutionalized. Hence the relative share of Mafdal in the various bureaucracies depends upon its maintaining its political strength and upon its continued participation in coalitions on all levels.

The educational levels of the ha-Po'el ha-Mizrahi membership (Table 4.2) correspond closely to occupational status. The bulk of the membership, some 43.5 percent, attained a maximal educational level of elementary school only, while another 16 percent or so completed only an elementary religious education, for a total of 59.5 percent. One can assume a close correlation between this figure and the 57.3 percent of the membership who are classified as workers.

At the other end of the educational ladder, a rather high percentage of the membership (almost 25 percent) possesses secular secondary or higher educational qualifications (which are neither free nor compulsory in Israel), while another 8.5 percent received higher religious (yeshivah) education (including rabbinical ordination), for a total of 33.5 percent, or one-third of the membership. Included among these are the professionals, teachers, and rabbis, who comprise about 13 percent of the membership; they generally have had higher education, whether religious or secular. The remaining 20 percent of the professional group probably is drawn from the white-collar members, many of whom have at least a secondary school background.

The educational statistics take on another dimension entirely when they are examined in the light of ethnic change. (While the survey uses the familiar euphemisms "new immigrants" and "veteran population," the meaning is really Sephardi and Ashkenazi.) It is interesting that almost identical percentages of both groups have had an elementary education. (This confirms our conclusion in Chapter 7 that the Mafdal education-socialization system has worked fairly efficiently on the elementary level.) The inter-group differences are far more egregious, however, on the secondary and higher levels, where the "new immigrants" fall far behind the "veterans" in their educational attainments. Mafdal long realized that the bottleneck in its educational system was the secondary school and that the casualties of the system were the Sephardi immigrant children, few of whom continued on to secondary school and even fewer to higher educational institutions; the ultimate result was fewer votes for Mafdal. As a result, both the religious and

Table 4.2. Educational Characteristics of Mafdal Membership

Education	ha-Po'elit ha-Mizrahi	"New Immigrants" (Sephardim)	"Veteran Population" (Ashkenazim)
No formal education	7.48	14.54	4.14
Elementary religious education	16.05	21.17	8.45
Secondary, higher religious education (including ordination)	8.50	6.42	11.28
Elementary general education	43.48	43.45	43.84
Secondary, higher, university education (including degree-holders)	24.49	14.40	32.27
Totals	100.00	99.98	99.98

Source: see Table 4.1.

political effectiveness of the Mafdal socialization system has been seriously weakened.

Indeed, the initial preference of many Sephardi immigrants for the religious education system reflects their traditional way of life, of which religion was only a part, though a central one, more than it does a commitment to the strict observance of a more rationalized orthodox religion in the Western sense and the political and party ramifications which this bears in the Israeli context. With their gradual secularization in Israel, their commitment to religion, religious education, and religious political parties began to decline. A sample of the religious and political attitudes in Israel taken in 1966, has shown that Sephardi immigrants are, in general, much more faithful in religious observance than their Ashkenazi colleagues, but the children of the former are significantly less observant than their fathers, while the children of the latter are about as observant as their parents.[45] Although their level of personal religious observance has declined, the tradition is strong enough for second-generation Sephardim to oppose separation of religion and state as forcefully as their fathers, while their Ashkenazi counterparts favor separation more than their elders.

The phenomenon uncovered here is a modified form of the modernization scheme. Sephardim are modernized and secularized to the point where personal religious observance declines, yet because of their residual traditionalism they still favor the retention of a traditional religious aura of legitimacy in the society. Whether this passive commitment to religion alone is sufficient to hold them in the ranks of a religious party, however, is questionable.

On the other hand, the already somewhat modernized Ashkenazim, whose religious observance, if any, is perhaps more in line with the Western idea of a voluntary, individual commitment to rationalized principles, have thereby already considered the idea of separation of religion and the public domain, and can more decisively accept or reject the idea and all that it implies for the religious parties, particularly Mafdal. That party, in turn, would prefer the latter type of individual. It hopes to breed such citizens in its education-socialization system, particularly in its secondary schools.

Because far fewer Sephardim attend high school, in the Mafdal system or elsewhere, Mafdal has not been successful quantitatively in imbuing many younger Sephardim with such a religious or political commitment. Of those small numbers of Sephardim who do go through high school and beyond, however, an unusually large percentage votes for religious parties. The survey cited above, which found a sharp decline in religious voting among Sephardim as they acquire education above the elementary level (16 percent of the elementary school graduates but only 7 percent of the high school ones vote religious), also found a reversal of that trend as educational levels increase further: 25 percent of Sephardim with more than high school education vote religious.[46] Apparently, the religious educational process, particularly that of Mafdal, is able to reverse the modernization scenario somewhat and provides an augmented, if rationalized, commitment to tradition along with higher education. Unless the efforts at increasing the percentage of Sephardim in its secondary schools and beyond are successful on a large scale, however, Mafdal can look forward to a decline in Sephardi membership and votership, as well as in pupil population—a decline which is in fact already taking place.

According to a rough estimate derived from the survey, the membership of Mafdal (more precisely, of ha-Po'el ha-Mizrahi) was approximately 45 percent Sephardi and 55 percent Ashkenazi as of 1966. This is something of a decline from the 1950s, when the mostly Sephardi immigrants were apportioned arbitrarily by the party key, yet it is more than the 40 vs. 60 percent that is regarded by most observers as a realistic estimate today. In order to stem the flow of Sephardi votes out of its ranks, Mafdal must not only promote and provide far greater educational opportunities for Sephardim in its educational system (as it has begun to do) but must also grant them greater access to positions of leadership in the party itself.

The party's old line East European Ashkenazi elite has been similarly unresponsive to another important but growing internal minority, youth. The formative experiences of native-born products of Mafdal's education-socialization system within an independent Jewish state, in the army, and so forth, are quite different from those the elite knew in their youth abroad. The generational conflicts had already engendered the rise of a youth faction, the Tze'irim. By 1966 some 40 percent of ha-Po'el ha-Mizrahi's membership was under thirty. This group could only be expected to grow, if for no other than natural causes, especially as the children of the large-scale immigration of the early fifties came of age. In fact, the party's membership was given an additional boost one year later by the Six Day War, in whose wake some five thousand new members, many of them young, joined ha-Po'el ha-Mizrahi. The 1969 party report attributes this sharp rise to the party's playing up its long-standing nationalistic tendencies, particularly vis-à-vis the question of the occupied territories.[47] The war may have helped in another way as well: the economic boom and full employment economy which replaced the prewar recession enabled more workers to afford the high monthly dues of ha-Po'el ha-Mizrahi, though, as noted above, this trend did not catch up as many professionals as the party had hoped.

As the party endeavors to increase the number of the better educated, younger ha-Po'el ha-Mizrahi members and to raise both the educational and occupational level of the party in the direction of higher socioeconomic status, the challenge for Mafdal is a complex one: the party must do its best to keep those better educated, upwardly mobile young people within the ranks of orthodoxy in general, and of Mafdal in particular, as it has apparently done with some success for a limited number of highly educated Sephardim. In order to do so, however, it must further readjust its ideology away from the earlier labor-left tenets embodied in the "historic partnership" with the Labor party and toward the middle-class and largely nationalistic values and aspirations of the younger members, who seek a far greater role for the party in the political and economic life of Israel than that alliance has traditionally allowed.

Further, the party elite must be active in promoting younger members into its ranks, something which it has been slow in doing in the past. It is precisely these values and political aspirations which have been embodied in the Tze'irim faction.

The elite has also been unresponsive to another large constituency in the membership, women. As noted above, the 1966 survey showed that there were about 22,000 working wives who held membership in ha-Po'el ha-Mizrahi, above and beyond non-working wives of members. The problem of the representation of and by women in the party was seen in religious terms at the very outset, and Mizrahi and ha-Po'el ha-Mizrahi have allowed women a far greater level of participation than have Agudah and PAY. But the representation of women in the party elite remains minimal.

The Leaders

Table 4.3,[48] a summary of some of the "vital statistics" on the men (and the woman) who have served as members of Kneset and/or cabinet ministers, provides objective criteria about the political elite of the religious parties. However, Kneset or cabinet membership may not be equally significant in all three parties, or even for each individual member. In Mafdal, because of the party's factional nature, Kneset membership is usually, though not always, related to leadership of one of the factions, but some individuals are placed in safe spots on the party's Kneset list for other reasons, such as ethnic (usually Sephardi) appeal. Such individuals are members of the party's symbolic elite, though not of its functional elite. A member who has been a minister or deputy minister is usually a member of the inner functional party elite. Other top party bureaucrats who wield great power and functionally can be considered members of that elite are omitted from the table because there are no objective criteria to decide which bureaucrats are or are not at any given time sufficiently influential to be considered in the group.

Because of PAY's very small size, its elite and Kneset delegation of two are identical. Rabbi Dr. Kalman Kahana, a member of Kneset, is president of PAY and editor-in-chief of its newspaper, *She'arim*. Avraham Werdiger, the other member, is secretary-general of the PAY labor organization.

Whether Agudah's Kneset delegation is simultaneously its elite is far more problematic. As a clerically dominated party, Agudah views its Council of Torah Greats as its symbolic leadership in several ways. First, the Council is regarded by Agudists as the ultimate repository of religious legitimacy, determining the "Torah position" on any given issue. In this sense, the Council's authority extends beyond the symbolic realm into the functional. Furthermore, many of the rabbis who comprise the Council are, at the same time, heads of the largest Hasidic sects, which are closely identified with national origin or ethnic groups. These groups are, in turn, the bases for the factions in Agudah. Thus these rabbis may rightly be considered the elite of the party. However, the Council and its member rabbis are not ordinarily involved in day-to-day political affairs. Barring a major issue of principle, they confine themselves to the legitimating and symbolic functions of leadership. The operational authority is delegated to the Kneset representatives, who may be considered the party's functional elite.

One salient characteristic of the elites of all three parties has been their advanced age, which is slowly changing under the inexorable pressure of death. As Table 4.4 shows, of all thirty-one individuals who have served as members of Kneset on the Mizrahi-ha-Po'el ha-Mizrahi–Mafdal ticket, twenty-four were born at least sixty years ago or more; only two of them were born between fifty and sixty years ago; only one is between forty and fifty years old; four are between thirty and forty years old. What we have, then, is a pattern wherein the old veteran leaders remain as long as possible, preventing the middle-aged leadership from taking power and the young elite members filling the gaps left by such attrition. The current average age of Mafdal Kneset members and ministers is 53.3 years; in 1973 it was 55.8; in 1970, before the deaths of Shapira and Ben-Meir senior, it was 56.8. This was slightly above the then overall average age of Kneset members of 54.5.[49]

As for PAY, three out of four men who have served as PAY Kneset members were born well over sixty years ago. One, Kahana, is still a member at age sixty-six. Benyamin Mintz died at fifty-five; Ya'akov Katz was killed in an auto accident at sixty-two. His replacement was Avraham Werdiger, fifty-five. The average age of the delegation is currently sixty.

Table 4.3. Characteristics of Individual Members of Religious Party Elites, 1949–76

Party	Year of Birth	Birthplace	Year of Immigration	Knesets Served In	Dates	Highest Education	Ordained	Stated Non-Political Occupation
Mafdal								
Abuhatzeira, A.	1938	Morocco	1949	8	1974–	univ.	no	educator
Avtebi, E.	1938	Iran	1950	8	1974–	agric. school	no	agriculturalist
Ben-Meir, S. Y.[1,2]	1910	Poland	1950	2–7	1952–71	J.S.D.	yes	rabbi, lawyer
Ben-Meir, Y.	1939	U.S.	1962	7, 8	1971–	Ph.D.	yes	psychologist
Burg, Yosef[1,3]	1909	Germany	1939	1–8	1949–	Ph.D.	yes	educator
Don Yihyeh, S.	1907	Latvia	1931	6	1965	n.a.[4]	no	journalist
Friedmann, S.	1911	Poland	1938	7, 8	1969–73, 1975–	high school, yeshivah	yes	agriculturalist
Genehovsky, E.	1901	Poland	1933	1–2	1949–55	n.a.	no	n.a.
Goldrat, A.	1911	Poland	1933	1	1949–51	n.a.	no	n.a.
Goldschmidt, Y.[2]	1907	Germany	1935	7	1969–73	univ., teacher's dipl.	no	educator
Greenberg, Y.	1900	Poland	1934	1, 3, 4–5	1949–51, 1955–63	yeshivah	no	n.a.
Hammer, Z.[2,3]	1936	Israel	—	7, 8	1969–	B.A.	no	educator
Hazani, M.[2,3]	1913	Poland	1932	2–8	1951–75	univ.	yes	agriculturalist
Kalmar, M.	1901	Poland	1921	1, 2, 3, 5	1949, 1951–59, 1963–65	n.a.	no	n.a.
Levi, D.	1917	Spanish N. Africa	1957	6–7	1965–73	univ.	no	businessman
Maimon, Y. L.[1,3]	1875	Russia	1913	1	1949–51	yeshivah	yes	rabbi
Melamed, A.	1924	Lithuania	1948	7, 8	1969–	univ.	yes	lawyer-economist, agriculturalist
Neriya, M. Z.	1913	Poland	1930	7	1969–73	yeshivah, teacher's sem.	yes	rabbi
Nurok, M.[1,3]	1884	Latvia	1947	1–5	1949–65	univ.	yes	rabbi
Pinkus, D.[1,3]	1895	Hungary	1925	1–2	1949–52	univ.	no	businessman
Refael, Y.[2,3]	1914	Poland	1935	2–8	1954–	M.A., doctorate	no	historian
Sanhedrai, T.	1906	Poland	1934	4–7	1959–73	high school	–	educator
Shaag, A.[1]	1886	Israel	—	1	1949–51	yeshivah	no	businessman
Shahor, B.[2]	1916	Israel	—	4–7	1959–73	yeshivah	no	"politician"

Name	Birth	Origin	Elected	Knesset	Term	Education	[4]	Occupation
Shaki, Avraham	1906	Yemen	1913	5	1961–65	n.a.	no	n.a.
Shaki, Avner[2]	1928	Israel	—	7	1970–73	J.S.D.	no	lawyer
Shapira, M. H.[3]	1902	Lithuania	1925	1–7	1949–70	yeshivah	no	"politician"
Sheinman, P.	1912	Poland	1948	8	1974–	univ.	no	businessman
Suaritz, F.	1907	Libya	1949	3–6	1955–69	yeshivah high school	yes	rabbi
Unna, M.[2]	1902	Germany	1927	1–6	1949–69	high school, agric. school	no	agriculturalist
Warhaftig, Z.[2,3]	1906	Poland	1947	1–8	1949–	J.S.D.	yes	lawyer
Agudat Yisrael								
Abramowitz, Y.	1913	Poland	1935	7, 8	1971–	yeshivah	yes	rabbi
Ben Ya'akov, Z.	1897	Poland	1935	2–3	1953–59	n.a.	n.a.	n.a.
Deutsch, A.	1889	Hungary	1945	2	1951–53	n.a.	n.a.	n.a.
Gross, S.	1908	Hungary	1950	3–7, 8	1955–72	yeshivah, high school	no	journalist
Levenstein, M.	1905	Denmark	1934	1	1949–51	n.a.	n.a.	businessman
Levin, Y. M.[3]	1893	Poland	1940	1–7	1949–71	yeshivah	yes	rabbi
Lorincz, S.	1918	Hungary	1939	2–8	1951–	yeshivah	yes	rabbi
Mazor, E.	1889	Poland	1940	1	1949–51	n.a.	n.a.	n.a.
Mizrahi, Y.	1922	Israel	—	7	1972–73	yeshivah	yes	rabbi
Porush, M.	1916	Israel	—	4–8	1959–76	yeshivah	yes	journalist
Po'alei Agudat Yisrael								
Kahana, K.[2]	1910	Poland	1938	1–8	1949–	Ph.D.	yes	rabbi
Katz, Y.	1906	Poland	1934	3–6	1955–68	n.a.	no	n.a.
Mintz, B.[3]	1903	Poland	1932	1–4	1949–61	n.a.	no	businessman
Werdiger, A.	1921	Poland	1949	6–8	1968–	univ.	no	"politician"

Sources: Mi va-Mi be Yisrael 1971–72 [Who's who in Israel, 1971–72] (Tel Aviv: Bronfman and Cohen, 1972); Yitzhak Refael, ed., *Entziklopediyah shel ha-tziyonut ha-Datit* [Encyclopedia of religious Zionism] (Jerusalem: Mosad ha-Rav Kook, 1958–71); State of Israel, *Government Yearbook* 5711 (1950) to 5732 (1972) (Jerusalem: Government Printer, 1950–72); David Tidhar, ed., *Entziklopediyah le-Halutzei ha-Yishuv u-Vonav* [Encyclopedia of the Yishuv and its builders] (Tel Aviv: Sefarim Rishmim, 1947–57); Asher Tzidon, *Beit ha-Nivharim* [The House of Representatives], 6th rev. ed. (Tel Aviv: Ahiasaf, 1971); *Who's Who in Israel and in the Work for Israel Abroad 1969–70* (Tel Aviv: Bronfman and Cohen, 1970); interviews.

[1]Mizrahi.

[2]Served as deputy minister.

[3]Served as minister, which at times has involved resignation of Kneset seat for purposes of elite circulation.

[4]Not available.

Table 4.4. Characteristics of Religious Party Elites, 1949–76

Party/Characteristic	Age		Year of Immigration		Highest Education[1]		Occupation[1,2]		Origin[4]	
Mafdal	60+	24	pre-1920	2	high school	1	educator	5	Poland	12
	50–60	2	1920s	4	agric. school	1	rabbi[3]	5(1)	Israel	4
	40–50	1	1930s	11	yeshivah	8	businessman	4	Germany	3
	30–40	4	pre-state 1940s	3	some univ. or	10	lawyer	3(1)	Lithuania	2
			post-state	7	equivalent		agriculturalist	3(1)	Latvia	2
			Israeli-born	4	doctorate	6	journalist	2	Russia	1
							politician	2	Hungary	1
							psychologist	1	Yemen	1
							historian	1	Libya	1
									Span. N. Africa	1
									Morocco	1
									Iran	1
									U.S.	1
PAY	60+	3	1930s	3	some univ.	1	rabbi	1	Poland	4
	50–60	1	pre-state 1940s	1	doctorate	1	businessman	1		
							politician	1		
Agudat Yisrael	60+	8	1930s	4	yeshivah	5	rabbi	4	Poland	4
	50–60	2	pre-state 1940s	3	high school	1	journalist	2	Hungary	3
			post-state	1			businessman	1	Israel	2
			Israeli-born	2					Denmark	1

Source: see Table 4.3.

[1] Where information is available.

[2] Secondary professions are listed in parentheses.

[3] Eleven were ordained rabbis, though only five considered the rabbinate their primary profession.

[4] In Mafdal, 25 Ashkenazim and 6 Sephardim; in PAY, all Ashkenazim; in Agudat Yisrael, 9 Ashkenazim and 1 Sephardi.

In 1973 the Agudah elite had dropped to its youngest level in many years, averaging 55.7. In 1971, before the death of patriarch Rabbi Yitzhak Meir Levin and the resignation of S. Y. Gross, the average age was a more characteristic (for Agudah) 61.2. With the exchange of Rabbi Menahem Porush for the older S. Y. Gross in an inter-factional squabble in 1976, and with the loss of a fourth Kneset seat as a result of the joint slate with PAY in the 1973 elections, the Agudah elite has now reached the venerable average age of sixty-three.

While the religious party Kneset members are slightly above the average age of members of that body in general, in the case of Mafdal, at least, they are getting younger with the slow but steady turnover. At the same time, the average age of Kneset members is increasing. The phenomenon is not due to any particular sudden concern of the religious parties for youth except where, as in the case of the Mafdal Tze'irim, their hand was forced—but reflects the fact that their elites were older to begin with, and are now being replaced by relatively younger ones. Inevitably, the same process will apply to both Agudah and PAY. The phenomenon of an aging elite is not confined to the religious parties but is endemic to the Israeli political system as a whole.

More revealing as to the social composition of the parties themselves are the origins of the elites. Because they were not indigenous, the parties have until recently had largely immigrant elites. Very few leaders (four out of thirty-one in Mafdal, two out of ten in Agudah) are native-born, slightly below the overall Kneset average of 24 percent Israeli-born.[50] The rate of increase of Israeli-born members in the parties' Kneset delegations is another indicator of the slow turnover of the elites.

Of the bulk of foreign-born members in Mafdal, the largest bloc of twelve is Polish-born, indicating the seminal importance of that once-great Jewish community in the development of Mizrahi and ha-Po'el ha-Mizrahi. Added to those twelve are two each from Lithuania and Latvia, and one from Russia. Thus sixteen, or over half the total, come from the former Russian Empire in eastern Europe. Once again, this is characteristic of the Kneset members as a whole, 55 percent of whom were born in eastern Europe.[51] The small but active Mizrahi and ha-Po'el ha-Mizrahi movement in Germany contributed three individuals to the Mafdal elite. The much larger orthodox community in Hungary, however, which historically was never receptive to Mizrahi ideology, preferring Agudist separatism, produced only one Mafdal (or, more precisely, Mizrahi) leader of note, David Tzvi Pinkus. The sole American-born Kneset member of Mafdal (or any religious party) is thirty-seven-year-old Dr. Yehudah Ben-Meir, son of the long-time Mizrahi member Rabbi S. Y. Ben-Meir (Rosenberg). Though Polish-born, Dr. Ben-Meir senior lived in the United States for some thirty years.

All these Mafdal members, plus three out of the four Israeli-born ones, are Ashkenazim. Of the six Sephardim, one was born in Yemen, one in Libya, one in Spanish North Africa, one in Morocco, one in Iran, and one in Israel (Dr. Avner Shaki, of Yemenite origin). The Sephardim are in fact notoriously under-represented in the Kneset delegations of all the parties, with the possible exception of Mapai.[52] But in Mafdal, a party whose votership is roughly half Sephardi and which counts heavily on retaining a large number of the traditionally minded Sephardim loyal to it, the inequity is particularly glaring.

Furthermore, none of those Sephardim who were placed in safe spots on the Mafdal Kneset list were given access to the inner elite and to positions of decision-making power. Rather, they were what Czudnowski calls "pseudo-representatives,"[53] symbolic or decorative figures put forth to attract or reward particular Sephardi ethnic voters. Four out of the six members seem to have been selected more for their appeal to their fellow immigrants than for any demonstrable political ability. None was given important committee assignments or a deputy ministerial portfolio, much less a ministerial one, with one possible exception: Dr. Avner Shaki, a highly educated and articulate young law professor who was co-opted onto the Mafdal list before the Seventh Kneset elections in 1969 and placed fifteenth, succeeding to a seat only with the death of Shapira in 1970. Sensitive to the criticism that Sephardi Kneset members were not given positions of responsibility, the party, by interfactional consensus, made Shaki deputy minister of education within one month after he assumed his Kneset seat. Given the great importance which Mafdal attaches to its own system of education and its autonomy, over which its deputy minister traditionally keeps guard, the appointment of a Sephardi, one who had no demonstrated party loyalty, was indeed a significant step.

Shaki, however, was to prove far too independent-minded for Mafdal. He devoted more energy to the advancement of Sephardi children, irrespective of educational track, then to defending the autonomy of the Mafdal educational system. This independence brought him into conflict with the Mafdal elite, which claimed his prior loyalty, and he broke with the party in 1972 when he voted for an Agudah bill proposing a change in the Law of Return. Mafdal, as a coalition member, found the timing of this bill, which limited the extension of immigrant status to those either born Jews or converted by religious law, embarrassing. Shaki was forced to resign his deputy ministership and later declared himself an independent. Needless to say, he did not appear on the Mafdal list for the Eighth Kneset elections in 1973. Given this experience, it may be many more years before Mafdal appoints a Sephardi to a position of power again.

Of the two current Sephardi Mafdal members, one, thirty-eight-year-old Eliezer Avtebi, born in Iran, is in fact the representative of the party's *moshav* movement rather than of any particular ethnic constituency or faction (though the *moshav* population is heavily Sephardi), and as such has limited political influence. The other, Aharon Abuhatzeira, also thirty-eight, is the scion of a Moroccan rabbinical clan which has close ties with Mafdal. He serves as mayor of Ramleh, a city with a large Sephardi population. As a member of the increasingly powerful Refael faction of Mafdal, which depends heavily on this ethnic vote, Abuhatzeira might become the first Sephardi in Mafdal to penetrate into the functional elite.

PAY's elite is entirely drawn from the Polish orthodoxy which sired it and still dominates its politics. While Secretary-General Avraham Werdiger somewhat optimistically estimates that 30 percent of PAY membership is now Sephardi,[54] the likelihood of a Sephardi being made a member of the two-man PAY Kneset delegation (or the PAY component of a joint list with Agudah) is minimal.

As for Agudah, its elite clearly reflects the major ethnic components of the party: the Polish and Hungarian orthodoxies, upon which the largest factions are built. The Polish contingent, in particular, is strongly identified with the Hasidic movement, and specifically with the dynasty of the rabbis of Gur. The late Rabbi Levin was the son-in-law of the late Rabbi of Gur, while his successor in the Kneset seat, Rabbi Abramowitz, is also predominantly identified with that group.

While Agudah has historically never been close to the Sephardim, it has found some adherents among them, particularly among the Yemenites, who are generally the most traditional of the eastern Jews. It has been estimated that 10 percent of Agudah is now Sephardi,[55] and, as elsewhere, this group has of late become more insistent upon representation in the party's elite, particularly in its Kneset delegation. Thus, veteran Kneset member S. Y. Gross agreed to resign his Kneset seat for the fourth and last year of the previous Seventh Kneset term in favor of Rabbi Ya'akov Mizrahi, of Yemenite extraction. Despite this gesture, however, Rabbi Mizrahi was merely a symbolic ethnic representative in the delegation. Furthermore, there are no Sephardi rabbis on the Council of Torah Greats. Much of the inner discussions of the Agudah elite are conducted in Yiddish rather than Hebrew, and the predominant cultural milieu of the elite is that of Polish and Hungarian orthodoxy. Thus there is little chance that even a symbolic Sephardi elite member can, as yet, exercise much influence in the Agudah elite.

Most of the Mafdal leadership arrived in Israel during the late 1930s as the Jewish economic position in Poland worsened and the political, economic, and social position of Jews in Germany deteriorated. This group of immigrants remains firmly entrenched at the helm of the party today, setting its tone and style. It includes all four of the most recent party ministers—Burg, Warhaftig, Refael, and the late Hazani, who also head all the major factions except, of course, the Tze'irim, whose leader, Zevulun Hammer, was recently minister of social welfare.

Only four of the elite had come to the country earlier. During the 1920s such *halutzi* types as Unna, Shapira, and Kalmar were among the actual founders of ha-Po'el ha-Mizrahi in Palestine. Going even further back, only two elite members, Rabbi Y. L. Maimon and Avraham Shaki, had come to Palestine in Ottoman times. Another three men arrived as refugees in the immediate postwar and pre-state period. Two of these individuals, Warhaftig and Nurok, had been top party leaders in Lithuania and Latvia, respectively, before, during, and after the war, and were co-opted into the party elite in Israel soon after their arrival. The post-state mass immigration brought two additional types of party leaders: ethnic figures from Sephardi groups (such as Suaritz and Levi) and immigrants from the United States who had been active in the movement there (Rabbi Ben-Meir and, later, his son).

Once again, virtually the entire PAY leadership is cut from the same cloth. All arrived in Palestine in the 1930s except Werdiger, who, born in Poland, came via France in 1947.

Consistent with its long anti-Zionist stand, most Agudah elite members arrived in Palestine/Israel as war refugees between 1939 and 1945 or later. A few did anticipate events, however, and arrived in the mid-1930s. This pattern is typical of all Israeli political leadership: some 40 percent of all Kneset members arrived in the country between 1932 and 1947, less than half that percentage between 1924 and 1931, and only a few before or since.[56]

Perhaps the different natures of the several religious parties, and their divergent views on the central question of the relationship between tradition and modernity (the crux of their ideological differences), is most clearly shown when the highest educational levels and occupations of their elites are examined (see Table 4.3). Mafdal, whose ideology has always been to develop a synthesis between Jewish tradition and modernity and which has included secular education within its purview, has a highly educated elite, with variegated career patterns. As of 1976 some six Mafdal elite members held doctoral degrees and another ten had other university-level education, for a total of 16, or over 50 percent. Eight more studied in higher *yeshivot;* only one listed high school as the highest level of education attained, and she is Mrs. Tovah Sanhedrai, who could not have attended yeshivah anyway. Some eleven were ordained rabbis in the course of their yeshivah studies, though only five actually listed the rabbinate as their profession (one listed it along with "lawyer").

Of the other persons for whom occupational data were available, five considered themselves educators, four were businessmen, another three were primarily lawyers (though one listed himself as also being an economist and agriculturalist), three were agriculturalists, two were journalists or writers, one was a psychologist, and one a historian. Two are legitimately considered "pure politicians," as Shahor termed himself, Shapira being the other. In fact, most of the Mafdal elite, particularly those functional leaders who have remained in their positions through more than one Kneset candidacy, are primarily professional politicians. Again, this pattern is characteristic: "The Kneset in Israel is composed predominantly of professional politicians."[57]

At the other end of the spectrum, all the members of the Agudah elite for whom data are available attended yeshivah as their highest level of education, and only one attended high school in addition. None is university-educated, reflecting Agudah's grim view of secular education in general. Five of six on whom information is available were ordained rabbis, and four of them retain this title. Two others consider themselves journalists, but they write largely for Agudah or Agudah-oriented publications. Like most of the Agudah elite, they are professional politicians just as much as Mafdal and other Kneset members are. Porush doubles as Jerusalem's deputy mayor, while Mizrahi is a member of the city council of Rehovot.

PAY again stands midway between Mafdal and Agudah. Of its current leaders, Kalman Kahana is an ordained rabbi and holds a Ph.D. degree from the University of Würzburg. He serves as rabbi of PAY's oldest and largest kibbutz, Hafetz Hayyim. Its other Kneset member, Avraham Werdiger, studied in yeshivah and attended the University of Paris, where he studied economics. As party secretary-general, he is a full-time professional politician, as were his predecessors, Ya'akov Katz and Benyamin Mintz (Mintz originally was a businessman, however).

Nearly all the elite members have long-standing personal associations with their respective parties. Many ties stretch back to childhood, when they were active in the various youth movements sponsored by the parties in the countries of their birth. This is particularly true for Mafdal, whose antecedent parties spawned numerous youth movements.

There are several discernible career patterns in Mafdal. One familiar avenue leads from leadership in a youth movement to entry into the party elite proper. Yitzhak Refael, for example, was active in the B'nei 'Akivah youth movement in Poland, and continued in it upon his immigration to Palestine as a student in 1935. Later he became national secretary of B'nei 'Akivah and then stepped into ha-Po'el ha-Mizrahi politics, representing the party in the Va'ad Leumi and Zionist congresses. He headed the immigration department of the Jewish Agency during the crucial years of mass immigration, from 1948 to 1954, when he entered the Kneset. His marriage to the daughter of the venerable Mizrahi patriarch Rabbi Y. L. Maimon further enhanced his status in the party.

A more recent example is the party's current *enfant terrible,* forty-year-old Zevulun Hammer. A typical product of the party's education-socialization system in Israel, Hammer attended religious state schools, a Mafdal-oriented religious high school, and the party-sponsored Bar-Ilan University. He has been active in B'nei 'Akivah since childhood and rose to be its national secretary. He then became head of the party's newly founded young adult auxiliary, ha-Mishmeret ha-Tze'irah ("The Young Guard"), from which the Tze'irim faction was born. In 1968, as a result of the Tze'irim agitation for new party elections, the faction gained the right to a safe spot on the party's upcoming Kneset list, and it was Hammer who was given the seat. In the 1972 party elections the Tze'irim proved that it was a permanent force within the party, one which expected positions of power commensurate with its strength, and its leader, Hammer, was named deputy minister of education to fill the seat vacated by Shaki. As mentioned above, he became minister of social welfare.

Another familiar avenue for Mafdal members to gain power is via leadership in one of the party's more important auxiliary bodies, particularly the agricultural and educational ones. The agricultural sector in Mafdal, especially the *kibbutzim,* as in most other Israeli political parties,[58] has long been over-represented both qualitatively and quantitatively in the elite relative to its numerical size within the party membership and votership. Veteran *moshavnik* Michael Hazani served in the Kneset from 1951 until his death in 1975, and was minister of social welfare. Earlier he had been head of the ha-Po'el ha-Mizrahi *moshav* organization and of the ha-Po'el ha-Mizrahi Agricultural Center, the umbrella organization for all Mafdal agricultural settlements. Moshe Unna, who served in the Kneset from 1949 to 1969, is a *kibbutznik* and founder of ha-Po'el ha-Mizrahi's ha-Kibbutz ha-Dati organization. He served as deputy minister of education for two years and held top assignments on the Kneset Foreign Affairs and Security committee and the chairmanship of the powerful Law, Constitution and Justice committee, the only chairmanship held by Mafdal. Upon his retirement, Unna was succeeded by one of the younger elite members, Avraham Melamed, a founding member of a ha-Po'el ha-Mizrahi *moshav shitufi* (a hybrid of *kibbutz* and *moshav* types) who identifies himself with the agricultural constituency, though he is also trained as a lawyer and an economist, and is an ordained rabbi.

Another route to power is via the educational ladder. Yosef Goldschmidt held a variety of posts in the party's educational system and eventually became director of the Religious Education Department in the Ministry of Education, a position which made him a virtual czar over Mafdal's educational-socialization system. Rabbi Moshe Tzvi Neriyah, who, like Goldschmidt, served in the Seventh Kneset, heads the elite yeshivah high school network affiliated with B'nei 'Akivah.

Needless to say, Mrs. Sanhedrai, the first and only woman ever to represent any of the religious parties in the Kneset, is head of the National Religious Women's Organization, the Mafdal women's auxiliary.

While all Mafdal Kneset members, like almost all Mafdal members, are also members of ha-Po'el ha-Mizrahi—the last old Mizrahist, the elder Ben-Meir, died in 1971—few, if any, are drawn from the ranks of the labor organization *per se*. The Shapiras and Kalmars have been replaced by highly educated professionals like the Shakis and Ben-Meirs. And while there has been a notable decline in the proportion of workers in the party membership and a commensurate rise in professionals, the elite is now lopsidedly weighted in favor of the latter. Of the fourteen members of the party elite in the Seventh Kneset, ten attended the university and five held doctoral degrees, a figure greatly at variance, for example, with the general educational level of the membership (see Table 4.2). In terms of occupation, ten of the fourteen were found in one of the three highest status categories—professionals, educators, and rabbis—which together comprise only some 13 percent of the party membership at large (see Table 4.1).

When queried as to their occupations, not a single member of the current Mafdal elite responded, "worker." (In fact, only 2 percent of all Kneset members do so, despite the dominance of labor parties in the political system.[59]) Mafdal is changing its image somewhat, de-emphasizing the specific interests of the workers as such and attempting to appeal to a wider audience. For a "party of religious workers" whose ideology is based at least in part on socialism and a majority of whose membership remains workers, the rapid professionalization of its elite indicates that the "contagion from the right," as Epstein calls it,[60] has affected it. From a mass socialist party limited only by its religious criteria, Mafdal has become a mass catchall type of party, at least for those with religious inclinations.

In Agudah, ethnic considerations still play the dominant role in elite selection, though Agudah's "youth" auxiliary, Tze'irei Agudat Yisrael, is represented by Rabbi Shlomo Lorincz in the Kneset. The small PAY elite is rather uniformly composed of those who have been active in the PAY labor organization. Perhaps it is more useful to view the PAY elite as originally part of the Agudah elite which was involved in its labor politics, and which then split off to form a new party.

Chapter 5
The Voters

A political party is defined not only as the expression of a particular ideology or world view, nor as merely the total of given historical influences. It cannot be evaluated solely by the strategy and tactics it employs in making certain policies, nor by its organizational structure, social composition, or elite characteristics. It is at least as much the instrument of practical politics, nominating candidates and competing in elections. Indeed, some political scientists define the political party primarily in terms of its function of running candidates for public office.[1] A party which is incapable of putting forth nominees and getting at least some of them elected—in a system where this is possible, of course—is destined to a short and ineffective political life. Hence electoral performance is an essential, if only a partial, tool in measuring the strength of any party or group of parties.

In Israel, the most satisfactory yardstick of the national performance of political parties in general, and of religious parties in particular, is the Kneset election, eight of which were held between 1949 and 1973. Because Israel is a small, highly centralized, unitary state, with a parliamentary system of government, there is but one governmental authority and but one set of nationwide elections, those held to elect its 120-member Kneset. Local elections are less satisfactory indices of party performance because the local units are considered subdivisions of the central government and are "often correctly seen as the weakest link in the state's political system."[2] Their elections are primarily of local importance and are even held simultaneously with those for the Kneset. There are complications in comparing the two types of elections in Israel. For while up to two dozen lists have competed for the Kneset, eight hundred or more local lists are not un-known, with the religious parties appearing separately, together, divided, under different labels, or not at all, depending on local conditions and coalitions. Despite the myriad combinations and permutations on the local level, the religious parties as a group have an almost identical pattern of support in both Kneset and local elections, more so than any other group of parties,[3] attesting to their loyal and stable followings.

Kneset election statistics are also far more reliable than party membership figures. Israel's highly regarded, non-partisan Central Bureau of Statistics compiles accurate and objective data, whereas the individual parties are free to exaggerate their membership figures in their literature. The Kneset election statistics are also far more accessible, internally consistent, and comparable than the parties' membership rolls, in that they indicate each party's strength in a given voting location, at a given same time, and, hence, under comparable conditions.

Furthermore, as Maurice Duverger points out,[4] a party's membership is neither identical with nor limited to its total voting support. In addition to party "militants" and "supporters," there are also "electors," who, though not formal members of the particular party, sympathize with and vote for it occasionally, if not regularly. Thus the Kneset returns are truer measures of real strength than party membership statistics.

The concept of party membership itself has a somewhat different connotation to the different religious parties. For Mafdal and PAY, which are built largely around labor organizations, it entails all the familiar duties and obligations (dues, membership cards, etc.), as well as the characteristic benefits (sick fund, job protection, placement, etc.), of a comprehensive union.[5] For Agudah the formalities of membership are of less importance. Its small workers' organization, Irgun ha-Po'alim, was appended only in 1961 after the breakaway of PAY and is largely composed of the party's own functionaries and employees, for whom it provides little in the way of social benefits.[6] Its overall internal structure remains traditional and clerically dominated.

In the analysis of the Kneset statistics here, the goal is to ascertain the numerical and percentile strength, and hence the resulting Kneset representation, of the religious parties, both cur-

rently and over time, as a group and individually. We are also
seeking to find their sources of electoral support, whether urban or
rural or in specific geographic areas. Finally, we hope to discern a
national pattern of voting behavior for the several religious parties
and to account for the development of such a phenomenon.

From Table 5.1[7] it is apparent that the religious parties had
increased their overall strength between the First Kneset elections
in 1949, when (running together as a United Religious Front) they
garnered some 12.2 percent of the vote and some 16 seats, and the
Seventh Kneset election in 1969, when (appearing as three separate
lists) they earned 14.7 percent and 18 seats. In view of the fact that
there were some 13 parties sharing the 120 seats in the Seventh
Kneset, a two-seat or 2.5 percent increase is significant. (Whether
the sharp decline to 12.1 percent and 15 seats is a one-time phenomenon attributable to the trauma of the 1973 Yom Kippur war,
in whose wake many Mafdal voters switched to the ultra-national-
ist Likud list, or whether it is symptomatic of a longer range decline will only be seen in the results of the upcoming Ninth Kneset
elections in May 1977.) Indeed, other parties originally comparable
in size to the combined religious parties such as the Marxian socialist Mapam, declined from a high of 14.7 percent and 19 Kneset
seats in 1949 to 6.6 percent and 8 seats in 1965. While this decline
is largely accounted for by the secession of Ahdut 'Avodah from
Mapam, similar splits are not unknown among the religious parties.
Taken as a whole, all the labor parties combined have declined
seriously—from 65 seats in 1949 to 51 in 1974—whereas the religious parties have remained remarkably stable, falling only one
seat below their 1949 figure in the wake of the extraordinary circumstances of the 1973 war.

In the Seventh Kneset the religious parties together held 18
Kneset seats. Thus they constituted the third largest bloc—assuming for the moment that they can be so considered—in that body,
trailing behind the Labor Party's 56 and Gahal's 26 but far ahead of
the nearest competition. Indeed, Mafdal, with 12 seats, was then
and remains today the third largest party. While all three religious
parties have increased their percentages over the twenty-year period 1949–69, Mafdal has gained the most. It went from 8.3 percent
and 10 seats in the Second Kneset (after the breakup of the URF,
when it appeared as two separate lists, Mizrahi and ha-Po'el ha-

Table 5.1. Number of Votes, Percentage of Votes, and Number of Kneset Seats of the Religious Parties, First–Eighth Knesets, 1949–73

Party	First Kneset 1949			Second Kneset 1951			Third Kneset 1955			Fourth Kneset 1959			Fifth Kneset 1961			Sixth Kneset 1965			Seventh Kneset 1969			Eighth Kneset 1973		
	votes	%	seats	votes	%	seats	votes	%	seats	votes	%	seats	votes	%	seats	votes	%	seats	votes	%	seats	votes	%	seats
Mizrahi				10,383	1.5	2																		
Ha-Po'el ha-Mizrahi				46,347	6.8	8	77,936	9.1	11	95,581	9.9	12	98,786	9.8	12	107,966	8.9	11	133,238	9.7	12	130,349	8.3	10
Agudat Yisrael	52,982	12.2	16	13,799	2.0	3	39,836	4.7	6	45,569	4.7	6	37,178	3.7	4	39,795	3.3	4	44,002	3.2	4	60,012	3.8	5
Po'alei Agudat Yisrael				11,194	1.6	2							19,428	1.9	2	22,066	1.8	2	24,968	1.8	2			
Totals		12.2	16		11.9	15		13.8	17		14.6	18		15.4	18		14.0	17		14.7	18		12.1	15

Sources: Central Bureau of Statistics, *Results of Elections to the Third Kneset and the Local Authorities* (Jerusalem: Central Bureau of Statistics, 1956) (includes First and Second Kneset statistics); *Results . . . Fourth Kneset* (Jerusalem: CBS, 1961); *Re-sults . . . Fifth Kneset* (Jerusalem: CBS, 1964); *Results . . . Sixth Kneset* (Jerusalem: CBS, 1967), 2 vols.; *Results . . . Seventh Kneset* (Jerusalem: CBS, 1970); *Results . . . Eighth Kneset* (Jerusalem: CBS, 1974).

Mizrahi) to 9.7 percent and 12 seats in the Seventh. This two-seat increase accounts for the entire rise in the religious parties' representation since the First Kneset and for two out of three additional seats since the Second. The two-seat decline experienced by Mafdal in the elections after the 1973 war may be an aberration from the pattern. Most votes lost were in the party's various West Bank settlements and among its voters of army age, many of whom switched to Likud under the pressure of the war and the imminence of negotiations over Israel's borders. With Mafdal's hawkish postwar stance—its insistence upon a referendum over West Bank negotiations as a precondition for its entering any government—and with the return to normalcy and the declining importance of security issues, many Mafdal voters are likely to return to the party in which they acquired their political orientation.

Agudah has risen from 2 percent and 3 seats in the Second Kneset to 3.2 percent and 4 seats in the Seventh. PAY has gone from 1.6 percent to 1.8 percent over the same period—not enough, however, to earn it a third seat. The fact that in 1973 the newly recombined Agudah-PAY list declined to 5 seats from the total of 6 the two had held is less a consequence of the war—since few Agudah or PAY voters "float" to secular parties—than a typical phenomenon in Israeli politics whereby mergers often decrease votership rather than increase it. Perhaps the union alienated true believers in both parties and caused them not to vote.

The fact that Israel's religious parties have grown over the twenty-year era of mass immigration, rapid modernization, and intense external pressures is a tribute to their adaptive abilities. These are exemplified by their systems of socialization and recruitment, particularly in the areas of education and immigrant absorption. This growth also belies the contention that with the increasing modernization of society there must necessarily occur a concomitant and undifferentiated secularization of peoples' attitudes as expressed in their political preferences.

Sources of Strength

As table 5.2 shows, Agudah's strength is overwhelmingly urban. Not even 5 percent of its national total derives from rural

Table 5.2. Urban vs. Rural Votes, Third–Seventh Knesets

Party and Kneset	Urban	Rural	National Total
Mafdal (Mizrahi- ha-Po'el ha-Mizrahi)			
Seventh	108,453	24,785	133,238
Sixth	88,004	19,962	107,966
Fifth	75,489	23,297	98,786
Fourth	71,330	24,251	95,581
Third	52,993	24,943	77,936
Agudat Yisrael			
Seventh	42,007	1,995	44,002
Sixth	37,993	1,862	39,795
Fifth	34,937	2,241	37,178
Fourth[1]	41,743	3,826	45,569
Third[1]	35,028	4,808	39,836
Po'alei Agudat Yisrael			
Seventh	22,154	2,814	24,968
Sixth	19,878	2,188	22,066
Fifth	17,001	2,417	19,428

Sources: see Table 5.1.
[1]Joint list with PAY.

sources. In light of the history of the party, this pattern of urban concentration is readily understandable. PAY, on the other hand, receives over one-tenth of its national vote from rural areas, largely from its own agricultural settlements.

Mafdal earns some 18 percent of its vote from rural areas. This strength, considerably higher than the 14 percent of Israel's total vote which comes from such sources, derives from the extensive system of rural settlements established by, and affiliated with, ha Po'el ha-Mizrahi—now the senior partner in Mafdal—over the last fifty years and from the party's closeness to the *halutziyut* ethic. But Mafdal's rural percentage has been declining gradually over the years, paralleling the overall decrease in the proportion of rural population in the country. In absolute terms, it, like Agudah and PAY, remains a heavily urban party.

Table 5.3 shows a more specific pattern for the Seventh Kneset, which is characteristic for the others as well. The more

Table 5.3. Percentage of Votes for Religious Parties by Area, Seventh Kneset

Area	Mafdal		Agudah		PAY	
Urban		9.4		3.6		1.9
Cities		*8.6*		*3.8*		*1.9*
Old Jewish[1]	8.5		4.2		1.9	
New Jewish[2]	9.6		2.5		2.1	
Non-Jewish	5.6		0.1		0.1	
Towns		12.6		2.8		2.1
Old Jewish	11.5		2.7		1.9	
New Jewish	13.8		3.1		2.4	
Non-Jewish	4.4		0.1		0.1	
Rural		11.8		1.0		1.3
Villages		*12.4*		*0.9*		*0.6*
Jewish	18.6		3.2		2.0	
Non-Jewish	10.3		0.1		0.2	
Moshavim	19.7		2.0		3.3	
Moshavim shitufiyyim	21.7		0.3		4.8	
Kibbutzim	3.4		0.0		0.5	
National		9.7		*3.2*		*1.8*

Source: see Table 5.1.
[1]Pre-state.
[2]Post-state.

citified and veteran (pre-state) a settlement is, the higher the Agudah percentage. Inversely, the newer and smaller the urban settlement—those mostly populated with new immigrants—the higher the Mafdal percentage. PAY varies but little in all types of Jewish urban areas.

In the 1969 elections, Agudah received 3.2 percent of the total national vote, 3.6 percent of the urban vote, 3.8 percent of the city vote, and 4.2 percent of the vote in long-established Jewish cities, but declined to about one-half that percentage in newer Jewish cities (2.5 percent) and in both older (2.7 percent) and newer (a somewhat more average 3 percent) towns, for an average of 2.8 percent in the towns. Mafdal's national percentage was 9.7, but its overall urban vote was only 9.4 percent. In the cities proper Mafdal took 8.6 percent and in the old established Jewish cities 8.5 percent. In the newer Jewish cities, the percentage jumped back up to 9.6, almost its national average, while in the towns it substantially exceeded its national average, receiving 12.6 percent, with some 11.5 percent in the older towns and 13.8 percent in the newer immigrant towns. PAY's urban percentage varied little from its national level of 1.8 percent, rising slightly to 1.9 percent in the urban areas in general as well as in the cities and in the veteran Jewish cities and towns. Somewhat higher percentages of 2.1 were to be found in both the newer Jewish cities and in the towns in general, reaching a high of 2.4 percent in the newer immigrant towns.

Although Agudah's rural vote is negligible (under 5 percent of its total and 1 percent of the total rural vote), it managed to maintain its national average of 3.2 percent in the non-ideologically organized, mostly privately owned, and older Jewish villages. The only other sizeable rural Agudah vote, the 2 percent that comes from the *moshavim,* is attributable not to any *moshav* network of its own—it has none—but rather to scattered votes from the other parties' *moshavim,* mostly from those of PAY. PAY's string of settlements returned that party impressive 4.8 and 3.3 percentages from among the country's *moshavim* and *moshavim shitufiyyim* ("collective cooperatives," a hybrid of the *kibbutz* and *moshav*), though its handful of *kibbutzim* only bring it 0.5 percent of the total *kibbutz* vote. Thus PAY's overall rural percentage was 1.3, not far below its 1.8 percent national figure. Mafdal, which has a higher percentage of rural voters than the percentage of rural voters in the total voting population, exceeded its own national average (of 9.7 percent) in the rural areas by garnering 11.8 percent of the vote there. Typically for Mafdal, the votes are fairly uniformly spread across the various types of rural settlements—unorganized villages (18.6 percent) or *moshavim* (19.7 percent) and *moshavim shitufiyyim* (21.7 percent) connected to ha-Po'el ha-Mizrahi's Iggud ha-Moshavim ("Union of *Moshavim*"), which comprise some sixty-four settlements,[8] and, though these are less significant, the *kibbutzim* (3.4 percent) of which ha-Po'el ha-Mizrahi has only twelve, organized in its ha-Kibbutz ha-Dati ("The Religious *Kibbutz*") movement.[9]

A more detailed examination of individual rural settlements would not prove useful because of their small size and their inherent ideological uniformity. To locate the parties' sources of strength geographically, the vote for the religious parties is broken down in Table 5.4 by the country's six administrative districts and

Table 5.4. Percentage of Votes for Religious Parties, by District and Sub-District, Seventh Kneset

District	Sub-District	Mafdal		Agudah		PAY		Total	
North			10.0		1.5		1.3		12.8
	Safad	12.1		1.7		2.4		16.2	
	Kineret	10.3		5.3		1.4		17.0	
	Jezreel	9.4		1.0		0.8		11.2	
	Acre	9.8		0.9		1.3		12.0	
Haifa			8.2		1.6		1.6		11.4
	Haifa	7.0		1.6		1.8		10.4	
	Haderah	12.3		1.7		0.7		14.7	
Merkaz			11.2		2.9		2.4		16.5
	Sharon	11.4		2.0		1.2		14.6	
	Petah Tiqvah	11.8		3.5		2.5		17.8	
	Ramleh	9.3		1.9		4.5		15.7	
	Rehovot	11.4		3.6		2.4		17.4	
Tel Aviv			8.0		3.5		1.4		12.9
Jerusalem			10.9		10.2		2.8		23.9
South			14.4		2.5		2.8		19.7
	Ashkelon	15.1		3.0		2.3		20.4	
	Beersheva	13.7		2.0		3.2		18.9	
National			9.7		3.2		1.8		14.7

Source: see Table 5.1.

by each sub-district (where one exists). Using the 1969 Kneset election as an example, the three religious parties as a whole received the highest percentage of a district's votes in the Jerusalem district, nearly 24 percent. But since the districts themselves are purely geographic-administrative units and their populations vary, a large percentage in a relatively small district, such as Jerusalem, may actually represent fewer votes than a smaller percentage in a larger, more heavily populated one, such as Tel Aviv, where the religious parties received only 13 percent of the district's vote. Thus, the three religious parties earned a total of 25,629 votes in the Jerusalem district, comprising approximately 13 percent of their combined national votes, while they garnered 59,193 votes in the Tel Aviv district, or nearly 30 percent of their combined national totals.

The individual parties' sources of strength are as different in geography as they are in ideology and political behavior, however, and an analysis of each is far more enlightening. For example, Mafdal fluctuated only moderately from its national average of 9.7 percent going from a low of 8.0 percent in the Tel Aviv district to 14.4 percent in the Southern district. Again, because the Tel Aviv district has such a large population, the 8 percent of its voters who support Mafdal constitute some 28 percent of that party's total national vote. Another 22 percent or so comes from the Merkaz (Central) district, and slightly under 15 percent each from the Northern, Southern, and Haifa districts, with the Jerusalem district supplying a mere 8 percent of the Mafdal total. Its religious and nationalist significance notwithstanding, Jerusalem is politically of only moderate importance for Mafdal as a source of voting strength.

Agudah exhibits a completely different and much more erratic pattern of voting support. While its national average was 3.2 percent, there were wild swings in the percentage of its voters by district. In the Haifa and Northern districts, for example, Agudah received one-half or less (1.6 percent and 1.5 percent, respectively) of its national average, while in the Merkaz and Southern districts it did somewhat better (2.9 and 2.5 percent), though still below its national par. In the Tel Aviv district Agudah exceeded its national percentile slightly (3.5 percent), while in Jerusalem, the only district in the country where it attained such "major-league" proportions, it trebled that figure (10.2 percent).

Adjusting for the differences in the sizes of the populations of the districts, Agudah's picture changes somewhat, but not radically. Thus, Jerusalem supplied the party with one-quarter of its nationwide vote, the much larger Tel Aviv district provided another third, and the Merkaz a sixth—all three are highly urbanized areas—while the Northern, Southern, and Haifa districts fill in with smaller amounts of from 5 to 8 percent. For Agudah, then, Jerusalem is of particular importance as a source of votes.

The pattern of PAY voting more clearly resembles the evenly spread one of Mafdal than the erratic highs and lows of its erstwhile parent party, Agudah. Thus, with a national average of 1.8 percent, PAY's district percentages ran as follows: 1.3 percent

Northern, 1.4 percent Tel Aviv, 1.6 percent Haifa, 2.4 percent
Merkaz, 2.8 percent Jerusalem and Southern. Nowhere did its
strength fall to half of its national average, as is true for Agudah,
nor did it ever reach double, let alone triple, proportions, again as
is true for Agudah.

Adjusting these district percentages of PAY in light of the
voting populations in each, the pattern of support resembles that of
Mafdal in terms of the percentages which each geographic area
contributed to the party's overall tally. PAY received one-quarter
of its votes from each of the Tel Aviv and Merkaz districts and
some 15 percent from each of the Haifa and Southern districts,
with slightly more than 10 percent in the Jerusalem district and
slightly less in the Northern district. For PAY, as for Mafdal, Jerusalem is of relatively less vote-getting significance than for Agudah.

Table 5.5 presents the numerical and percentile totals received by each of the religious lists in the Seventh Kneset elections, which did not substantively change from the previous six, in
each of Israel's (currently) ten largest cities proper, as distinct from
the larger districts: Jerusalem (Jerusalem district), Haifa (Haifa district), Beersheva (Southern district), Netanya and Petah Tiqvah
(Merkaz district), and Tel Aviv and its satellite cities of B'nei Braq,
Holon, Bat Yam, and Ramat Gan (Tel Aviv district). It is evident
that Mafdal strength in any given city never fell to one-half of its
national average of 9.7 percent—the lowest being in Haifa, where it
was 5.7 percent—and that it never quite doubled—its highest level
being in B'nei Braq, where it was 18.8 percent. This is roughly the
pattern seen in the much coarser district-by-district breakdown,
though the smaller the unit of analysis—and the more urbanized—
the more pronounced and exaggerated the variations within the
trend.

The same holds true for Agudah. Whereas in the district
breakdown it dropped as low as one-half its national strength of 3.2
percent in some districts, in the city-by-city breakdown it hit a new
low of about one-third that figure in Holon, Bat Yam, and Ramat
Gan and one-half that figure in Haifa. On the other hand, the figure
rose almost three and one-half times in the city of Jerusalem and
seven times in B'nei Braq, indicating the highly concentrated nature of the party following.

On the city-wide level, PAY deviates from the Mafdal-like

Table 5.5. Percentage and Number of Votes for Religious Parties in Ten Largest Cities, Seventh Kneset

City	Mafdal		Agudah		PAY	
	%	no.	%	no.	%	no.
Jerusalem	10.1	9,591	11.0	10,492	3.0	2,848
Tel Aviv	7.1	14,922	2.6	5,433	0.9	1,967
Haifa	5.7	6,732	1.6	1,897	1.8	2,153
Beersheva	11.8	3,470	2.9	845	4.3	1,259
B'nei Braq	18.8	6,479	21.6	7,448	8.9	3,080
Bat Yam	7.5	2,880	1.0	373	0.6	219
Holon	6.1	2,698	1.1	480	0.4	170
Netanya	12.8	3,986	3.2	997	2.0	624
Petah Tiqvah	10.1	4,358	3.4	1,482	3.2	1,360
Ramat Gan	7.2	4,534	1.2	765	0.6	364
National	*9.7*	*133,238*	*3.2*	*44,002*	*1.8*	*24,968*

Source: see Table 5.1.

pattern of evenly spread support on both the national and district levels. For such a small party, what appears to be evenly spread support within the districts is, in fact, concentrated within them in certain locales. Thus, PAY's fragmentation is even greater than Agudah's, while it never quite achieves the same high levels of concentration. For example, its support dropped to a low of one-quarter of its already tiny 1.8 percent national average in Holon and one-third in Ramat Gan and Bat Yam; it rose to two and one-half times its national average in Beersheva and five times the average in B'nei Braq. In Jerusalem, it received 3.2 percent, or less than twice its national average.

A comparison of the number and the percentage of votes achieved by each of the parties in the cities (Table 5.5) versus those received in the entire district in which the city is located (Table 5.4) simply reconfirms this pattern. The Agudah and, less significantly, the PAY vote rose in the cities but declined in the district as a whole (which includes the surrounding rural areas), while Mafdal's support rose in the districts but declined in the cities proper. This again reflects Mafdal's relatively strong rural settlement network.

This pattern seems to be contradicted in the Tel Aviv district, where all three religious parties—not only Mafdal, as to be expected, but also the highly urbanized Agudah and PAY—received fewer votes in the city of Tel Aviv proper than in the overall district. This is explained by the presence of the city of B'nei Braq within the boundaries of this district. Founded in the 1920s by orthodox immigrants from Poland, B'nei Braq has become a major center of traditional orthodox life in Israel.

While all three religious parties received disproportionately high percentages of the vote in B'nei Braq (Mafdal twice its national average, PAY five times, Agudah seven times), PAY and Agudah reaped the most political profits. In fact, Agudah and PAY earned substantially more votes in this city, whose voting population is 43,000, than they did in the neighboring metropolis of Tel Aviv, which has some 282,000 voters. For Agudah, B'nei Braq constituted the second largest reservoir of votes in Israel (about 17 percent of its total), next to importance only to Jerusalem (25 percent), with Tel Aviv third (12 percent). For PAY, B'nei Braq was the largest single source of votes (12 percent of its total), slightly ahead of the city of Jerusalem (11 percent) and followed by Haifa (over 8 percent) and Tel Aviv (under 8 percent). For Mafdal, B'nei Braq was of relatively minor vote-getting importance, supplying slightly under 5 percent of the Mafdal national total, trailing behind Haifa (over 5 percent), Jerusalem (7 percent), and Tel Aviv (11 percent). Again, PAY stood between the Mafdal and Agudah patterns, though closer to Mafdal: while B'nei Braq was its largest single source of support, the city was not much more important to PAY than Mafdal's largest source, Tel Aviv, was to that party, and in no case was it as disproportionately significant to PAY as was Agudah's citadel, Jerusalem, to that party.

Aside from Jerusalem's immense religious and nationalist significance to Jews, it also provided a considerable number of votes to each of the religious parties. This is particularly true of Agudah and, to a lesser extent, of PAY. As compared to the national averages of these two parties, Jerusalem constituted something of an exception, being one of their high points of concentration. Viewed in relation to its own neighborhoods, however, the city replicated, in miniature, the national pattern of religious party support.

Thus, Mafdal, whose national average is 9.7 percent and whose Jerusalem average is only slightly higher, 10.1 percent,

maintained an even level of support throughout Jerusalem's variegated neighborhoods (see Table 5.6), much as it did nationally.
For example, its strength ranged from 8.6 in the poor, working-
class neighborhoods of Romema, Lifta, and Giv'at Shaul to 15.5
percent in even poorer Musrarah, one of the city's worst slum
districts. Nevertheless, Mafdal also had a respectable following in
Jerusalem's fashionable, upper-middle-class neighborhoods—11.9
percent in Rehaviah and Qiryat Shmuel, 9.6 percent in Talbieh,
and 10.9 percent in Qiryat Moshe, Beit ha-Kerem, and Bayit ve-
Gan. The party fared equally well in sociologically traditional
quarters like Beit Yisrael, Sanhedriah, Bukharim, and Meah
She'arim (10.7 percent) and Geulah, Kerem Avraham, and Meqor
Barukh (9.6 percent), and particularly well in neighborhoods
populated heavily with Sephardi immigrants, such as Shikunei
Gonen (Qatamon) (12.3 percent) and Giv'at Mordekhai and
Rassco (12.9 percent).

Agudah, whose national percentage was only 3.2, received
some 11 percent of the Jerusalem vote, which constituted about
one-quarter of its total national support. But Agudah's support
was, if anything, even more concentrated in the capital than in the
country at large. Thus, whereas Agudah earned 11 percent in Jerusalem, as opposed to 3.2 percent nationally, in the Beit Yisrael,
Sanhedriah, Bukharim, and Meah She'arim quarters it earned 30.6
percent, while in the adjacent Geulah, Kerem Avraham, and Meqor
Barukh it earned 31.6 percent. These two sections of the city alone
comprised some 35 percent of Agudah's total vote in Jerusalem, or
nearly 9 percent of its entire national vote. Lying side by side along
the northern limits of the city, they constitute a "religious belt" of
traditional neighborhoods, much like the "red belt" of solidly communist suburbs ringing Paris (no invidious comparison is intended
here). The density and intensity of religious (particularly Agudah)
strength in these quarters are so high as to render them virtually
impervious to, and to insulate their inhabitants from, the appeals of
other parties almost entirely.

The extreme example of this phenomenon of concentration
and insulation is the fifteenth election district in Jerusalem. It is
located in the heart of the Meah She'arim quarter, which, like most
of the others in the "religious belt," was among the first to be built
by Old Yishuv Jews outside the Old City wall during the nineteenth

Table 5.6. Percentage and Number of Votes for Religious Parties in Jerusalem, Selected Neighborhoods, Fourth-Seventh Knesets

| | Fourth Kneset | | | | Fifth Kneset | | | | | |
| | Mafdal | | Agudah-PAY | | Mafdal | | Agudah | | PAY | |
Neighborhood	%	no.	%	no.	%	no.	%	no.	%	no.
Beit Yisrael, Sanhedriah, Bukharim, Meah She'arim	11.6	949	42.0	3,433	10.2	766	38.8	2,925	5.4	410
Geulah, Kerem Avraham, Meqor Barukh	12.3	1,186	24.4	2,362	10.5	982	23.9	2,238	3.0	281
Downtown	10.5	395	7.8	295	9.2	337	7.5	274	2.4	87
Musrarah, Sham'ah	10.3	394	10.5	403	10.5	380	12.5	451	1.2	43
Mehaneh Yehudah, Nahlaot, Sha'arei Hesed	9.9	1,104	12.7	1,415	9.3	977	12.7	1,325	2.5	258
Rehaviah, Qiryat Shmuel	12.1	665	5.6	310	11.6	558	4.1	198	2.7	132
Romema, Lifta, Giv'at Shaul	11.4	276	13.4	326	11.8	285	11.3	273	3.6	88
Qiryat Moshe, Beit ha-Kerem, Bayit ve-Gan	11.8	404	9.9	272	11.6	484	4.6	192	2.9	122
'Ein Karem, Qiryat ha-Yovel, Qiryat Menahem, Manhat	12.3	514	3.0	127	11.8	651	3.3	182	1.4	78
Shikunei Gonen, Giv'at Mordekhai, Rassco	9.7	544	11.5	641	10.7	697	9.9	643	1.8	115
Talbieh, Yimka	8.0	156	3.3	65	7.1	159	3.2	71	0.8	18
Gonen, Moshavah Germanit, Moshavah Yevanit	7.7	464	10.8	657	8.6	503	9.7	568	2.7	161
City-wide totals	*10.8*	*7,578*	*15.0*	*10,537*	*10.4*	*7,372*	*13.6*	*9,591*	*2.6*	*1,853*

Sources: see Table 5.1.

century and before the advent of the Zionist movement. In this one district, then, Agudah, which received its highest percentage here—76—competes not with the other religious parties (PAY got 9 percent, Mafdal 2 percent) or with the secular parties (Gahal got 7 percent, Labor 4 percent), but rather with that remnant of the Old Yishuv population which never reconciled itself to Zionism or Israel, i.e., the Neturei Qarta. Of course, it does not participate in the "Zionist state" elections, but its anti-state agitation insures that the percentage of eligible voters in the district actually casting ballots is low—only 53 percent in 1969, the second lowest among Jerusalem's 204 election districts (the lowest voter turnout, 49 percent, was recorded in the adjacent sixteenth election district, which is similar in composition and voting behavior).

Outside the "religious belt," Agudah had a few pockets of strength in other Old Yishuv pre-Zionist neighborhoods, like Sha'a-rei Hesed. Elsewhere in Jerusalem, its strength fluctuated markedly,

Table 5.6—*continued*

		Sixth Kneset						Seventh Kneset			
Mafdal		*Agudah*		*PAY*		*Mafdal*		*Agudah*		*PAY*	
%	*no.*	*%*	*no.*	*%*	*no.*	*%*	*no.*	*%*	*no.*	*%*	*no.*
8.9	709	33.4	2,665	6.4	514	10.7	962	30.6	2,744	6.4	575
9.5	874	29.1	2,678	5.1	471	9.6	863	31.6	2,852	5.2	468
9.2	531	6.8	392	2.7	156	9.2	499	6.3	343	3.0	161
8.5	203	13.3	320	1.8	43	15.5	335	7.8	168	3.3	71
9.2	892	14.2	1,374	2.6	250	8.7	789	13.6	1,233	2.5	227
9.7	566	2.9	168	3.6	213	11.9	710	2.6	154	2.9	171
8.4	283	11.0	371	4.1	138	8.6	384	14.8	662	5.9	232
9.2	592	4.4	283	3.9	251	10.9	950	4.8	417	3.2	279
7.7	717	6.9	644	1.9	181	8.8	1,155	3.1	410	1.6	208
9.9	694	11.2	788	1.3	88	12.3	1,039	7.7	649	1.1	91
12.7	285	3.8	84	3.3	75	12.9	411	2.6	83	2.7	85
6.7	167	2.7	66	1.6	41	9.6	259	2.0	54	1.3	36
7.3	387	5.8	498	1.7	154	9.5	538	4.1	427	1.4	135
8.8	*7,372*	*12.7*	*10,692*	*3.2*	*2,686*	*10.1*	*9,591*	*11.0*	*10,492*	*3.0*	*2,848*

being higher in poorer, more traditional areas (14.8 percent, for example, in Romema, Lifta, and Giv'at Shaul) and drastically lower in the more affluent ones (2 percent in Talbieh). Thus, in Jerusalem, as elsewhere in Israel, its electoral support is circumscribed within definite geographic confines and limited largely to members of those socioeconomic groups which sired it some sixty years ago.

PAY, whose national average of the vote is 1.8 percent and whose Jerusalem average is 3 percent (and which in turn represents 11 percent of its national vote), also does well in the city's traditional religious neighborhoods, though its concentrations are not as high as those of Agudah. For example, it garnered some 6.4 percent, or slightly more than double its city-wide average, in the Beit Yisrael, Sanhedriah, Bukharim, and Meah She'arim quarters, as compared to Agudah which almost tripled its city-wide average there. PAY dropped to 5.2 percent in the neighboring Geulah, Kerem Avraham, and Meqor Barukh communities, where Agudah strength increased slightly. PAY, however, also maintained this percentage in the poor working-class Romema, Lifta, and Giv'at

Shaul areas, while Agudah's vote declined there to one-half its level in the more traditional neighborhoods. Elsewhere in Jerusalem, PAY's strength was fairly evenly distributed. Like Mafdal, it did well (exceeding its national average) in both well-to-do Rehaviah and Qiryat Shmuel (2.9 percent), for example, as well as in slum-ridden Musrarah (3.3 percent).

Although numerically Tel Aviv contributes more votes to the religious parties as a whole, and to Mafdal in particular, than does Jerusalem it has no such extreme concentrations of religious party voters. Mafdal, which earned some 7.1 percent of the Tel Aviv vote, once again followed its evenly spread national pattern, never falling to one-half its city-wide figure (its low was 3.9 percent in Ramat Aviv and surrounding areas) but never quite doubling it either (it reached 13.6 percent in Kfar Shalem). Agudah, with only 2.6 percent of the Tel Aviv vote, also adhered to its national pattern of fragmentation and concentration, though by no means in Jerusalem-style proportions. Thus, it received only about one-fifth its city-wide average in the upper-middle-class northeast part of Tel Aviv, while doubling its city-wide average in the older, poorer Qiryah, Montefiore, and Rakevet quarters (6 percent) and in the ha-Tiqvah slum area (5.9 percent). Tiny PAY, with 0.9 percent of the Tel Aviv vote was again slightly less fractionated than Agudah (its low of 0.2 percent in one district was slightly less than a fourth of its city-wide total) but never reached the same level of concentration (its high of 2.2 percent was only two and a half times its city-wide average).

The absence of any religious "ghettos" in the Tel Aviv municipality, as compared with Jerusalem, which has no adjacent cities, is more than amply made up for by the presence of the city of B'nei Braq within the district, as noted earlier. Although numerically it provides more votes for Agudah than for PAY, B'nei Braq is of greater importance to the latter in percentage terms. It is not a stronghold of the Old Yishuv, which fathered Agudah, since it did not exist until well into the Zionist period. Indeed, it was founded and developed by the same Polish orthodox immigrants who first brought PAY to Palestine and then effected the major changes in Agudah itself during the 1930s.

By way of summary, clear patterns of voting behavior and support for the three religious political parties of Israel have emerged. Mafdal has a large and stable vote, widely and evenly

spread throughout the country's districts, cities, and neighborhoods thereof, both rich and poor, traditional and modern, as well
as a substantial percentage of rural support. These factors combine
to make it a party of truly national scope, with broad geographic as
well as class appeal, limited only by its religious orientation. In
contrast, Agudat Yisrael's small though secure vote is highly fractionated and concentrated, is almost entirely urban, and is confined
to certain districts, cities, and neighborhoods which are mostly
traditional, religious, and poor. Because of this pattern Agudah is
not a truly national party. It is only as a result of Israel's very pure
proportional representation system that it is projected onto the
national political stage. The pattern of support for Po'alei Agudat
Yisrael is less concentrated, localized, and urbanized than that of
Agudah but more so than that of Mafdal. Notwithstanding its
somewhat broader geographic and class appeal than that of Agudah, its miniscule size precludes its classification as a national political party, and it too remains in the Kneset by the grace of God
and proportional representation.

Electoral Reform

Radical electoral reform would be alien to Israel's political
and ideological traditions. Ben-Gurion, for example, failed to impose a single-member district majority electoral system, which he
hoped would induce an instant two-party system. But more gradual
types of reform might modify Israel's virtually pure system of representation, thus eliminating splinter parties and encouraging the
coalescence of the others about two or three poles.

Since the Second Kneset in 1951 a minimum of 1 percent of
the valid national vote was required for a party to participate in the
allocation of Kneset seats. The raising of the minimal percentage to
2, as has recently been contemplated, would entirely eliminate
PAY, with its 1.8 percent, as an independent party. Raising the
cutoff point to 4 or 5 percent, as, for example, in the German
Federal Republic, would eliminate Agudah as an independent
party. Raising the minimal percentage to 10, as suggested twenty
years ago by the then Mapai and General Zionist parties, today
could eliminate even Mafdal, though the possibility of a reconsti-

tuted United Religious Front, under such circumstances, must be kept in mind; in that case, the religious parties together could garner a total of between 12 and 14.7 percent.

A more likely modification of the Israeli electoral system would be a division of the country into districts in which a modified proportional representation system would be applied. Such a system would have the advantage of preserving the Israeli belief in pure democracy by representing minority opinions. On the other hand, it would eliminate small parties by fragmenting their votes still further among the various election districts; those "wasted" votes would not be enough to elect a representative anywhere in the country.

The precise effect of such reform on the religious parties will, of course, depend on the specific nature of the system that is ultimately set up. It must be remembered, however, that the long-range intent of any such electoral reform is the elimination of small parties, such as the religious ones. According to one possible method, the new electoral districts would be drawn geographically, roughly along the lines of the present administrative districts and sub-districts, without regard to the size of their populations. If, for example, there were to be ten new electoral districts, each would elect one-tenth of the 120 Kneset seats. In order to gain one seat, then, a party would have to muster one-twelfth, or roughly 8 percent, of the vote in a given district.

This system would have a deleterious effect on Agudah, for only in the Jerusalem district, where it received 10.2 percent of the vote in 1969 could it acquire anything close to the 8 percent necessary for one seat, whereas its aggregate vote in the nation as a whole enabled it to gain some four seats in the Seventh Kneset. Agudah votes in other areas, even in B'nei Braq, under the new system would be insufficient to elect any members. Thus most of its votes would be wasted, and it would be transformed into a purely localized party.

The impact on Mafdal would be far less serious, since that party has currently been receiving at least 8 percent in every sub-district except the Haifa one, where it gets 7 percent. Thus, Mafdal would be likely to get at least one representative in every one of the ten new districts, for a total of twelve seats, the same as its current total. If there were to be twelve new electoral districts, with ten representatives alloted to each, thus requiring 10 percent of the district's vote per seat, Mafdal would fare less well but would still have a substantial representation; it earns over 10 percent in most of the sub-districts, and at least close to that figure in three others, which, after the elimination of the smaller parties, would be enough to earn it one seat in each. Under this system, however, Mafdal would probably not earn a seat in either Tel Aviv or Haifa districts, where it received only 8 and 7 percent, respectively, in 1969.

If, on the other hand, the districts were drawn roughly equal to population, and closer both to the one-man-one-vote principle and to the traditionally pure "every vote counts" Israeli system, Mafdal would suffer less. Indeed, Tel Aviv would loom even larger in the electoral picture because of its huge population, and Mafdal, whose numerical strength there is higher than in Jerusalem, would stand to gain. On the other hand, Agudah, whose numerical strength is concentrated in less populated Jerusalem, would only decline further.

However the districts are composed, as the number of representatives per district decreases and the percentage required to elect one representative increases, it becomes more difficult for the religious parties, even Mafdal, to survive. An electoral reform plan proposed in November 1968 by the Labor party envisioned the establishment of thirty new electoral districts with three representatives each, plus 30 representatives elected at large. Each of the 90 members elected from districts, then, would have to have attracted one-third of the district's vote. None of the religious parties ever command anything like such a following in any sizeable area. The few representatives they would be able to elect would be among the 30 at-large seats, each of which would require 3 percent of the national vote. On this basis, Mafdal could hope for 3 seats and Agudah for 1. The religious parties were saved from this fate only by the decline in Labor party strength in the Seventh Kneset elections, which dashed Labor's hope for a majority for electoral reform.

No matter how the districts are drawn, how many districts there are, how many seats per district, or what percentage is necessary to win a seat, the effect on PAY would be fatal. Nowhere does the party have sufficient votes to gain even one seat under such a system. Even by tallying every one of its far-flung votes nationwide, it has never managed to elect more than two members.

The only alternative, if the three religious parties are to survive

qua parties in the face of electoral reform, would lie in a combination of the three along the lines of the old URF. Even if PAY could
see its way clear to rejoining Agudah in an electoral alliance (which
in fact occurred in anticipation of the 1973 Kneset elections), their
total strength would be unlikely to change matters much. In some
areas a full coalition might conceivably add enough votes to those of
Mafdal which would otherwise be wasted to add a seat or two (particularly in the south and in Merkaz), but even this would not make
up for the loss of three or four of Agudah's current seats and PAY's
two.

In summation, any type of electoral reform along modified
proportional representation-district lines would at best leave Mafdal with the same number of Kneset seats, if not fewer; it would
also set a precedent for farther-reaching and, from the religious
parties' point of view, more damaging electoral reform. As for
Agudah and PAY, even moderate electoral reform would perma-
nently cripple the former and eliminate the latter as independent
political entities. It is no wonder, then, that the religious parties are
ardent foes of electoral reform in Israel. Mafdal, of course, would
prefer a URF under the present electoral system, affording it domination of a potential combined religious vote of nearly 15 percent
and some 18 Kneset seats, but given the religious parties' long-
standing antagonisms and differences, this remains unlikely.

The Arab Voter

Historically, the attitude of the religious parties toward the
Arabs has been indifferent at best, and in general suspicious and
hostile. In the pre-state era, Agudah did occasionally make common cause with the Arabs, who were anti-Zionist for their own
reasons. Since the establishment of the state, however, neither
Agudah nor PAY has run lists in Arab areas, as the two largely
traditional communities share no ideological ground or practical
interests. Agudah generally takes a militant stance—at least in principle—on such questions as the occupied areas, speaking of the
God-given boundaries of the land of Israel. In practice, the party
generally defers in this, as in other matters of foreign policy and
security, to Labor.

Arab relations are even more strained with the religious Zion ist parties, Mizrahi and ha-Po'el ha-Mizrahi. Indeed, despite the latter's "socialist" leanings, both took stands close to that of the right-wing Revisionists on the integral unity of Eretz Yisrael and against its partition into separate Jewish and Arab states. These long-held, stridently nationalist sentiments were reawakened by the 1967 Six Day War, in whose wake Mafdal called for the settlement of the question of "the liberated areas in light of the religious and historical rights of the Jewish people."[10] Indeed, many of the new settlements established in these areas, particularly on the West Bank, are affiliated with Mafdal. The retention of these settlements since the 1973 war has become a key obstacle to a negotiated settlement between Israel and Jordan in particular.

Mafdal is also under strong pressure on the settlement issue from the Gush Emunim movement, which developed largely out of Mafdal's Tze'irim faction in the period beginning after the 1967 war and crystallizing after the 1973 war. The Gush, which is now independent and includes both religious and non-religious nationalists, is opposed to the return of any of the territories to the Arabs and actively promotes Jewish settlement there. The militancy of the Gush threatens to embarrass and upstage Mafdal's own nationalist stance, which, say Gush members, is purely propagandistic and is in any event tainted by the party's participation in a coalition which is willing to contemplate territorial compromise. The Gush also points to the reservations of such Mafdal leaders as Yosef Burg, the late Michael Hazani, and even Yitzhak Refael on at least the political advisability, if not the religious significance, of the retention of all the territories. Worse yet, they consider the views of such leading dovish Mafdal intellectuals as former Kneset member Moshe Unna and writer Zvi Yaron, who have formed a small counter-group called Oz ve-Shalom ("Power and Peace"), as evidence of the party's softness on the territorial issue.[11]

Nevertheless, while maintaining an ostensibly strongly nationalist stance vis-à-vis the Arabs externally, Mafdal has effected a significant change in its internal attitude toward the Arab citizens of Israel, who increasingly have reciprocated. These new-found relationships are based on pragmatic rather than ideological grounds; Mafdal is seeking new sources of votes, while Arab voters need certain bureaucratic favors which Mafdal ministries can provide and also seek campaign funds for local Arab lists.[12] A common interest in the preservation of religious traditions and institutions does exist, however, particularly among the traditional leaders whom Mafdal first began to court. The latter were interested in preservation of the *shar'iah* (Muslim religious) court system, in the building and maintenance of mosques, in control over *awqaf* (Muslim religious trusts), and so on, all of which Mafdal's Ministry of Religions was uniquely suited to supply. They also wanted a variety of local government services, which Mafdal's Ministry of the Interior and Ministry of Social Welfare were instrumental in obtaining for them.[13]

The initial response to these efforts—Mafdal formally established a Minorities Department to deal with Arab affairs in 1959—was modestly encouraging. Mafdal received 1,620 Arab votes in the Kneset election of 1955 and 2,600 in 1959.[14] Impatient with this response, it tried another approach, directly appealing to Arab workers, both blue- and white-collar, via the ha-Po'el ha-Mizrahi labor organization rather than through the traditional elite. In this respect, Mafdal has been an agent of modernization, offering the services of a modern comprehensive labor organization to the Arab community. This time results were better. In the 1961 elections Mafdal earned 4,800 Arab votes, in 1965 5,700, and in 1969 almost 11,000, roughly enough to add one Kneset seat. This constituted 8.7 percent of the Arab vote,[15] or only slightly less than Mafdal's 9.7 percent of the general electorate that year. Mafdal-affiliated Arab officeholders sit in some forty local councils. The party has recently set up permanent branches in the larger Arab population centers. Like the Histadrut and the Labor party, ha-Po'el ha-Mizrahi and Mafdal have recently overcome earlier Zionist inhibitions and authorized the establishment of Arab sections within the labor organization and party to admit Arabs to full membership.[16]

Since the 1973 war however, this carefully nurtured relationship may have been disturbed. The militant nationalist stance taken by Mafdal—the Gush notwithstanding—on questions relating to negotiations with the Arab states, and particularly its opposition to a return of the West Bank to Arab control, only broadens the ideological gap between the party and its new-found Arab constituency. The effect of these developments may well have contributed to the decline in Mafdal votes in the December 1973 elections. The 1977 elections will tell whether the Arab voter's relationship with Mafdal is still viable.

Part III
The Parties
in the System

Chapter 6
Mafdal and the
Nationalization of Religion

With the establishment of the state in 1948, the major task for the Mizrahi and ha-Po'el ha-Mizrahi parties was the nationalization of religion. The former Kneset Yisrael religious structures and procedures were to be absorbed into the institutional and fiscal network of the new state, with full recognition and extension of their powers, and new structures and arrangements would have to be established to satisfy unmet needs. The process of nationalization was facilitated by the colonization or domination of these institutions by Mafdal.

Where possible, the nationalization was accomplished by the enactment of appropriate legislation. Elsewhere it depended on less formal arrangements, collectively referred to as the status quo. Mizrahi and ha-Po'el ha-Mizrahi (later Mafdal), true to their traditional pattern of behavior, accomplished the goals incrementally, deftly exploiting their pivotal coalition position as the most convenient partner for Mapai-Labor. Nevertheless, despite its long-standing domination of the religious establishment—which had been granted it by Mapai in return for its support in other areas—Mafdal has recently met with an increasingly effective challenge to and penetration of its position by Mapai-Labor itself, the dominant party in Israel.

The Ministry of Religions

The key tool in, and indeed itself a prime example of, the nationalization of religion in Israel is the Ministry of Religions

(Misrad ha-Datot). Mizrahi and ha-Po'el ha-Mizrahi realized that to strengthen and expand the role of official religion, an institutional basis would have to serve as the focal point for its domination of the religious establishment. Thus, they insisted upon the immediate establishment of such a ministry.[1] (The Ben-Gurion government was also under external pressure from non-Jewish international religious bodies and states with interests in the Holy Land to set up such a ministry.) This was, in fact, decreed by the Provisional Council in 1948, and Mizrahi and ha-Po'el ha-Mizrahi (later Mafdal) have held the portfolio except in the period 1958–61 and briefly in the post-1973-war Meir and Rabin governments. The minister has been a top party leader (e.g., Maimon, Shapira, Warhaftig, Refael), and the large majority of the ministry's officials and appointees are Mafdal members. Clearly, Mafdal attaches great importance to the ministry.

The significance of the Ministry of Religions for Mafdal is threefold. On the first level are the largely administrative, supervisory (and less political) powers over and technical services for all the various religious sects in Israel. Such tasks, inherited from the mandatory government, have since been expanded. In the dominant Jewish community, the ministry, along with the chief rabbinate, supervises the *kashrut* of those public institutions not under the supervision of the local rabbinate and of imported foodstuffs, especially meat. It participates in the financing of the building of synagogues and *mikva'ot*; distributes religious articles and literature to synagogues, institutions and needy individuals; supervises the activities of burial societies; administers holy sites, notably the Western Wall; fosters the development of *yeshivot*; and in general promotes religious life. It also handles the administrative and financial affairs of the rabbinical courts and of the chief rabbinate. The ministry exercises authority of a much more limited and supervisory nature over the various religious minorities in Israel.[2]

On the next, and more specifically political, level, the ministry is the chief source and implementor of legislation on religious affairs in the state. Thus Mafdal has enormous influence on the character of such legislation.

Perhaps most important, and most explicitly political, the ministry is directly involved in the selection of the personnel of virtually all the other religious institutions in the state, both Jewish and non-Jewish. Thus Mafdal has an abundant source of patronage and the loyal party character of such institutions is secure. In the dominant Jewish community, these organs include the chief rabbinate and the local rabbinates, the rabbinical courts, and the religious councils, as well as the state religious educational system. Mafdal's dominance of the religious establishment—and, conversely, the exclusion of the other religious parties from it—only reinforces the separatist tendencies of Agudah, which is now unabashedly calling for the elimination of the chief rabbinate, much as it had done in the days of the mandate.

Contested Nationalization:
The Chief Rabbinate

One of the major accomplishments of Mizrahi during the mandatory period was the institutionalization of a chief rabbinate.[3] Although the original electoral arrangements remained in effect, their legal foundations were shaky, for they were based on the 1936 regulations of Kneset Yisrael, and their continued validity was denied by the Supreme Court. A validation act was finally passed by the Kneset in 1953.[4]

In 1955 the original Religious Communities Ordinance (Organization) of 1926 (Chief Rabbinate Council of Israel) was amended. The role formerly played by the Va'ad Leumi—i.e., the appointment of four of the eight members of the Electoral Committee, which in turn appointed the forty-two rabbis in the Electoral College (the other four committee members were appointed by the Chief Rabbinate Council itself)—was now assumed by the Ministry of Religions.[5] As the Ministry of Religions was dominated by Mafdal, and as the Chief Rabbinate Council itself appointed half the members of the Electoral Committee, the party was now in a position to dominate the chief rabbinate election process, and it did so.

Given Mapai's reluctance to institutionalize Mafdal's domination over the chief rabbinate and Mafdal's determination to accept nothing less, no permanent law on chief rabbinate elections existed until 1972. Upon the expiration of each five-year term, the minister of religions had to request of the Kneset a new temporary law in order to arrange new elections and a temporary extension of the rabbinate's authority. Each of these occasions served to reopen the controversy over the control of the rabbinate elections and, indeed, over the rabbinate itself.

One of the two most notorious controversies over the chief rabbinate elections, and one in which Mapai challenged Mafdal's continued domination over the chief rabbinate and the Ministry of Religions itself, occurred in 1959, when Ashkenazi Chief Rabbi Herzog died. Mafdal was not in control of the Ministry of Religions at that time, having left the government over the issue of "who is a Jew." Rabbi Ya'akov Toledano was appointed by Prime Minister Ben-Gurion to take over the portfolio of religions vacated by Mafdal's Moshe Shapira. He had been a member of Mafdal for decades but had been passed over for the post of chief rabbi, and had therefore accepted the ministry from the hands of Mapai.

Toledano proceeded, with Ben-Gurion's blessing, to issue regulations for the next chief rabbinate elections which were designed to ensure the success of the candidate more favorable to Mapai (Rabbi Shlomo Goren, then chief military chaplain and now chief rabbi, known for his liberal interpretation of *halakhah* [religious law]) and the failure of the two candidates likely to be put forward by Mafdal. A rule making retirement mandatory at the age of seventy-five was to render the chief rabbi of Tel Aviv, Isser Yehudah Unterman, aged seventy-one and one of Mafdal's two likely choices for the post, ineligible for a five-year term. A regulation making Israeli citizenship mandatory for candidates was to eliminate a second Mafdal choice, Rabbi Joseph B. Soloveichik, of the United States. In opposing the regulations, Mafdal was fighting for the preservation of its domination over the chief rabbinate and, indirectly, for the restoration of the chief rabbinate's control over the Ministry of Religions.

In view of the public storm that raged about the rabbinate issue, in no small part fanned by Mafdal, as well as the delaying tactics the party had devised, it seemed inauspicious, if not impossible, to hold elections. In October of 1960, Rabbi Toledano died, and Prime Minister Ben-Gurion himself temporarily assumed the Ministry of Religions portfolio.

Once again fortune came to Mafdal's rescue. The government fell in January of 1961, when Ben-Gurion resigned amid the renewed controversy over the Lavon affair. Mafdal used the nine-month interregnum of caretaker government, when Mapai was on the defensive, to strengthen its position vis-à-vis both the chief rabbinate and the Ministry of Religions. It sponsored in the Kneset another temporary extension of the chief rabbinate's legal authority until new elections were held, scheduled within six months.[6]

The coalition negotiations took longer than envisioned, but Mafdal nevertheless emerged in November 1961 with the greater prize, the Ministry of Religions. The new minister, Dr. Zerah War-haftig, changed the regulations for chief rabbinate elections in a way more favorable to Mafdal and freed them of the restrictions of age and citizenship.[7] When, under the new regulations, elections were finally held in March of 1964, Rabbi Unterman was elected Ashkenazi chief rabbi by a close margin over Rabbi Goren, while the incumbent Sephardi chief rabbi, Yitzhak Nissim, handily won re-election.

Both of the chief rabbis elected remained in office well beyond the expiration of their five-year term and into 1972. Mafdal was by now determined that any new law on chief rabbinate elections should be permanent, allowing future elections to be held automatically at the expiration of a chief rabbinate term, under regulations to be issued by the Minister of Religions. This would keep the issue out of the political arena of the Kneset and within Mafdal circles—i.e., the Ministry of Religions, the chief rabbinate itself, and the Mafdal-dominated electoral college—thereby insulating the process from Labor influence.

The Labor party, for its part, was particularly interested in increasing its influence over the chief rabbinate because of a number of public controversies—such as the prohibition of marriages of *mamzerim* to other Jews (*mamzerim* are children of marriages considered adulterous or incestuous under Jewish law)—which were directly related to the chief rabbinate and its supreme *halakhic* authority. There were also signs of a general public impatience with the inability of the chief rabbinate to address itself to the solution of such pressing current problems, or at least to do so to Labor's satisfaction. Mafdal felt that its preferred choice for the Ashkenazi chief rabbi, once again Rabbi Goren, would best fulfill its expectations. Thus, Labor's disagreement with the demand for a permanent elections law for the chief rabbinate did not affect its increasing influence vis-à-vis Mafdal in the electoral process through the new regulations issued under the law.[8]

Under those regulations,[9] the traditional two-to-one proportion of rabbis to lay members in the electoral college was somewhat readjusted in favor of the latter, with eighty rabbis versus seventy laymen. Of the seventy lay representatives, twelve were to be the mayors of the twelve largest towns, or their appointees, and thirty-four were to be representatives of other mayors and local council heads elected in a conference of such politicians. As the overwhelming majority of local government heads in Israel are Labor men, the dominant party was thus ensured strong representation in the electoral college. Of the remaining twenty-four lay representatives, twelve were to be the heads of the religious councils of the twelve largest towns, or their nominees, and twelve were to be elected by assemblies of all the other religious councils in the country. While Mafdal had long dominated the religious councils, Labor made significant inroads here too, using similar tactics. Thus, a percentage of the religious council members of the electoral college would be either Labor party officials or party sympathizers.

Labor would have less influence among the eighty rabbinical delegates to the electoral college, who were composed as follows: sixteen rabbis of the largest towns; twenty-four rabbis from smaller towns and villages, each elected at a local assembly of such rabbis; five neighborhood rabbis from the three largest cities (three from Tel Aviv and one each from Jerusalem and Haifa), each elected at an assembly of such rabbis in his city; fourteen rabbis of *kibbutzim* and *moshavim* chosen at the appropriate assembly; nine *dayanim* (religious judges) picked by a *dayanim* assembly; two army chaplains; and ten rabbis appointed by the minister of religions, officially to redress the balance between Ashkenazim and Sephardim but unofficially to reinforce Mafdal's influence in the electoral college.

The elections committee also reflected increased Labor influence. Its membership was reduced to five; two members appointed by the chief rabbinate and two members appointed by the government were to choose a chairman. This time Labor insisted that one of the two cabinet appointees be its representative, and the chairman subsequently selected by the committee was a Labor member of the Kneset. Clearly, the Labor party was determined to exert its maximal influence to ensure the election of Rabbi Goren.

Not only the Labor party but most of the Mafdal leadership were now supporting Rabbi Goren, whether for reasons of ideology (his more modern outlook and his liberal interpretation of *halakhah*) or expediency (his relative youth). His popular appeal would dampen public pressure for the elimination of the chief rabbinate, and, not least important, his acceptability to Labor might forestall any further Labor penetration into Mafdal's fief. Yet the aging Rabbi Unterman maintained strong support among the more conservative Mafdal wings, particularly in those rabbinical circles which would participate in the chief rabbinate elections. They were more sensitive to criticism and pressure from Agudah, which, while it lacked direct institutional access to the election process, nevertheless had influence over it through rabbinical channels and public opinion. Agudah viewed Rabbi Goren as a reformist threat to *halakhah*.

After numerous delays and postponements, the elections were held in October 1972. Rabbi Goren soundly defeated Rabbi Unterman for the post of Ashkenazi chief rabbi, and another younger figure, 'Ovadyah Yosef, the Sephardi chief rabbi of Tel Aviv, aged fifty-one, defeated the incumbent Sephardi chief rabbi, Yitzhak Nissim. While it cannot be said that Labor votes decided the election, since most electoral college members were Mafdal men, Labor influence over the chief rabbinate elections, and ultimately over the chief rabbinate itself, was clear. For Mafdal, Labor's partial victory was a calculated risk inherent in the nationalization of religion. For Agudah, it was the inevitable consequence of allowing secular government intervention in religious affairs.

The chief rabbinate was recognized as the supreme *halakhic* authority and under the mandate also doubled as the Supreme Rabbinical Court of Appeals. With the establishment of the state, however, and the separation of the rabbinical courts from the rabbinate, it ceased to serve as a judicial body. Thus, its remaining functions in the realm of Jewish law are confined to the development of *halakhah* via innovative interpretation.[10] Although it might set new guidelines for the actual day-to-day judicial work carried out by the rabbinical courts, very little innovation has in fact come forth from the chief rabbinate. Goren's election was supposed to remedy this major flaw. This hope is as yet largely unfulfilled because of the continued politicization of the chief rabbinate and personal enmity between Goren and Yosef.

For the most part the chief rabbinate has occupied itself with administrative and symbolic tasks.[11] Its administrative functions in particular provide further links in the Mafdal-dominated web of relationships that constitute the religious establishment in Israel, for these tasks are concerned primarily with the appointments of religious functionaries and are carried out in close cooperation with the Ministry of Religions.

The chief rabbinate tests and must certify any rabbi who wishes to be a candidate for a *dayan,* for a city, town, local, or neighborhood rabbi, or for a *shohet* (ritual slaughterer). It thus exercises crucial influence over the appointments, and hence the careers, of such individuals and can exclude those whose religious or political leanings are not to its liking.

Wholesale Nationalization:
The Rabbinical Courts

At the time of the founding of the state, Mizrahi and ha-Po'el ha-Mizrahi demanded the preservation and expansion of religious control over personal status law. Under the mandate this law for Jews, with certain limitations, was adjudicated by the rabbinical courts, and it continues to be so decided today. Although the rabbinical courts are now independent from the chief rabbinate, they are intimately linked to it and indirectly, to Mafdal. All *dayanim* have to be approved by the chief rabbinate. The two chief rabbis themselves serve, until age seventy-five, as presidents of the Supreme Rabbinical Court of Appeals, while other members of the Chief Rabbinate Council are often judges of that court as well. Finally, the chief rabbinate establishes the rules of procedure of the rabbinical courts.

A series of laws was designed by Mizrahi and ha-Po'el ha-Mizrahi (later Mafdal) not only to secure but also to expand the authority of the rabbinical courts and to grant them equal status with the civil courts.[12] Several major loopholes in the authority of the rabbinical courts were created with the establishment of the state. In general, the King's Order in Council 1922, the basic constitutional document of the mandate, provided for broader authority in matters of personal status to non-Jewish religious courts, particularly Muslim ones, than to rabbinical ones. The rectification of this disparity had long been a Mizrahi demand.

Specific challenges to the rabbinical courts' jurisdiction focused on the exclusion of foreign citizens (paragraph 53 of the King's Order) and the definition of citizenship as Palestinian (paragraph 59, King's Order amended 1935). Both of these caused confusion in a new state populated largely by recent arrivals and in which there was as yet no citizenship law at all.[13] Lacking a legal definition of citizenship, some civil courts ruled that the rabbinical courts had legal jurisdiction over no one. With the passage of the Citizenship Law of 1952, the problem of jurisdiction over Israeli Jewish citizens was solved. The question of Jewish foreign nationals, however, remained. A further difficulty arose out of the fact that many of the new *dayanim* in the post-state era were ad hoc appointees of the minister of religions and the chief rabbinate. Hence they lacked formal legal authority. The passage of the Rabbinical Courts Law (Confirmation of Appointments) in 1952 remedied this anomaly and was made retroactive.

A more fundamental challenge to the continued authority of the rabbinical courts was the fact that mandatory courts (and later Israel's Supreme Court) had recognized the rabbinical courts' authority only over members of Kneset Yisrael, but the last Kneset Yisrael membership list had been published in 1944, and no new one was possible, since the establishment of the state superseded the voluntary Kneset Yisrael community. Thus, Jews who came of age or who immigrated to Palestine-Israel after that time—some two-thirds of Israeli Jews—were not recognized as subject to the rabbinical courts' jurisdiction.

In the face of these challenges Mizrahi and ha-Po'el ha-Mizrahi sought a new law clearly delineating the authority of the rabbinical courts. Thus was born the Rabbinical Courts Law (Marriage and Divorce) of 1953, which states:

> 1. All matters of marriage and divorce of Jews in Israel, whether citizens of the state or its residents, are in the exclusive jurisdiction of the rabbinical courts.
> 2. Marriage and divorce of Jews will be conducted in Israel according to Torah law.[14]

The first paragraph solves the problem of Jewish nationals of foreign citizenship, as all Jews, citizens or residents, are subject to rabbinical courts in questions of marriage and divorce. Mizrahi and ha-Po'el ha-Mizrahi insisted that this declaration appear before the statement on Torah law (the government had proposed the reverse order) so that no question of who determined Torah law would arise (i.e., no non-orthodox interpretations would be recognized). The law does not specify what the Torah law is on these questions, but merely incorporates it, as interpreted by the rabbinical courts, into the corpus of Israeli jurisprudence. The law goes on to delineate other areas of the courts' competence, including such financial questions as that of wife and child support arising from a divorce suit.

While strengthening and clarifying the rabbinical courts' jurisdiction, the law also narrows it by granting parallel authority to the civil courts in matters of personal status where such matters come up indirectly in the course of adjudicating another issue (despite attempts by the religious parties to remove this provision). Thus, a civil court, in the course of hearing a suit for wife support (not related to divorce), can decide, incidentally, as it were, whether in fact the marriage was valid.

Mizrahi and ha-Po'el ha-Mizrahi promoted the passage of several related laws which rounded out the authority, as well as the autonomy, of the rabbinical courts. The most important of these was the *Dayanim* Law of 1955. With the establishment of the state the need was felt to separate the rabbinate from the *"dayanate,"* and no legal procedures existed to appoint *dayanim* per se.[15] In its broad outlines the law follows the Judges Law of 1953, giving equal legal status to the *dayanim* and guaranteeing their freedom from political intervention. But the qualifications to be *dayanim* are established by the chief rabbinate, not by the law, as in the case of judges. Further ensuring his autonomy, the *dayan* is bound only by the strictures of *halakhah* of the case which is before him, and not by the law of the state in general, as are judges. Similarly, whereas a judge must swear allegiance to the state and its laws, the *Dayanim* Law provides for an oath of allegiance to the state only.

The rabbinical courts system is composed of twenty district courts and the Supreme Rabbinical Court of Appeals in Jerusalem.[16] Appeal on substantive questions can be made only to the Supreme Rabbinical Court of Appeals, whose verdict is final. Nevertheless, the Israeli Supreme Court, in its capacity as the High Court of Justice, does retain, according to the Court Law 1957, the mandatory right to determine whether the rabbinical courts have jurisdiction in a given matter. By precedent it also has the right to intervene in cases where it believes the principles of "natural law" have been violated by the rabbinical court.[17] In practice, the overall effect of the Supreme Court's residual authority over the rabbinical courts has been to limit their authority.[18]

Despite these limitations on the authority and autonomy of the rabbinical courts, they have exclusive jurisdiction over all Jewish citizens in the most crucial areas of personal status law. Thus party influence on the courts and their activities, though not on their composition, has been neutralized.

Shared Nationalization: The Religious Councils

The local religious councils were established on Mizrahi's instigation in the 1920s to provide religious services, paid for in part by use taxes but largely funded by the local community. The local rabbis nominated candidates for appointment, and the local council selected half of those candidates. Thus there was no national control over the religious councils. Since most of the local council authorities were controlled by non-religious parties, particularly Mapai, they were often reluctant to budget, or later disburse, such funds, leaving the religious councils weak. Furthermore, while the rabbis who nominated candidates were most often Mizrahi or ha-Po'el ha-Mizrahi members,[19] insuring their religious conformity and party loyalty, much discretion was granted to the local councils.

Mizrahi and ha-Po'el ha-Mizrahi hoped to ensure greater party control over these bodies via appointments (colonization), to provide them with national government financing (nationalization), to expand the number of such religious councils to cover every Jewish locality, and to strenghten their legal bases and increase their scope of activities. Once again, the ideal instrumentality for accomplishing these aims was the Ministry of Religions, but it had to be authorized by appropriate legislation.

Although the Jewish Religious Services Budget Law of 1949[20] was temporary—it had to be renewed periodically by the Kneset until a permanent law was passed (some eighteen years later)—it did set up the framework for a new system of relationships vis-à-vis the religious councils. The law provided for the automatic transformation of all existing local *shehitah* councils into religious councils which would inherit all the powers they had had since the mandatory period. The minister of religions was authorized to make additional appointments to existing councils and to select new religious councils in those places where no local authorities existed. Where local authorities did exist, those authorities were empowered to make the selection. The effect of these provisions was also to spread rapidly the establishment of religious councils in all Jewish settlements. To accomplish what may have been government financing of the religious councils, the law provided that their budgets, once approved by the local authority, were to be funded two-thirds by that authority and one-third by the government, i.e., the Ministry of Religions.

While some of the major aims in relation to the religious councils were achieved by this law, it contained numerous flaws from Mizrahi's and ha-Po'el ha-Mizrahi's point of view. First, the temporary authority of the religious councils had to be renewed annually in the Kneset, where it was exposed to the usual barrage of anti-religious invective. Second, the partial funding by the central government left the religious councils at the mercy of the often hostile local authorities. Further, while the minister of religions and, via him, the party had gained access to the religious council appointment process, the local authorities, largely dominated by the secular parties, still controlled the ultimate selection of religious council members. Finally, no provision was made for the renewal or replacement of religious council members.

The correction of these faults required a coalition agreement between Mizrahi–ha-Po'el ha-Mizrahi and its Mapai partner. As far back as the 1954 coalition agreement,[21] the partners had agreed in principle upon the necessity of enacting a more permanent law on religious councils. Mapai, however, was reluctant to perpetuate a system which gave control of this arm of the religious establishment to Mizrahi and ha-Po'el ha-Mizrahi. It supplied religious services directly to the population at large, was a lucrative source of patronage, and participated in the selection of the local rabbi. Since Mapai was interested in penetrating this Mafdal stronghold when the time was right, no progress towards a permanent religious councils law was made until the early 1960s, when circumstances appeared more propitious.

In 1959 Mapai's *moshav* movement set up a department, in cooperation with the religious department of the Histadrut, to cater to the religious needs of some sixty-four of its *moshavim,* representing a population of some ten thousand, mostly Sephardi, immigrants, which were officially classified as religious settlements. Soon after, the Mapai Religious Circles were organized. Among their aims were the establishment of a religious department in Mapai itself, the provision of some type of alternative to that of the Mafdal-controlled religious state education, and the penetration and capture of the local rabbinates and especially of the religious councils, where Mapai generally had a 30 percent representation.[22]

At the same time Mapai found allies in the other religious parties. Agudah and, in particular, PAY had by now overcome some of their ideological inhibitions about participating in "official" religious bodies. They also objected to Mafdal's domination of the local religious councils, which, they felt, resulted in their exclusion from fair representation on these local bodies.[23] With PAY's entry into the government in 1960—a vote on which Mafdal abstained in the Kneset—Mapai's hand was strengthened. It altered the political and legal framework of the religious councils in a way that both satisfied some of Mafdal's demands for greater institutionalization and nationalization and promoted its own desire, and that of PAY and Agudah, for greater influence over and representation in the councils.

In 1963 an agreement between Mapai and Mafdal on the religious councils provided for new regulations which allowed the extension of the existing religious councils' authority for four years, after which a permanent religious council law would be passed. The agreement also provided, however, for a new system of composition of the religious councils, whereby Mapai, and to a lesser extent the other religious parties, were guaranteed a share therein. Thus, under the new regulations, 45 percent of the religious council members were to be named by the (Mafdal) minister of religions, another 45 percent by the (usually Mapai) local authority, and 10 percent by the (usually Mafdal) local rabbi.

The appointments under this system are supposed to reflect accurately the various groups in the local population who have an interest in the religious councils, such as ethnic groups and political parties. In practice, the municipality's share is usually divided up in accordance with the proportion of each party in the municipal government. Mapai (since expanded to Labor) usually leads, but the opposition parties and the religious parties, whether they are in the coalition or the opposition, are also considered. The rabbi's appointees are usually Mafdal, and those of the minister are used to balance the conflicting interests of the various groups. Often they are in fact utilized to keep the balance as favorable to Mafdal as possible.

While the new system still left Mafdal, as the largest bloc, in a position to dominate the religious councils in most places, the local authorities now had direct influence over nearly half the religious council members in many places. Since these authorities were usually Labor, for the first time a secular party had institutionalized influence over the religious councils. Furthermore, the agreement also provided that while all religious council members were to be personally religious, and while a majority of the religious council members were to be representatives of the religious parties, this majority was now to include the other religious parties, PAY and Agudah.[24] Thus, in effect, Mafdal. domination was seriously challenged from the right as well as from the left.

In accordance with the subsequent coalition agreement of 1966 between the Labor Alignment and Mafdal,[25] a permanent religious councils law was passed on March 29, 1967, as an amendment to the Religious Services Law. It provided for the automatic re-composition of the religious councils every four years. While the secular parties, particularly Labor, have gained a strong foothold in the religious councils under the new law, the majority of the council heads are still Mafdal men,[26] as are the majority of religious council employees. Thus, nationalization of the religious councils took a long time and exacted a high price in terms of party influence shared with Labor and, to a lesser extent, with the other religious parties.

The Failure of Sabbath Legislation

Mafdal's successful nationalization of these autonomous religious realms within the framework of a newly independent, highly centralized, and nationalistic state whose dominant party was headed by a dynamic and charismatic leader bent on *mamlakht-iyut* ("statism") is indeed among its most impressive accomplishments in terms of its goals. It should be noted that after Agudah and PAY departed from the government in 1952, their influence over or initiative in the field of legislation, religious or otherwise, was negligible.

Mafdal realized that, as Samuel Huntington would have it,[27] those religious interests which were successfully institutionalized and colonized, preferably by legislation and as soon in the new state's existence as possible, would be, despite recurrent problems of implementation, the ones most likely to be nationalized and to endure. Subsequently they would, in effect, create their own self-perpetuating public interests somewhat independent of the party, a process for which Mafdal was willing to pay a high price. But not all questions could be equally easily solved through institutionalization and nationalization. In general, those institutions which were not already substantially institutionalized by the time of the establishment of the state have progressed little, if any, from pre-state days, and Mafdal has found it difficult to overcome the centripetal force of *mamlakhtiyut*.

A prime example is the case of Sabbath legislation. Under the Mandate's continuation of the Ottoman *millet* system of religious autonomy, each religious community's Sabbath was given recognition, but no attempt was made at government enforcement of religious Sabbath rules. In 1934 municipalities and in 1941 local authorities were given the discretionary authority to enact various local ordinances, including Sabbath laws.[28] Their enactment and enforcement was uneven at best and depended on the relative influence of the religious population and the religious parties locally. Thus in Jerusalem public transportation stopped and cafes were closed on the Sabbath, but in Tel Aviv only transportation stopped and in Haifa both operated as usual. Because no uniform country-wide law was established in the pre-state period, this area was unlikely to be brought under central control at a later time.

With the rise of the Jewish state, the first of the four minimal religious demands presented by the United Religious Front[29] was the recognition of the Jewish Sabbath and holidays as official days of rest. Satisfaction of this demand came swiftly in the Order of Government and the Law of 1948.[30] This legislation, however, did not specify any prohibition of labor on the official days of rest. In 1951 the outgoing First Kneset passed the Hours of Work and Rest Law during the interregnum before the Second Kneset elections—elections caused by the fall of the government over the question of religious education in the immigrant camps. The coalition agreements, therefore, were no longer valid, and Mapai rode roughshod over the religious sensibilities of its erstwhile partners. The law reiterated that for Jews the Sabbath was an integral part of the compulsory thirty-six-hour weekly rest period, and that the employment of Jews during such periods was prohibited.[31]

The hours law met some of the minimal requirements that the religious parties would have demanded had they been party to it. Unlike the Religious Services Law, however, it was not conceived as religious legislation per se, but rather as a piece of general social legislation. Second, the minister of labor was in charge of the enforcement of its provisions, not the minister of religions, as Mizrahi and ha-Po'el ha-Mizrahi had demanded, or the rabbis, as Agudah had proposed.[32] Third, the law set up no enforcement machinery so that its implementation was rendered problematic at best. Furthermore, it was limited in scope. It applied only to employees, not to employers, self-employed people (professionals, storekeepers, etc.), members of cooperatives, and so forth, thereby excluding a large and growing sector of the Israeli work force. And permits could be obtained from the Ministry of Labor to employ workers during the weekly rest period if the minister was satisfied that the interruption of such work would endanger the security or economy of the state or hinder essential services. Even though blanket permits of a general nature were not supposed to be issued except by a ministerial committee composed of the prime minister, the minister of labor, and the minister of religions, the broad discretion of the minister of labor to grant work permits precluded frequent resort to the ministerial committee. And within that committee, the position of the Mafdal minister of religions was a permanent minority of one.

The law also provided for a higher wage scale for Sabbath and holiday work. The religious parties had hoped thereby to discourage employers from employing their workers on the Sabbath.[33] Instead, the additional payment became an incentive for workers to seek Sabbath jobs.

In 1955 the first of many coalition agreements[34] providing for the enactment of a separate Sabbath law to include stores and businesses, industries and crafts, and employees and employers was signed. It was never implemented, however. The knotty question of public transportation on the Sabbath was specifically excluded from the agreement,[35] so as not to upset the status quo in Haifa.

Once again in 1960 a paragraph on a Sabbath Law appeared in the coalition agreement (Fourth Kneset).[36] This time Mafdal had prepared a comprehensive draft law, the Sabbath and Holidays Law (Prohibition of Business) 1959,[37] which would have forbidden all forms of business on the Sabbath and holidays, including public transportation and entertainment. The inclusion of public transportation doomed the bill to a certain death, but Mafdal insisted upon this under pressure from the chief rabbinate. Mafdal was also under pressure from its ha-Po'el ha-Mizrahi labor organization to limit more effectively the number of industrial plants open on the Sabbath and hence effectively closed to workers observing the Sabbath.[38]

The coalition agreement of 1961 (Fifth Kneset) promised a Sabbath bill which would include entertainment but would specifically exclude public transportation.[39] The Ministry of Labor was also to seek new scientific and technical means to minimize violations of the Sabbath in those plants given work permits, thereby limiting the number of jobs closed to Mafdal members. On the basis of this agreement, in 1964 the minister of religions, Dr. Zerah Warhaftig, proposed the Sabbath and Holidays (Prohibition of Business) Basic Law.[40] The bill would have closed virtually all businesses on the Sabbath and holidays. By omitting the question of public transportation from the draft, Mafdal hoped for a more limited and realistic victory.

Opposition to the bill came from both religious and secular quarters. The chief rabbinate, and more particularly the Haifa rabbinate, objected to a Sabbath law that tacitly agreed to the status quo on public transportation in Haifa. More direct opposition from the Ahdut 'Avodah minister of labor, Yigal Allon, was based on the hours law. He claimed as his prerogative proposing legislation regarding days and hours of work and rest. Prime Minister Levi Eshkol then appointed a committee to work out a compromise bill, and it proposed that all businesses, including entertainment, be closed on the Sabbath. The implementation of the bill, however, was placed under the minister of labor, who would retain the power to grant permits which he had had under the hours law. This provision satisfied the secular labor parties. The government accepted the joint bill, with slight modifications, in June of 1965, and its passage in the Kneset seemed likely.

One week later Minister of Labor Allon proposed his own bill, which excluded such broad economic activities as *kibbutz* industry, entertainment and sports facilities, and gasoline stations from compulsory Sabbath closing. With the introduction of Allon's proposal, the government reversed its stand and refused to honor its previous decision accepting the compromise bill. Mapai's change of heart was due in part to its solicitiousness for its new partner in the Labor Alignment, Ahdut 'Avodah. Thus, despite cries of foul play by the Mafdal ministers, no Sabbath bill was presented to the Fifth Kneset.

In the Sixth Kneset coalition agreement[41] there was no provision for a separate Sabbath law. Mafdal no longer saw the possibility of passing such a law. Instead, the party sufficed itself with proposing an amendment to the original hours law[42] which included independent artisans, industrial proprietors, storekeepers, members of industrial or craft cooperatives, and so forth, in the prohibition against work on the Sabbath, and allowed members of agricultural cooperatives to perform only those tasks essential to the settlement's welfare. Outside the amendment's purview were entertainment and sports facilities. Gasoline stations were excluded from the definition of a "store," and hence from the application of the amendment,[43] thus permitting and promoting motor traffic on the Sabbath. The proposed amendment was ultimately passed in March of 1969.[44] Beyond that, a patchwork of local Sabbath ordinances still remains. In the subsequent Seventh Kneset coalition agreement and in the current Eighth the demand for a comprehensive Sabbath law has been dropped. Mafdal has merely asked for a reactivation of the inter-ministerial committee which is supposed to grant Sabbath work permits with an eye to minimizing them.[45] (In the military forces Sabbath observance, insofar as consistent with national defense needs, is guaranteed by a standing order of the general staff and is implemented by the military rabbinate.)

The failure of the amended hours law to include a more comprehensive list of businesses and occupations is not Mafdal's most serious shortcoming in the nationalization of religion, however. Such flaws could have been remedied incrementally, in good Mafdal fashion, by additional legislation or administrative regulation if this religious interest had been successfully institutionalized and satisfactorily colonized by Mafdal. Neither precondition was satisfied.

Chapter 7
Education

In analyzing the cardinal importance of education for the religious parties today, it will be recalled that questions of education acted as catalysts in the formation of both Mizrahi and Agudah. The high importance of education as the chief means of socialization placed such questions outside the realm of legitimate political compromise for these parties, and some measure of autonomy for religious education was inevitable. Thus, despite *mamlakhtiyut,* "from the very outset it was clear that Mapai would have to compromise on the demand for one unified educational system throughout the state."[1]

Different educational philosophies had different outlooks on meeting the challenge of the modern world, particularly on the question of whether and how secular knowledge was to be introduced into the traditional religious curriculum. Roughly six conflicting attitudes were prevalent in orthodox Jewish thinking at the time of the formation of the parties:[2]

1. No secular education is permitted in school; learning a craft necessary to earn a living is permitted, but only outside the school.

2. Secular education in the school is permitted if it is necessary to earn a living.

3. Secular education is permitted, although not desirable per se, not only when necessary to acquire the skills to earn a living but also when the government requires it.

4. Secular studies are necessary to the proper understanding of religious studies.

5. Secular studies have independent value of their own, as another, complementary means of understanding the greatness of God and His creation.

6. Secular studies, indeed, the entire Western culture, are to be
accepted as equal in importance to religious studies (this last is, in
essence, the *Torah 'im Derekh Eretz* philosophy of Rabbi S. R.
Hirsch).

The views within the religious parties varied widely. In Agudat Yisrael the extreme views were markedly different. The first
attitude listed above was the dominant one of Agudah's two major
constituencies, Hungarian and Russian-Polish orthodox Jews, as
well as that of the Old Yishuv, whose descendants still maintain
separate, Yiddish-speaking religious schools outside the Israeli
educational system. It shaped both the institutional scope and substantive content of Agudah education. On the elementary level,
however, Agudah has accepted the implications of both the second
and third attitudes above. In PAY circles, particularly in its *kibbutzim,* the fourth attitude predominates, as evidenced by the establishment of a scientific institute for the study of agriculture according to Torah under PAY auspices.

At the opposite extreme of Agudist opinion, and decidedly in
the minority, stood the liberal educational views of Rabbi Hirsch,
whose device of communal separatism Agudah adopted. But while
the Hirsch outlook survived in the small German orthodox community, its impact on the world Agudah organization, and on the
Palestine Agudah in particular, was minimal. Purified of its anti-
Zionist implications, it was more acceptable to the educational
principles of Mizrahi,[3] which under Reines and others had begun to
introduce secular studies into the traditional curriculum in the late
nineteenth century.

Yet the equality of religious and secular knowledge was not
wholly acceptable to Mizrahi either. While attitudes varied, leading
Mizrahi educators took a decidedly instrumental view of secular
studies, which were seen as necessary and desirable not for and in
themselves but for the accomplishment of Mizrahi's religious-
nationalist goals. The Mizrahi philosophy of education, as compared to that of Agudah, is summed up by the movement's leading
educator, Rabbi Ya'akov Berman, as follows:

The disagreement [between Mizrahi and Agudah] concerns the
political and practical work which leads to the building of a modern

Eretz Yisrael and to the return of [the people of] Israel and the preparation of the new generation for the return to its land. And on this point the people of Agudah disagree with Mizrahi as follows: modern political and practical work in order to organize a people and to build a land requires the undertaking of "dangerous" things. It demands modern education in languages, both modern Hebrew and foreign languages. It demands development of ways of life, in literature and art, of scientific concepts and specialization in modern technology; and the public initiative to give children an active, real life education must also be developed. Political ties with non-Jews must be made; and mutual relations and joint public works must be undertaken with all segments of the nation, even with the non-religious. We must develop the will to work, to develop the qualities of initiative and action, to develop the body and the ability to do.

Most of these attributes are lacking in the students of the traditional *beit midrash* [study hall], those who devote day and night to the Book. In the realization of the Redemption and the Return and the rebuilding theré is of course the danger of an imperfection in faith by dint of leaving the confines of the Law and prayer.

And what does Mizrahi believe? That without Redemption and without Zion[ism] the future is quite bleak.[4]

On the basis of this educational philosophy, Mizrahi developed both the content and the scope of its educational institutions.

Because of their fundamental divergence on the question of Zionism, Mizrahi was able to develop its educational system within the institutional framework of the Zionist Kneset Yisrael, whereas Agudah remained outside that framework. Thus the Mizrahi system had far greater financial means and access to new immigrants.

The "Trends"

Education in the Yishuv was firmly politicized at an early stage. In the wake of World War I, the Zionist executive assumed chief financial responsibility for all Zionist-oriented Jewish schools in Palestine, including those of Mizrahi (though the various parties themselves contributed to their own schools' maintenance and development). At the Zionist conference in London in 1920, Mizrahi obtained recognition of its educational system as an autonomous zerem, or "trend," separate and distinct from the "General" trend dominated by the General Zionist party. In 1926, a third trend, Labor, itself an umbrella for the various subtrends of the sundry socialist parties in the Histadrut, was afforded similar recognition.

In 1932 overall financial responsibility for this triple trend system was transferred to the Va'ad Leumi, the executive organ of Kneset Yisrael. The Va'ad Leumi appointed a board of directors whose executive arm, the Department of Education, was also composed by trend. Under this umbrella each of the trends had substantial autonomy. Each had its own Board of Supervisors, which devised the curriculum for its schools and appointed or dismissed teachers, principals, and school inspectors. The trend system applied to all levels of education from kindergarten through teachers' seminaries.[5] It was understood that the particular political party or parties whose ideological outlook each trend represented was to exercise paramount control over it, both in terms of content and appointments.

Although the trends have been officially abolished, education in Israel remains largely a confederation of sectarian systems of education.[6] However, Agudah did not participate in the Zionist Organization or in Kneset Yisrael and was therefore entirely outside the purview of the Va'ad Leumi's trend system. Its educational network consisted of traditional religious elementary schools (hadarim) and higher religious schools of learning (yeshivot), concentrated largely in the places of residence of the Old Yishuv in the larger cities. These were financed by contributions from Jews in Palestine and especially from abroad.

From 1941 on, the Agudah schools were recognized by the Mandatory government and received some financial subsidies, without interference in their educational autonomy.[7] This move was wholly consistent with Agudah's operational ideology. The Mandatory authorities were viewed as a neutral secular government which neither made demands on nor presented any threats to its autonomy. Kneset Yisrael, however, was seen as a voluntary organization of secularized Jews whose influence on their traditions Agudah feared, and whose authority it denied. Once that voluntary organization was transformed into the new sovereign government of Israel, which Agudah recognized de facto, the party was forced to reconcile its anti-Zionism with its need for government support for its educational institutions. It thus opted for inclusion as an independent fourth trend in the former Zionist educational system, which was about to be adopted by the state via the Compulsory Education Law of 1949. It thereby obtained a virtual blanket state subsidy, but at the price of greater state involvement.

Agudah chose trend status for several reasons.[8] For one, the financial condition of its schools had always been precarious, depending upon charitable donations, and state financing was a great temptation. This was particularly true if Agudah was to absorb and socialize any part of the thousands of immigrants who had begun to flow into the new state. With such prospects Agudah was unwilling to overcome its differences with Mizrahi and submerge its educational network in Mizrahi's. It preferred the separate but equal status of an independent trend. Furthermore, the autonomy of the trends could be relied upon to prevent undue interference in the content of its education. As a precondition to trend status, however, the Agudah schools had to meet such minimal requirements as fixed hours of study and set curricula.

The Contest for the Immigrants

The conflict inherent in Mapai's ambition to dominate the educational and thereby the socialization system versus the desire of the religious parties to preserve and expand their carefully nurtured autonomy was apparent from the outset. Thus, while the Compulsory Education Law of 1949[9] ostensibly preserved the trends, its implementation was fraught with difficulties. The law made free and compulsory the attendance of all children aged five to thirteen in a school of one of the four trends. As an alternative, it allowed attendance in a school "recognized" by the minister of education, i.e., a school which met certain minimal standards. The law empowered the minister to exempt children who attended certain non-recognized schools, including the traditional *hadarim* of the 'Eidah Haredit and other orthodox groups, who still allow no secular instruction. These schools, encompassing over five thousand children, receive no government support and are subject to no government supervision whatsoever.

The parents' right to choose among the various types of

education available was stipulated in the law. After the sudden injection of hundreds of thousands of unsocialized immigrants into the political system, however, the complex educational network was subject to such partisan abuse that freedom of parental choice became meaningless, and structural change was inevitable. Furthermore, since most of the immigrants in this period were from the Islamic countries of the Middle East and were therefore, in varying degrees, traditionally religious, the religious parties gained special impetus. Their educational systems had decided advantages over the other trends in the attempts to socialize the immigrants. Tacit evidence of this was given by the sudden mushrooming of a network of religious schools within the Labor trend itself, under the auspices of the Histadrut's splinter religious faction, ha-'Oved ha-Dati. The religious parties viewed this development as a ruse by which Mapai, the dominant party of the Histadrut and of the Labor trend, could siphon off what those parties considered to be their own natural constituency. True religious education, they felt, could only be provided in schools where the staff and the school atmosphere, as well as the curriculum, were religious.

Mapai was not about to abandon the socialization of the masses of the immigrants to the religious parties, especially since it had distinct organizational advantages. Most of the immigrants were at first quartered, for lack of more permanent housing, in camps or *mahanot* that were divided among the various parties by the familiar device of party key, in which every object of patronage is apportioned on the basis of party strength in a particular area. Most of the camps were put under the aegis of the largest party, Mapai. Only some 23 percent were under the tutelage of ha-Po'el ha-Mizrahi. Given the highly dependent condition of these largely indigent immigrants, the party in control of a camp wielded enormous influence over its inhabitants and their decisions, including their choice of educational trends.

The religious parties charged, and a government-appointed investigating committee subsequently affirmed,[10] that various forms of pressure and coercion were being applied by Histadrut and Mapai operatives to dissuade immigrant parents from choosing religious education, thereby effectively excluding the religious trends from immigrant camps. In January 1950 the United Religious Front

(URF) demanded, under the shadow of a boycott of cabinet meetings by its ministers and the threat of its resignation from the government (which would mean the government's fall), the immediate cessation of such pressures on parents.[11] It insisted that religious education should be available to all who desired it and that the continued autonomy of the trends should be guaranteed.[12] In response, the government appointed a ministerial committee of five, including ha-Po'el ha-Mizrahi's Shapira and Agudah's Levin, to examine the question. The committee recommended that religious education be provided to all concentrated ethnic immigrant groups, under the permanent supervision of a ministerial committee of four, to be made up of two ministers of the URF, the minister of education, and one additional minister.[13]

The recommendations of the committee were rejected outright by the Mapai leadership, which instead proposed that a referendum be held in the immigrant camps to consult the parents themselves as to which trend they preferred.[14] In the light of its administrative control over most of the camps and of the confusing division of religious education into three competing systems—Mizrahi, Agudah, and ha-'Oved ha-Dati—Mapai stood to benefit from such a referendum. In a burst of unprecedented unity, the three religious networks announced their merger into one religious educational system in the camps, thereby presenting the immigrant with a clear-cut distinction between religious and non-religious education. Upon this move, Mapai withdrew its referendum proposal.[15]

After exhaustive negotiations, a compromise reached on March 14, 1950, was presented to the Kneset and passed as an amendment to the 1949 law.[16] This provided that education in the Yemenite camps was to be exclusively religious, under the supervision of a panel of four religious individuals representing each of the four trends. In other camps, two types of schools were to be established, one religious and one non-religious. The subsequent registration showed some 80 percent of the parents choosing religious education.[17]

The intent of the agreement was once again flouted by its application. While the religious schools were set up in the Yemenite camps, only two such schools were established in any of the other camps.[18] More important, many of the immigrants were being transferred from the *mahanot* to *ma'abarot* (literally, "transit camps''), where the system applicable elsewhere in the country, the trends, was instituted.[19] Because of political and economic pressure prevalent in the *ma'abarot,* and because parents were unaware of the intricacies of the trend system, many children were registered for the Labor trend school, which was, in any case, the only one available in most of the *ma'abarot.*

The URF vehemently protested these actions. It felt that the agreement did indeed apply to the *ma'abarot,* and that the Mapai minister's unilateral decision that it did not was based at best on a technicality. In any event, as the 1949 law forbade the transfer of students from one trend to another in mid-year, it demanded that those former students of the joint religious schools in the *mahanot* be allowed to continue in religious schools to be set up in the *ma'abarot,* at least until new and fair registration procedures could be implemented for the following academic year.

In the midst of this crisis the ministerial committee presented its new recommendations. These included the establishment of religious schools in all the Yemenite camps, as well as in other camps where no such schools then existed; the participation of a religious representative in registration in all the camps; and the establishment of a ministerial committee of three, including the prime minister, the minister of education, and the minister of religions, to supervise the implementation of these recommendations. The majority of the cabinet approved these proposals and prepared to bring them before the Kneset, but the URF cabinet ministers opposed them because of the provision that religious schools be established in immigrant camps where none existed.[20] These, they feared, would be ha-'Oved ha-Dati schools rather than the joint religious trend institutions like those which had already been established in the Yemenite camps. Furthermore, the institutionalization of an arrangement in education whereby the religious party representatives would be in a permanent minority vis-à-vis the Mapai prime minister and minister of education was anathema.

It was no surprise, therefore, that the URF voted with the opposition when the committee recommendations came before the Kneset on February 14, 1951. As a result, Ben-Gurion announced the government's resignation. New elections were held some five months later.

Nationalization and Independence

As the Second Kneset elections approached, a change in the policy of most parties toward the conflict-ridden trend system appeared because of inter- as well as intra-party pressures. Mapai now favored the nationalization of the entire educational system, so long advocated by the General Zionist party, for a variety of reasons. Externally, it was interested in courting the General Zionists as potential coalition partners in addition to, or in place of, the religious parties for whom the trends had been sacrosanct. What better way to accomplish this goal than to favor one of the General Zionists' central planks, the nationalization of education? Under such a scheme the Ministry of Education would provide a uniform basic curriculum for all the schools, with some provision for optional supplementary religious education.[21]

Developments internal to Mapai and to its related Labor trend also motivated it to seek the nationalization of education. A clear pattern emerged in the application of its *mamlakhtiyut* philosophy. In general, Mapai favored the nationalization of those of its particularistic preserves over which it could maintain, if not augment, its substantial control via the newly established government bureaucracy, as in the case of the labor exchanges. On the other hand, it opposed the nationalization of such preserves as the Histadrut's Qupat Holim sick fund, which, it felt, would reduce its power over a particular area.[22]

As long as the Labor trend was clearly smaller than the General (Zionists') trend, the latter could with some justification claim a dominant position in the Ministry of Education bureaucracy, if not the post of minister itself, and could play an important role in decisions concerning the content of a unified educational system. Table 7.1 shows that the Labor trend—thanks in no small part to its successful absorption of masses of immigrants—dramatically increased its percentage of the school population in a relatively short period of time, largely at the expense of the General trend. As Kleinberger notes, "Under these circumstances there was no longer any danger that State education would merge the Labour trend in the General trend and cause it to lose its distinct identity. On the contrary, the Labour trend, supported by Mapai's dominant position in the Government, had every chance of imprinting its

Table 7.1. Percentage of Pupils in Primary Education, by Trend, 1947–53

Trend	1947–48	1948–49	1949–50	1950–51	1951–52	1952–53
Labor	24.8	26.3	27.3	30.9	35.8	43.4
General	50.1	47.7	41.9	38.3	33.2	27.1
Mizrahi	25.0	25.9	24.4	22.3	20.9	19.1
Agudah	n.a.	n.a.	5.7	5.8	7.2	8.3
Non-trend	0.1	0.1	0.7	2.7	2.9	2.1

Sources: J. A. Bentwich, *Ha-Hinukh bi-Medinat Yisrael* [Education in the state of Israel] (Tel Aviv: Chachik Publishing House, 1960), p. 72; *Report to Nineteenth World Convention,* p. 78.

Table 7.2. Number of Pupils in Primary Education, by Type of School, 1953–72

Year	State	Religious State	Hinukh 'Atzmai	Total
1953–54	150,118	53,573	15,438	219,129
1954–55	162,098	55,525	16,710	234,333
1955–56	176,994	61,696	16,754	255,444
1956–57	196,178	71,212	18,536	285,926
1957–58	220,416	81,354	19,573	321,343
1958–59	232,382	88,477	21,586	342,445
1959–60	239,330	94,763	23,551	357,644
1960–61	240,970	96,437	24,300	361,707
1961–62	243,755	100,495	24,398	368,648
1962–63	247,549	107,435	25,412	380,396
1963–64	253,814	112,863	25,967	392,644
1964–65	254,960	115,554	27,407	397,921
1965–66	255,163	113,375	27,363	395,901
1966–67	253,170	112,685	26,707	392,562
1967–68	248,010	110,887	26,692	385,589
1968–69	248,283	108,745	25,853	382,881
1969–70	246,293	104,294	24,947	375,534
1970–71	245,716	99,663	24,426	369,805
1971–72	267,811	103,810	23,779	395,400

Sources: Central Bureau of Statistics, *Statistical Abstract of Israel,* No. 10 (Jerusalem: CBS, 1958–59), p. 359; No. 13 (Jerusalem: CBS, 1962), p. 486; No. 14 (Jerusalem: CBS, 1963), p. 636; No. 15 (Jerusalem: CBS, 1964), p. 509; No. 19 (Jerusalem: CBS, 1968), p. 533; No. 20 (Jerusalem: CBS, 1969), p. 556; No. 21 (Jerusalem: CBS, 1970), p. 553; No. 22 (Jerusalem: CBS, 1971), p. 553; *Din ve-Heshbon Mugash le-Tzirei ha-Ve'idah ha-'Olamit ha-Kaf Bet shel ha-Mizrahi veha-Po'el ha-Mizrahi* [Report presented to the delegates to the twenty-second Mizrahi and ha-Po'el ha-Mizrahi world convention, pt. 2: education] (Jerusalem: Ha-Merkaz ha-'Olami shel ha-Mizrahi veha-Po'el ha-Mizrahi, 1973), p. 8.

Table 7.3. Percentage of Pupils in Primary Education, by Type of School, 1953–75

School	1953–54	1955–56	1956–57	1960–61	1964–65	1965–66	1967–68	1968–69	1969–70	1970–71	1973–74	1974–75
State	68.5	69.3	68.6	66.6	64.1	64.5	64.4	64.8	65.5	66.4	69.8	70.7
Religious state	24.5	23.9	24.8	26.7	29.0	28.6	28.8	28.5	28.0	27.0	24.1	23.3
Recognized independent[1]	7.0	6.7	6.6	6.7	6.9	6.9	6.8	6.7	6.5	6.6	6.1	6.0

Sources: Central Bureau of Statistics, *Statistical Abstract of Israel*, No. 18 (Jerusalem: CBS, 1967), p. 529; No. 25 (Jerusalem: CBS, 1974), p. 617; No. 26 (Jerusalem: CBS, 1975), p. 612; *Israel Government Yearbook*, 1957, p. 173; 1958, p. 162; 1965, p. 174; 1966, p. 181; 1967, p. 159; 1968, p. 196; 1970, p. 153; 1971, p. 156; 1972, p. 148.

[1] *Hinukh 'Atzmai*.

characteristic aims and values on the educational system as a whole.''[23]

The Labor trend itself was becoming less ideological because the old socialist (and even Zionist) slogans had little or no appeal to the masses of new immigrants. Thus serious doubt was cast on the advisability of maintaining it as a separate entity. Mapai met strong opposition from its more ideologically oriented junior partners in the Labor trend, Ahdut 'Avodah and Mapam, who feared that abandonment of their educational system would herald their political decline. Hence, both smaller parties favored the continuance of the separate Labor trend: "Mapai . . . could profit more by State education. For its predominant position in the Government in general and in the Ministry of Education in particular would enable Mapai to introduce the fundamental principles and values of Labor education throughout the system of State education.''[24]

The religious parties also began re-thinking their positions for internal as well as external and ideological as well as pragmatic reasons. Both Mizrahi and ha-Po'el ha-Mizrahi were alarmed not only by the steadily declining percentage of the Mizrahi trend and the concomitant rise of the Labor trend but also, and perhaps more distressingly, by the new Agudah trend.[25]

State education divided into separate secular and religious sections, such as Mizrahi and ha-Po'el ha-Mizrahi now advocated in their Second Kneset platform, would eliminate all the Mizrahi trend's rivals. The Labor trend and its religious offshoot would be merged into some type of general state education, while the Agudah trend would either be absorbed by Mizrahi or would be denationalized completely. As a result, the decline of the Mizrahi educational system would be arrested. Furthermore, by accepting a modified plan of state education, Mizrahi and ha-Po'el ha-Mizrahi once again made themselves attractive coalition partners for Mapai.

Agudah, along with Mapam and Ahdut 'Avodah on the far left, was one of the few parties to favor the continuation of the trend system, and for good reason. Its newly established trend had grown impressively, and it rejected Mizrahi's bid for merger.[26] Just as understandably, it was opposed to a single state religious education system under Mizrahi domination; such a system would mean either the submergence of its trend or its total exclusion from official status and financing. Furthermore, the government financing of its educational system and the substantial autonomy afforded by the trend system were ideally suited to Agudah's long-standing separatist ideology.

Thus Agudah's conditions for joining any government in the newly elected Second Kneset were a two-year moratorium on the question of changes in the educational system and a one-year moratorium on the question of National Service for religious women; it hoped thereby to defer indefinitely legislative action on both issues.[27] Only a one-year moratorium was accepted by Mapai, during which time it proceeded to plan such legislative initiatives as per Article 20 of the Basic Principles of the Government Program presented to the Kneset on October 7, 1951.[28] With the moratorium about to expire, and government action on these two fundamental questions imminent, Agudah (and PAY) resigned from the government on September 18, 1952.

With the elimination of Agudah and PAY, Mapai established a broadened coalition, which included the General Zionists and Progressives, who had long advocated the elimination of the trends. With conditional approval for the move by Mizrahi and ha-Po'el ha-Mizrahi, the way was clear for the nationalization of the educational system.

The nationalization itself was effected by the State Education Law of 1953,[29] passed on August 12 of that year. The law explicitly (Section 27) eliminated the trends and substituted state education, which it defined as "education provided by the State on the basis of the curriculum, without attachment to a party or communal body or any other organization outside the Government, and under the supervision of the Minister, or a person authorized by him in that behalf."[30]

Thus far the law would seem to strike a fatal blow at the religious parties and their hitherto autonomous trends. However, the separation of education and schools into two categories, "state" and "religious state" is the leitmotif of the whole law.[31] Religious state education is defined as a state educational system whose way of life, curriculum, teachers, and inspectors are religious.[32] Since institutionalization of this vital religious interest, preferably under Mizrahi–ha-Po'el ha-Mizrahi colonization, was necessary if the two parties were to agree to the nationalization,[33] the law and the regulations issued under it provided carefully delineated institutional structures which gave substantial autonomy to religious state education and assured continued domination of the system by Mizrahi and ha-Po'el ha-Mizrahi.

Among the most important of these structures is the Council for Religious State Education. Its very composition indicates the continued dominant influence of Mafdal in religious state education. Its fourteen members are nominally appointed by the minister of education for four-year terms with the approval of the cabinet, where Mafdal ministers can oppose objectionable appointments. Only two members, however, are actually appointed by the minister of education himself. Six others, the largest bloc on the council, are chosen by him from a list of twelve drawn up by the minister of religions, who, as we have seen, has almost invariably been a leading Mafdal member. Three other members are chosen from a list of six proposed by the (Mafdal-oriented) religious teachers association. The final three are the religious members of the overall Education Committee, a far less autonomous institution which advises the minister on matters of state education: "In sum, the statutory composition of the Council for Religious State Education guarantees that at least nine of its fourteen members will be nominees of the National Religious Party and that this political faction effectively controls the entire personnel of religious State Education."[34]

The far-reaching powers granted to the council reflect the autonomy of religious state education. The law stipulates that the minister of education must consult with the council before exercising any of the powers vested in him, including the appointment of the director of the Religious Education Department within the ministry and of inspectors, principals, and teachers for the state religious schools.

The council may disqualify a person from appointment or continued service as a teacher, principal, or inspector in the religious educational system on purely religious grounds, whether related to public or private life.[35] Thus, in order to be hired, a candidate and his spouse must live a religious life, defined as regular participation in public worship and so forth, and must also take an active part in the religious aspects of public life, a requirement which can be interpreted as participation in a particular religious party. In fact, the political significance of the personnel of the religious state education network for Mafdal is great, especially on the local level.[36] The marriage of a teacher to a non-religious person or the education of a teacher's child in an institution other than a state religious one is cause for dismissal. The net result is that most employees of the religious state system, especially its higher officials, are Mafdal members. Over the years, the council has expanded its authority to such matters as the supervision of curricula, coeducation, supplementary education, teacher education, structural changes in the educational system, budgetary decisions, and so on.[37]

The other important structure established at Mizrahi and ha-Po-el ha-Mizrahi's insistence in order to preserve the autonomy of their former trend is the Religious Department of the Ministry of Education. The appointment of the director of this executive arm of religious state education must be passed on by the council, as noted earlier. While only mentioned in passing in the 1953 law, the very considerable powers of this department and its director were delineated in the State Education Rules (Procedures of Inspection) set forth by the minister of education in 1956, by authority of Section 34 of the law.[38] They specify that the director shall be "the supreme pedagogic authority as far as religious State schools are concerned."[39]

The enormous political significance of this position to Mafdal, which is, in effect, the head of the party's system of socialization, is evidenced by the fact that its long-time occupant, Yosef Goldschmidt, held the position from its inception in 1953 until 1968, shortly before he was elected to the Kneset on the Mafdal list. Mr. Goldschmidt is a member of the party's Central Faction headed by Dr. Zerah Warhaftig, who, as long-time minister of religions, wielded great influence on the state religious education system via appointments.

The 1953 State Education Law envisaged that state religious education would apply to both the Mizrahi and the Agudah trends, with two separated "tracks," one "general religious," and the other "Torah religious," thereby making some accommodation for the Agudah schools.[40] But when the state religious education system was established, all former Mizrahi schools and most of the religious Labor trend schools joined, but only 21 of some 104 Agudah schools did so, and of these most were in PAY agricultural settlements.[41]

The rest of the Agudah schools were organized under a sepa-

rate framework called Hinukh 'Atzmai ("independent education").
Section 11 of the State Education Law[42] gave the minister of education discretionary power to declare non-official schools to be
"recognized" educational institutions if they followed a minimum
program under the ministry's supervision, and to grant them budgetary support. The reasons for this move are not hard to discern.
Agudah agreed to enter the government education system in 1949
only as long as the trend system, which assured it maximum autonomy and government support with minimum government supervision, applied. With the abolition of the trends and the nationalization of education, the Agudah system would have had to accept far
greater government intervention. And with the simultaneous establishment of the religious state education network, it would have
had to subordinate its system of socialization to that of Mizrahi-ha-
Po'el ha-Mizrahi, which dominated the new machinery, offers and
assurances of a "separate track" notwithstanding.

The administrative structure and staff of Hinukh 'Atzmai are
even more clearly related to its parent party, Agudah, than those of
religious state education are to Mafdal.[43] The Hinukh 'Atzmai
center is headed by a directorate of rabbis, most of whom are also
members of Agudah's Council of Torah Greats. A smaller executive committee included the late Rabbi Yitzhak Meir Levin, a
Kneset member and head of Agudat Yisrael, and Rabbi Menahem
Porush, an Agudah Kneset member.

Despite its "nonofficial" character, Agudah's Hinukh 'Atzmai has more influence over educational content, administrative
supervision, and personnel practices than the State Education Law
would imply. At the same time, Hinukh 'Atzmai has received
larger and larger government subsidies despite its minimal subordi-
nation to government. The actual percentage of government sub-
vention of Hinukh 'Atzmai's budget has risen from 60 in 1953, to
66 in 1956, to 75 in 1957, to 85 in 1960, which remains the current
figure. The increases have often been granted by Mapai, whose
education minister holds the discretionary power, in return for
Agudah's political support, despite its non-participation in the coalition, in instances where coalition partners defected over such
sensitive issues as the continuation of military rule in Arab areas of
the country in the early 1960s.[44]

Two minimal conditions have been imposed on Hinukh 'Atz-

mai by the ministry:[45] that its teachers must possess formal qualifications equal to those in official schools, and that the language of
instruction, except for Talmud, be Hebrew, as opposed to Yiddish,
still the *lingua franca* of many of the traditional *hadarim* and *yeshivot* today.

The new arrangements were ideal for Agudah in still another
way. Both the Compulsory Education Law of 1949 and the State
Education Law of 1953 deal only with elementary, and not secondary, education, which is neither entirely free nor compulsory in
Israel as yet. Agudah sees secondary education as unnecessary
and/or undesirable, and thus finds the structure set up under these
laws entirely adequate. The Hinukh 'Atzmai system itself is limited
almost exclusively to kindergartens and elementary schools, divided into Talmudei Torah or *hadarim* for boys and Beit Ya'akov
schools for girls. For those who continue their education to the
secondary level, the traditional yeshivah education is the rule for
boys. For girls there are a handful of secondary schools and three
teachers' seminaries.

So satisfied is Agudah with the confinement of compulsory
education to the elementary level that when a government commission proposed educational reform of the structure in 1965, including
the establishment of junior high schools through the ninth grade,
thereby making the first year of secondary school compulsory, Agudah felt its educational system threatened. The reform meant, in
effect, the imposition of an additional year of what Agudah considered unnecessary secular studies at the expense of Talmud study
in the *yeshivot*. Agudah successfully evaded the dictum and de-
fended its institutions by receiving permission from the Ministry of
Education to provide the additional year of compulsory education
within its existing framework. Once it had obtained these assurances, Agudah proceeded to vote for the reform in the Kneset.

The legal structure of education was far less adequate for
Mafdal, whose educational philosophy was based on an acceptance
of at least the utility of modern secular education and whose educational institutions were far more extensive than those of Agudah.
Mafdal-related education included not only the kindergartens and
elementary schools of the government-funded religious state educational system but also secondary schools of various types: academic, vocational, agricultural, and evening (for working youth);

"programmatic" *yeshivot* (*megamatiyot*), which combine the traditional curriculum with academic (*yeshivot tikhoniyot*), vocational
(*yeshivot miktzo'iyot*), or agricultural (*yeshivot haklaiyot*) curricula;
parallel institutions for girls called *ulpanot*; and regular *yeshivot,*
teachers' seminaries, and the related Bar-Ilan University.

The lack of government recognition, supervision, and in particular, funding of this post-primary network was, therefore, a far
greater problem for Mafdal than for the much smaller system of
Agudah, for it meant, in effect, that the party had to finance an
extensive and expensive network of education, particularly on the
secondary level. As a result, a far smaller percentage of the pupil
population (about half) originally attended Mafdal-related high
schools than attended the state religious elementary schools, a gap
which intensive efforts have all but closed. Nevertheless, roughly
30 percent of the school population has attended religious state
schools over the years, but only about 15 percent (again half) votes
for the religious parties, which indicates a serious failure of their
system of socialization.

Mafdal believed that it was in the secondary school that the
religious and political habits of the next generation were firmly
molded[46] and that the largest reservoir of potential voters was
among its own high school graduates.[47] Therefore the party advocated the extension of nationalization to its secondary schools. But
there was no pre-existing institutional framework applicable to secondary education in general in Israel, and certainly no niche
therein for Mafdal. The party had to resort to the far less satisfactory alternative of reliance on coalition agreements, administrative
regulations, and other less concrete means to secure at least the
semi-nationalization of religious secondary education. It was not
until June 5, 1962,[48] that the minister of education issued regulations for religious secondary schools that closely followed the pattern of supervision established for the religious state primary
schools. The state subsidy remained limited to the first year of
compulsory high school, with sliding-scale tuition support beyond
that. Yet, with the promulgation of these regulations, Mafdal considered that "we have arrived at, thank God, the *de jure* recognition by the State of the entire religious educational system in its
various sectors, from kindergarten up until higher education."[49]

This "educational reform" was as strenuously opposed by

Mafdal as by Agudah, but for entirely different reasons. Mafdal did not disagree with the extension of compulsory free education per se: indeed, it had long advocated such a move. But it did oppose the method chosen, which focused on the intermediate school. Transferring the seventh and eighth grades from the elementary school to the secondary level placed the burden on the weakest link in the Mafdal-related educational network. Mafdal saw the new system as particularly threatening to its *yeshivot tikhoniyot*,[50] highly selective boarding institutions based on a four-year program of intensive and rigidly structured study as well as immersion in a religious way of life.[51] Once the reform was voted into law, with Mafdal's abstention, a solution was worked out: two-year (seventh and eighth grades) junior high schools were appended to the *yeshivot tikhoniyot*.

The Socialization of Values

Both the religious educational systems are quantitatively far more heavily weighted in favor of religious and Jewish subjects than are the regular state schools.

Taking the seventh- and eighth-grade curricula,[52] for example, the secular state schools provide four hours per week for Bible study—which is not necessarily a religious subject in Israel— while the religious state schools allocate five hours and the independent religious schools seven hours to the same subject. The study of Talmud is only perfunctorily undertaken in the general schools, with one hour per week, whereas in both religious systems it occupies the largest single bloc of time (seven and eight hours, respectively). Some subjects, such as religious laws and customs and prayer, are absent entirely from the general curriculum, while they play a prominent role, either as part of the prescribed curriculum or as a mandatory extracurricular activity, in both religious systems.

There is another group of subjects, more neutral in nature, which occupy approximately the same amount of time in the seventh and eighth grades of all three school systems. These subjects include Hebrew language and literature (three hours) and mathematics (four hours). However, because of the time devoted to religious studies, the religious schools have fewer hours to devote to certain secular subjects that may be deemed more sensitive or less practical. These subjects include natural sciences, history, art, music, agriculture, handicrafts, and physical education, some of which seldom appear in the religious school curricula.

As a result of the weaker emphasis on secular studies, students from religious schools have generally scored less well than others on the Seker, the national survey test of eighth-graders which determines admission to high school and hence access to government tuition aid.[53] This fact does not trouble Hinukh 'Atzmai greatly because few of its graduates continue on to secondary schools, but it is a source of vexation to those within the Mafdal-related system.

Bible study is a compulsory subject which is given almost equal weight in both secular and religious state schools. In the former it is approached more as a source of national literature and history and as the basis of universal social and moral ideals than as the revealed word of God.[54] In the religious schools, however, "the written Torah and its oral interpretation that was given to Israel by God, and God's work in the hands of the Prophets and in the Hagiographa that were written with the Divine Spirit, comprise the central [factor] in the life of the people of Israel, both as a book of instructions for every detail of an individual's behavior, and as a treasury of its wisdom and culture."[55] The aims of Bible instruction in the religious schools, then, are not only to instill belief in the divine and literal truth of the Bible, and the authoritative interpretation thereof by the oral law and rabbinical literature, but also to encourage observance of its commandments.[56] In other words, the objective is to socialize the students in the values and behavior patterns of Mafdal.

The differences between state religious and non-religious schools are not limited to subjects of a religious nature. In history, for example, the religious schools emphasize the "observance of the divine law," while the non-religious institutions stress the "sublime principles of Israel's religion."[57] In science, the religious schools are careful to instill the belief in the divine creation,[58] and religious criteria are used in the selection of Hebrew literature to be read.[59] Similarly, the religious ties between the Jewish people and its land are underscored in yedi'ot ha-aretz ("homeland study").[60] Indeed,

while the curriculum in all Israeli schools is ethnocentric and nationalistic, often to the point of chauvinism, studies have shown that "in
all these respects the ethno-centric attitudes among teachers and
pupils in the religious schools were significantly stronger than in
secular schools. This is not surprising, since the notion of the
'chosen people' derives from religious tradition."[61] The implications of these findings for the strongly nationalistic tendencies of the
religious parties, particularly of Mafdal and especially of its younger
elements, the Tze'irim, cannot be ignored.

There may seem to be little difference between the state religious and the Hinukh 'Atzmai systems of education, yet the two
networks reflect the ideological and sociological differences of the
political parties which founded them. The fundamental question
remains that of accommodation to the modern age and its corol-
lary, modern political nationalism, or Zionism. The Mafdal outlook
attempts to reconcile the challenges of modern life with a continued adherence to religious observance. The Agudah approach
tries to stave off the effects of such challenges insofar as possible,
and to maintain both a high level of religious observance and a
highly traditional way of life.

Take the question of military service. The religious state
schools are based on the tenets of religious Zionism: the state itself
is seen as a positive manifestation of the divine will and the beginning of the redemption of the Jewish people. Inasmuch as the state
is regarded as something holy, the necessity to defend it by service
in the army becomes not only an obligation of good citizenship, but
a positive religious duty as well. Thus, there is a clearly positive
attitude in the religious state schools toward military service, at
least for boys, and there is substantial, though by no means uniform, support in Mafdal for the implementation of a voluntary system of civilian national service for religious girls as a substitute for
military service.

These values are not shared by the Hinukh 'Atzmai system.
Since it never accepted the Zionist vision, Agudah does not view
the Israeli state as holy, but rather as a secular human creation.
The allegiance owed the state by each citizen does not override
supreme religious values, which in this case dictate the continuation of yeshivah study for boys without the interruption of military
service. Thus, the attitude toward military service for boys in Hin-

ukh 'Atzmai schools is negative. As for girls' military or alternative service, the attitude is completely hostile.

Other differences between the systems reflect their values. In Hinukh 'Atzmai schools, religious studies are carried on in one solid bloc of time, beginning in the morning, and secular studies are confined to the end of the compulsory school day, indicating their lesser importance. In religious state schools, religious and secular subjects alternate throughout the school day. Hinukh 'Atzmai schools are never coeducational; religious state schools are partially coeducational. Personal appearance and dress of teachers and students in Hinukh 'Atzmai schools are more traditional than in the religious state schools.

The apparently stronger traditionalism of the Hinukh 'Atzmai schools gives the impression that they are therefore more "religious." As a far larger and official state education system, the religious state system has had to absorb many children of parents, particularly Sephardi immigrants, who, though themselves not religiously observant, are attracted to the religious system because of a general interest in a traditional life. This infusion has led in many cases to a dilution of both the religious and the educational levels of the religious state schools and, in turn, to the demand of some parents for a separate Torah education track within the state system, or, alternatively, to choosing Hinukh 'Atzmai education for their children. Mafdal condemned parents, some of them active party members, who chose Hinukh 'Atzmai, thereby in effect choosing to socialize their children into another value system and, ultimately, into another party.[62] The rapid growth of and emphasis on developing Mafdal-oriented secondary schools in general, and *yeshivot* in particular, is an attempt to counter the image of Agudah's schools as more religious and to ensure the religious and political socialization of the next generation. As a result of these efforts, the percentage of pupils in Mafdal-related secondary schools of all types rose from 16 in 1953 to 19 in 1962 to 22 in 1967 to over 25 in 1972. Enrollment was 13,000 in 1962, 26,000 in 1967, 30,000 in 1968, and 35,000 in 1972.[63]

In measuring the effectiveness of the religious aspects of the two systems, a survey of graduates of Mafdal-related secondary schools (no such information is available on Hinukh 'Atzmai) found that about three-quarters of the respondents reported personal religious observance, as measured by such criteria as wearing of a *kipah* (skullcap), non-travel on Saturday, socializing or marriage within religious circles, attendance at synagogue on Saturday, and so on.[64] However, the survey found a significant difference among Ashkenazi graduates, who were consistently more observant than Sephardi graduates. If one considers that only 20 percent of religious high school graduates are Sephardi, as opposed to some 75 percent of the students of the much larger state religious elementary school system, it is apparent that Mafdal's socialization system has been qualitatively less successful in regard to the Sephardim, who constitute the numerical bulk of the religious state elementary school system, and a major portion of the Mafdal membership and votership itself.

The lower level of religious observance for Sephardim tends to augur ill for their continued participation in the religious state education system. Indeed, the decline from the highs of the mid-1960s already in evidence (see Tables 7.2 and 7.3) is due in no small part to the fact that second-generation Sephardim do not send their children to religious state schools. This pattern is unfavorable to their continued adherence to Mafdal, and Mafdal is making strenuous efforts to increase the percentage of Sephardi students in its secondary schools, despite the higher costs involved in subsidizing them.

To examine the effectiveness of the political aspects of the socialization process, our primary concern here, we may put the question thus: why is it that while about one-third of Israeli schoolchildren attend religious schools, the religious parties receive only half that number, or some 15 percent of the vote? The contrast is even sharper when one compares the voting strength of the individual religious parties with the size of their respective education-socialization systems. Thus Mafdal (plus half of PAY, which has no separate education system but shares both) received some 10.6 percent of the vote in the 1969 Kneset elections, while Agudah (and the other half of PAY) received some 4.1 percent. The percentage of the population enrolled in religious state schools at the time was 27, nearly three times the Mafdal vote, while the percentage of the population in the Hinukh 'Atzmai system was 5.5, only slightly more than the Agudah vote. Adjusting for the fact that there are more children than parents-voters, especially in Agudah-oriented families, the Agudah votership and educational system are well synchronized. In general, those who vote Agudah also educate their children in Hinukh 'Atzmai schools, and vice versa.

The relationship between Mafdal and its related education-socialization system is more problematic. Even assuming that there is no overt party propaganda in its schools, as stipulated by the state education law,[65] the religious-nationalist values taught in the system are identical with those of Mafdal, the chief political patron, protector, promoter, and provider of staff of the religious state education system. Why has Mafdal not made further inroads into its natural hinterland, the religious state education system, and attracted more political support from among those it has educated? Why has its political socialization system failed to a marked degree?

Several factors contribute to this relative failure. Although many parents favor religious education for reasons of tradition or sentiment, they are not necessarily religiously observant themselves and apparently give higher priority to economic, political, or personality considerations when it comes to voting. This tendency is reinforced by Mafdal's image of primary, if not sole, concern with religious matters, which leaves the important questions of economic or foreign policy in the hands of its long-time senior coalition partner, Labor. It is precisely this image which the Tze'irim have set out to change. For those who vote for the opposition Likud, Mafdal's close association with the Establishment makes it an unattractive choice. Thus, ironically, Mafdal's very success in nationalizing so much of the religious establishment, including education, has left marginal voters free to pursue other political inclinations.

The typical Mafdal voter, then, either regards religious issues as the most salient ones or is organizationally and financially tied to the party by dint of membership in it or employment by it, which are often synonymous. Indeed, there is little floating vote attracted to Mafdal. For example, while there were roughly 100,000 members (including spouses) of ha-Po'el ha-Mizrahi, the core of Mafdal membership, at the time of the Seventh Kneset election in 1969, the party's total popular vote that year was only 133,000. Further, the party has not devoted much effort to the political organization of the parents of religious state schoolchildren,[66] and only lately has it shifted its emphasis from the rapid quantitative expansion of religious state elementary schools to their qualitative development, and to the expansion of its high school system, the principal source of future voters.

Mafdal's partial failure to penetrate into and politically social-ize broader social groups does not negate the fact that it has main-tained and even slightly increased its voting strength over the first two decades of statehood (though it experienced a decline to its 1949 level in the wake of the 1973 war). Whether the party will continue to hold its own depends largely on the effectiveness of its education-socialization system. From statistical evidence (see Ta-bles 7.2 and 7.3), however, it appears that there has been a gradual, if steady, decline in both the absolute numbers of pupils and the percentage in both the religious education systems. If unchecked, this phenomenon could show up in another ten years or so as a declining votership as well.

Chapter 8
"Who Is a Jew?"

The question of who is a Jew in Israeli politics is not limited to any one specific instance or case. Rather, it is a manifestation of one of those underlying, long-term, unresolved, fundamental problems in a polity—perhaps like the civil rights issue in the United States—which recur periodically with great intensity and in a variety of different forms and guises: court cases, administrative rulings, laws, coalition agreements, public protests, and the like. Our purpose here is not to detail the controversy but to delineate the importance of the issue to the Israeli political system as a whole, to the religious parties in particular, and to Mafdal specifically. The issue raises a serious challenge to the basic operational ideology fundamental to Mafdal, the nationalization of religion; as Agudah does not subscribe to this principle, it is less directly involved in the issue.

The roots of the problem lie in the early debates in the World Zionist Organization over the "cultural question," i.e., whether the WZO, or its offspring, the state of Israel, had the right to intervene in religious-cultural questions which many orthodox Jews felt to be beyond the legitimate bounds of secular state authority.

Mafdal, whose antecedent, Mizrahi, arose because of this very issue, felt that the determination of who is a Jew is a purely *halakhic* question, to be ascertained by the competent rabbinic authorities. Once this is done, the state could render its judgment on the civil rights and duties that do or do not arise. The claim to prior rights of religious authorities over the state is a serious challenge to the sovereignty of the state and has broad ramifications. Questions such as the obligation of military service, especially for women, present the issue dramatically: does the pressing need of

the state for a defense force override the decision of religious authorities that such service is prohibited for women? The state, for
its part, claims the right to make its own determination of who is or
is not a Jew insofar as it is necessary to decide on an individual's
obligations and privileges vis-à-vis the state, a determination which
it feels is entirely independent of the religious one.

These are, of course, the extreme positions. Actually, each
side has recognized its vested interest in the other—the religionists
in the survival of the state, the statists in the maintenance of the
state's ties to tradition, ties which give it legitimacy and preserve
national unity both in Israel and among Jews abroad. Based on this
mutual recognition of the need for each other, the arrangements
collectively known as the status quo have been worked out. Thus
the state has long since ceded its sovereign right to determine the
personal status of its citizens to the religious courts, though agitation for the institution of secular marriage and divorce in Israel, a
related question, flares up regularly. Whether or not the determination of who is a Jew for purposes other than those of marriage,
divorce, and the like is part of that grant of autonomy to the religious authorities or whether it is a residual right of the state is the
crux of the problem.

Legislative Definitions

Basically, the question of who is a Jew is a latter-day version
of the centuries-old conflict between religious authority and the
state, a conflict familiar in both cultural contexts in which the
Israeli political system operates, the western Christian and the
Middle Eastern Islamic. It is one of the fundamental conflicts, like
that between central and local authority (or center vs. periphery),
the resolution of which affects the types and stability of the political system. Yet only in the last twenty-eight years has Judaism had
to come to grips with a sovereign state which claims it as the
source of its legitimacy.

The question arises most frequently in connection with the
laws relating to immigration and population registry, particularly in
filling in the categories of *le'om* (nationality or ethnic group) and
dat (religion) on the appropriate documents. In the absence of clear

legislative guidance, the Ministry of Interior, which is charged with the application of these laws, must either make an administrative determination of its own or follow that of the rabbinical authorities on who is a Jew. The issue is somewhat less complicated in the case of most people married in Israel and that of their children, as the rabbinate and rabbinical courts in charge of these affairs prevent intermarriage, thereby avoiding most complicated and controversial problems of the determination of Jewishness. However, immigrants whose marriages, divorces, and the like, took place abroad, and which therefore may or may not have been *halakhically* valid, may find that the rabbinical authorities differ from the Ministry of Interior as to their Jewishness.

Under the 1950 Law of Return, all Jews, with certain limited exceptions such as criminals and others whose presence would endanger the welfare or security of the state, were guaranteed the right to immigrate to Israel. Subsequent legislation and administrative regulation provided automatic citizenship (unless waived) and a variety of material aids and incentives for the new immigrant. The law does not specify, however, who is to be considered a Jew for purposes of determining immigrant status and rights. Such a determination is left to the ministry in charge of implementing the law, the Ministry of Interior.

Although Mafdal attaches particular importance to the control of this ministry, precisely because of its influence over such matters, one of the most notorious episodes in the saga of who is a Jew arose in 1958, when the ministry was in the hands of Mr. Bar-Yehudah of Ahdut 'Avodah, a small, secularist, socialist party since absorbed into the Labor party. In March Bar-Yehudah issued new regulations under which a person was to be registered as Jewish on the strength of his own declaration, irrespective of whether he or she would be deemed Jewish under rabbinical law. Further, a declaration by parents that a child is Jewish was to be sufficient grounds for registering him as such, even when the mother was a non-Jew, a blatant contradiction of religious law. The rationale given in the regulations was that the religious and secular definitions of a Jew differ, and that one can be considered a Jew in the èyes of the secular law of the state while not being considered so under *halakhah*.[1]

Mafdal swiftly raised several objections to the regulations.[2]

On the level of practical politics, the party contended that the regulations violated the religious status quo enshrined in the coalition agreement. On the level of operational ideology, the regulations, although ostensibly applicable only to questions of population registry and not binding upon the rabbinical courts, would by their nature infringe upon the exclusive authority of the latter to determine the personal status of Israeli Jews. On the still higher plane of ultimate ideology, Mafdal's Warhaftig asserted that adherence to the regulations would split the Jewish people into two groups, those who were genuine *halakhic* Jews and those who were not, with intermarriage between the two prohibited by religious law.

Inter-party negotiations resulted in only a slight modification of the regulations—a person's declaration that he was a Jew had to be made in good faith, and he had to declare also that he was not an adherent of another faith—and Mafdal, for the first time, left the government. Its ministers, Shapira and Burg, and deputy ministers, Warhaftig, Ben-Meir, and Unna, resigned their positions. Agudah and PAY, who were already in the opposition, joined Mafdal in protesting the regulations, and in an unsuccessful no-confidence vote in the Kneset. Chief Rabbi Herzog issued a strongly worded condemnation and reaffirmed the inseparable nature of the religious and national definitions of a Jew.[3] A storm of protest among orthodox Jews in Israel and abroad ensued.

In an effort to defuse the opposition, Ben-Gurion sent inquiries to some forty-five Jewish sages in Israel and abroad asking for their opinion on the question. When the responses came back in the summer of 1959, it was apparent that the overwhelming majority supported the traditional orthodox definition. Mafdal's position was thus strengthened. When the government fell in July 1959 because left-wing Mapam and Ahdut 'Avodah opposed arms sales to Germany, Mafdal was able to recover control of the Ministry of Interior in the new government formed after the Fourth Kneset elections in December 1959, and also obtained a change in registration policy. A child of a mixed marriage was not registered as to its religion or nationality, but those of its parents were noted. This obviated the possibility of non-Jews ultimately marrying Jews on the strength of a judgment made by a government bureaucrat rather than by the rabbinate.

Court Rulings

It was not long before a new manifestation of the who is a Jew dilemma arose, this time in the Supreme Court (sitting as the High Court of Justice). While the court's ultimate decision was favorable to Mafdal's position, the grounds for that decision were distinctly inimical to the conception of religiously determined nationality.

Brother Daniel Rufeisen, a Polish-born Jew who had become a Carmelite monk, attempted to be registered as a Jew in order to receive the same status and privileges under law as any other Jewish immigrant. The interior minister, Mafdal's Shapira, based his refusal to do so, ostensibly, at least, on the earlier cabinet decision in 1958, then still valid, that a Jew is one who sincerely declares himself to be so and, what is more important, is not a member of another religion. Rufeisen claimed that despite his conversion he remained ethnically a Jew and hence was entitled to be classified as such under the *le'om* category.

Once again, the indivisibility of the religious and national aspects of being Jewish, which Mafdal upheld, and the right of rabbinical authorities to determine questions of personal status on the basis of *halakhah* were being fundamentally challenged. This time, however, the onus of *halakhic* proof was on Mafdal and those who adhered to its position, for under *halakhah,* Rufeisen, having been born of Jewish parents, was still a Jew. Hence, Mafdal spokesmen endeavored to emphasize the limitations on the Jewish status of a convert to another religion, particularly in the area of inheritance, which is the basis for the Law of Return.

The majority of the Supreme Court, however, insisted upon a strict interpretation of *halakhah* by which Rufeisen would be deemed technically a Jew. Their denial of his appeal was based on grounds that the *halakhic* and secular definitions of a Jew are not necessarily the same, and that the state is bound only by the former. In secular parlance, a convert from Judaism is no longer considered a Jew, and therefore Rufeisen ought to be, and was, denied his request.[4] While the practical result of the case was satisfactory to both camps, the basis for the decision augured ill for Mafdal and its ideological conception of state and religion, for it tended to transfer the power of deciding who is a Jew from the rabbinate and its *halakhah* to some vaguely defined popular will, as interpreted by the Supreme Court.

Perhaps the high point in the developments inimical to Mafdal's stand came in the first Shalit case in 1968.[5] Briefly, the facts were as follows: Benjamin Shalit, a Jew born in Israel, a naval officer, married a non-Jewish woman abroad and returned home. Difficulties arose between Shalit and the Ministry of Interior when he requested that his two children be formally registered as Jews under the *le'om* category. Following the procedures enacted in 1960 after Mafdal rejoined the government, which provided for leaving blank, in such cases, the category on the official, legally mandated registration forms, the ministry refused to accede to Shalit's demand. As for the "religion" category, the parents were content to have that left blank, as they said that they were atheists.

On the precedent of the Rufeisen case, the Supreme Court, by a five to four margin, ruled that Shalit was entitled to register his children as Jews by nationality, though not by religion. There is a significant difference between the cases of Rufeisen and Shalit, however, one which the court itself alluded to indirectly, for whereas in the first case the court took upon itself the right to decide the "Jewishness" of a born Jew whose *halakhic* status was now somewhat cloudy because of his subsequent conversion, in the second it ruled that two individuals who were clearly not Jewish in a *halakhic* sense were to be considered Jews, at least ethnically. While the court did take pains to point out that the thrust of its decision was not to detract from the authority of the rabbinical courts to decide questions of marriage, divorce, and the like, this blatant violation of *halakhah* grated not only on the sensibilities of Mafdal members and other orthodox Jews but of many Israeli citizens who felt that the court was overstepping its bounds.

New Regulations

Led by Mafdal, but with broad inter-party support, momentum gathered in the Kneset to amend the Law of Return and the Population Registry Law to define more clearly Jewishness and to limit the power of the court to make determinations in this area which are alien to Jewish tradition. How much of this sentiment was motivated by genuine religious or nationalist considerations and how much by pragmatic political concerns for the continued unity of the coalition after the 1969 Seventh Kneset elections (the amendment was part of the new coalition agreement) is hard to tell. Nevertheless, the laws were amended by Kneset legislation in 1970. The definition of a Jew for the purposes of these laws— immigration and population registry—is now essentially the *halakhic* one: a Jew is one born to a Jewish mother or one who was converted. To prevent the recurrence of the Brother Daniel incident, the amendment excludes those who have adopted another religion. The law, however, does allow non-Jewish family members of Jewish immigrants to enjoy the same privileges of citizenship and immigrant status as their Jewish relatives, again excluding only Jews who have converted to other religions. The awarding of immigration privileges to non-Jews was particularly distasteful to the religious parties, but apparently was the price Mafdal had to pay for the amendment as a whole.

While some loopholes remained, and caused problems later, the amendment was clearly a victory for Mafdal and for the other orthodox elements, as well as for those in the population, or at least in the political parties, who objected to a definition of Jewishness far removed even from the traditional folk conception inherent in the secularist position, especially as expressed by the Supreme Court. Indeed, the revision of the law marked a period of rethinking and reversal on this question among many Israeli public officials which extended even to the level of the Supreme Court.

In 1972 Benjamin Shalit's non-Jewish wife had another child, and while his first two children were registered as Jewish by nationality under the Supreme Court decision, the status of the third child, to whom the amended Population Registry Law defining a Jew in essentially *halakhic* terms applied, was now in question. Cognizant of the amended definition now part of the law, Shalit attempted to circumvent it by requesting that the child be registered in official government documents such as its birth certificate, identity card, and passport not as a Jewish but as a "Hebrew" national. (In the area of citizenship the registration itself is of limited significance to those born in Israel, who are all automatically Israeli citizens, as opposed to immigrants, among whom Jews have privileged status under the Law of Return. Similarly, in the realm of personal status, it is the religious courts which determine rights. Nevertheless, there are areas of law, such as military service—which is limited to Jews and certain small religious minorities—where one's status as Jew or non-Jew determines legal obligations.) Had the Supreme Court been interested in flouting the traditional definition of a Jew embodied in the amended law, it could very well have seized upon Shalit's argument as a means of doing so. In fact, the court this time ruled against Shalit, stating that his attempt to register his child as of Hebrew nationality was merely an effort to circumvent the law, as the terms Jewish and Hebrew in this context are synonymous.[6]

The court's newfound solicitousness for the traditional definition of a Jew may have been motivated by the sort of soul-searching that has affected many thoughtful Israelis who are concerned with the values of Israeli society and which had led many leading Israeli educators, for example, to attempt to introduce Jewish (as opposed to purely Israeli) consciousness programs, which seek to promote the knowledge of and identity with traditional Jewish values, into non-religious state schools.

The court may have been impelled to uphold an essentially religious definition of a Jew because it realized that once the traditional, social, and fairly objective *halakhic* tests thereof are removed, serious, if not dangerous, consequences for Israel's survival may follow. For example, a group of American blacks arrived in Israel beginning late in 1969 and into the early 1970s as tourists and then demanded immigrant status under the Law of Return, claiming to be "Hebrews" by virtue of their professed adherence to at least part of the laws of Moses and Israel. Adopting a very strict interpretation of the Law of Return, the court ruled that as these individuals neither claimed to have been born of Jewish mothers in the usual meaning of the word nor to have been formally converted to Judaism, they could not be considered Jews or Hebrews and hence could not enjoy the rights of Jewish immigrants. As they enjoyed no vested right of entry into Israel, the Ministry of Interior was free to expel them, having earlier refused to renew their tourist visas.[7] The implications of this case are very broad indeed. Had not the Supreme Court upheld the traditional and *halakhic* definition of a Jew, any group could define itself as Jews and could demand the right to return to the Jewish land, the most fundamental of principles upon which Zionism and the state of Israel are based.

A third reaffirmation by the Supreme Court of the traditional definition of a Jew was significant for several reasons. In a pure test case, Dr. George Tamarin, a psychologist and a Jew, asked, for reasons of his own, to have his nationality classification changed from Jew to "Israeli." The change would not have affected his citizenship or immigrant rights but would have demonstrated the existence of an "Israeli" nationality, as opposed to the traditional Jewish one. Tamarin based his case on a number of recent social scientific works which indicated, he argued, that such a nationality group did in fact exist.

Rejecting Tamarin's appeal, the court denied the existence of a separate Israeli nationality, pointed out how antagonistic such a claim was to the Zionist dream and to the legitimacy of the state, and reaffirmed the traditional definition of a Jew as embodied in the amended laws.[8] Nevertheless, the issue is far from resolved, as witnessed by the Schick case of several years ago, where the court ruled that a citizen might voluntarily delete the classification of Jewish nationality from his identity card, asserting that both religion and nationality "are subject to a man's heart, faith, and personal philosophy."[9]

The Continuing Problem

Plainly, there has been an increased, if far from unanimous, recognition of the importance of the traditional definition of who is a Jew both in the legislative realm, which is more sensitive to political party pressures, and in the judicial, which is substantially less so. This is not to say, however, that the current situation satisfies all religionists or secularists—quite the contrary, as two cases will illustrate.

The small Independent Liberal party has led a concerted effort, supported by the left in the Labor Alignment, the civil rights movement, and others on various points along the political spectrum, to force the issue of civil marriage, at least for those unable to wed under *halakhic* restrictions. The ultimate aim here is to eliminate the control of the rabbinate (or, more precisely, the rabbinical courts) over personal status questions. The issue was only temporarily shelved with the election of the more liberal Rabbi Shlomo Goren to the chief rabbinate, which, it was hoped, would herald more flexible handling of the more egregious cases of couples unable to marry. Public ire had been particularly roused by the Langer case, where a brother and sister serving in the Israel Defense Forces were deemed *mamzerim* (in this instance, children of the second marriage of a mother who had not been properly divorced from her first husband) and hence prohibited to marry Jews, a decision which Goren later ruled void on factual grounds (arguing that the first husband had never been properly converted to Judaism in Poland and hence that marriage was never valid).

At the other end of the spectrum, some religionists called for a revision of the religious status quo in the opposite direction. More specifically, they—and on this issue, Goren, too[10]—demanded that the Law of Return define more precisely its reference to conversion and to state that it is dealing only with conversion according to *halakhah,* thereby excluding from the definition of Jews, and hence from eligibility as Jewish immigrants under the Law of Return, those persons converted to Judaism by non-orthodox rabbis. The issue became particularly relevant in light of the large-scale immigration of Soviet Jews, many of whom have non-Jewish spouses who may not have been properly converted according to *halakhah.*

The two opposition religious parties, Agudah and PAY, seized upon this issue in the summer of 1972, largely to force their old antagonist, Mafdal, into a crisis with its Labor allies. Agudah's Rabbi Lorincz and PAY's Rabbi Kahana introduced almost identical private member bills to amend the Law of Return to stipulate conversion according to *halakhah* as the only recognized type of conversion for purposes of immigrant status. Lorincz introduced another bill to remove immigrant privileges from non-Jewish family members of Jewish immigrants. As opposition motions in a highly disciplined legislature, the two bills stood no chance of passage, which was Mafdal's argument for not voting for them. When, in fact, the vote in the Kneset was taken on July 12, 1972, Mafdal as a bloc abstained (with the sole exception of Dr. Avner Shaki, a maverick Mafdal member, who voted for the Lorincz bill), with Agudah and PAY, predictably, charging that it had betrayed its principles.

After the 1972 fiasco, Mafdal committed itself not to join the next coalition (presumably after the elections scheduled for October of 1973) without iron-clad assurances that a provision for conversion according to *halakhah* would be inserted into the amended Law of Return. That election was postponed until December of 1973 by the October war. In the interim, Mafdal, under pressure from its militantly nationalist Tze'irim faction, had added to its demands the establishment of a broad-based National Unity government, which would include the nationalist Likud opposition, and assurances that the West Bank would not be returned and that more settlements would be established there.

While Prime Minister Golda Meir's government rejected the wall-to-wall coalition, it did, in essence, accept Mafdal demands on the West Bank by agreeing to hold new elections when and if any part of the West Bank was to be returned, and by investing a substantial sum in settlements there. Deprived of these *causes célèbres,* the Tze'irim then agitated for the acceptance of a conversion according to *halakhah* amendment. Here too the weak Labor government offered a compromise. It would announce, in presenting the government program to the Kneset for its approval, that conversion was understood as an *halakhic* term; that it was forming a cabinet committee to work on a revision of the Law of Return; and that the administration of these matters by the (Mafdal-controlled) Ministry of Interior would continue for the one-year moratorium on the issue, during which the committee was to work out an acceptable compromise.

Unwilling to accept this package, the Tze'irim demanded that the chief rabbis be asked whether Mafdal could join a coalition which did not commit itself to an amendment to the Law of Return stipulating conversion according to *halakhah.* This was in itself an aberration from traditional Mafdal practice. As indicated above, Mafdal, while a religious party with strong ties to the chief rabbinate (the party in fact was instrumental in its establishment), has always been dominated by its secular leaders. The leaders of Mafdal's other factions—Burg, Hazani, and Refael, but not Warhaftig—concurred in putting the question to the chief rabbis, hoping to receive their blessing for joining the coalition and thereby to counter any criticism of the party for violating its promise to uphold the "according to *halakhah*" revision.

As it turned out, Sephardi Chief Rabbi 'Ovadyah Yosef, while insisting that "according to *halakhah*" was the only acceptable formula, nevertheless upheld the party's right to make an essentially political decision. Ashkenazi Chief Rabbi Shlomo Goren, however, under heavy pressure from Agudah and the more traditional rabbinical circles, convened the Chief Rabbinical Council and ruled that it could not sanction Mafdal's entry into the coalition without such assurances, thereby deepening Mafdal's dilemma. Only the somewhat contrived threat of an imminent outbreak of war on the Syrian front in March 1974 provided the opportunity for Mafdal to violate the rabbinate's dictum by joining the coalition, rationalizing the act on the basis that military exigencies justified it and that, in any case, it was not expressly prohibited but merely not sanctioned.

The Meir government, however, was short-lived; one month later, in the aftermath of the Agranat Commission report revealing the government's inadequacies in the 1973 war, it resigned. Once again Mafdal was confronted with the possibility of negotiating another coalition agreement with the new prime minister, Yitzhak Rabin. As the latter was no more inclined to accept a more restrictive definition of who is a Jew than his predecessor, nor more willing to establish a National Unity Government, despite his narrow parliamentary base (61 votes out of 120), Mafdal initially remained out of the government, though three cabinet seats were held open for it. It was a particularly inopportune time to be absent from the coalition, which now contained the small but vociferously anti-religious Civil Rights Movement, which had extracted an agreement from Labor stating that within three months, if Mafdal had not returned to the government, it could begin to revise existing religious legislation. With that and other threats to the hard-won religious status quo imminent, Mafdal overcame its internal factional conflicts and ideological inhibitions and returned to the coalition in October of 1974, where it remained until its expulsion in December 1976.

While still committed in principle to a revision of the Law of Return to stipulate conversion "according to *halakhah*," Mafdal is unlikely to press the issue to the point of refusing to join a government coalition over the question of who is a Jew in the foreseeable future.

In retrospect, it is clear that Mafdal has traditionally focused on cooperation and participation as a means to achieve its ultimate ideological goals via incremental change. When, as we have seen in the wake of the 1973 war, the party makes the immediate resolution of questions of ideology, such as conversion according to *halakhah,* a condition for joining the government and as a result stays out of the coalition for a time, it is abandoning a long tradition of effective participation. Agudah, not sharing the tradition, and PAY, not sharing it entirely, as evidenced by their long presence in the opposition, utilize other tactics in pursuing their ideological goals. The differences between these several religious parties are accentuated and highlighted by the issue of who is a Jew.

Chapter 9
Conclusion: Religious
Parties in a Modern State

In their important essay on "The Origin and Development of Political Parties," Joseph LaPalombara and Myron Weiner[1] discern three major approaches: the institutional, which focuses primarily upon the rise of parties in relation to parliaments and secondarily on parties as torchbearers of specific ideologies; the historical-situational, which relates party development to certain "crises"—such as legitimacy, integration, and participation—in a given political system; and the modernization approach, which relates party growth to the overall pattern of socioeconomic change that is commonly referred to as "modernization." In analyzing the religious parties of Israel, an eclectic approach has proven most useful.

The religious parties of Israel arose within, or in reaction to, the World Zionist Organization, which can be legitimately considered the legislative body of a state-in-the-making. Their unique ideological positions were developed largely in response to the challenges of modernization, as embodied by the WZO and Kneset Yisrael in Palestine. The ideological tenets formulated by the "founding fathers" influenced and guided the subsequent political behavior of the parties.

The nascent religious parties also encountered the historical crises of party development. For example, the crisis of legitimacy, the right of the government to rule, is one which has not yet been fully resolved as far as Agudat Yisrael is concerned, much as the extreme left and right oppositions in France have yet to reconcile themselves to the legitimacy of that regime.[2] Agudah's participation in the Israeli political system is limited to those minimal political duties incumbent upon citizens, like voting and taxpaying, which do not conflict with its overriding religious principles, as does military service, for instance. Its integration into the fabric of the Israeli society and polity is incomplete and conditional at best, as manifested by its separatist institutions, especially its educational system, and by the geographic concentration of its adherents. Virtually all the secondary characteristics of organization, political behavior, and the like, emanated from and were ultimately subject to each party's ideological accommodation to modernity or avoidance or rejection of it.

Responses to Nationalist Modernization

Once it had accepted the idea of modernization (with reservations) Mizrahi felt that cooperation with non-religious Jews in the rapid nationalist modernization that was Zionism, with all its attendant "dangers," was necessary. In order to protect and promote its particular blend of modernity and tradition, Mizrahi organized itself politically within the proto-parliament of the WZO and later of Kneset Yisrael. In Maurice Duverger's terms, it was typical of an "internally created" party[3] and displayed all the characteristics of responsibility he attributes to such parties of notables, which, in effect, the old Mizrahi was. On the other hand, the mass, trade-union-based ha-Po'el ha-Mizrahi, which later overtook and overwhelmed its Mizrahi predecessor, closely resembles Duverger's characterization of the externally created parties,[4] particularly of the western European socialist labor type. It must be remembered, however, that despite its early militancy, ha-Po'el ha-Mizrahi has always remained within the Zionist consensus.

Agudat Yisrael might seem a better example of an externally created party. But it did not, as Duverger would have it, remain external to the political system because of any inherent organizational flaws or because it was a late arrival on the scene.[5] Its exclusion was voluntary and ideological in nature. It never accepted—or, more precisely, it rejected or avoided insofar as possible—the challenge embodied in the nationalist mobilization effort of Zionism. Thus it was free to be militant toward or critical of the system it rejected, and, because of its negativistic, defensive posture, it never developed the kind of organizational centralization, coherence, and discipline that Duverger imputes to such parties.[6] Anti-modern in both ideology and organization, Agudat Yisrael recoils from the idea of a true mass party, though it makes masterful use of the technique of the mass demonstration. Hence, despite its external origins, it is a classical "cadre" party,[7] one which is based on a qualitative, ascriptive elite and has no real membership as such. Furthermore, as our analyses of voters and members have shown, "in cadre parties the counting of electors provides the only possible measure of the party community."[8]

In ha-Po'el ha-Mizrahi, and later in Mafdal, the correlation between the membership and votership is much closer precisely because they have accepted the challenges of modernity. Given the increasing division of labor in society, the party has also accepted the implication that it must provide the same broad range of social services that comprehensive labor organizations elsewhere, and the Histadrut in Israel, offer. A mass party evolved from this mass labor organization base.

With the establishment of the state and its nationalization (*mamlakhtiyut*) of many of the former particularistic party preserves, Mafdal has been subject to a measure of de-ideologization, destratification, and professionalization of leadership. This phenomenon has been described by Otto Kirchheimer[9] and Leon Epstein[10] as "contagion from the right," replacing Duverger's once historically valid "contagion from the left." Nevertheless, the mass base of labor organization remains.

Ideology, however, has not come to an end in Israel, at least as far as the religious parties are concerned.[11] Although Mafdal toned down some of its more ideological appeals in the face of *mamlakhtiyut* and the mass immigration of the fifties, it still perceives issues and formulates goals in much the same ideological terms as it has for decades. In multiparty systems the decline of ideological intensity, as Giovanni Sartori properly cautions, should not be confused with the decline of ideology itself,[12] and the change in Mafdal may be more appearance than reality. The transitory nature of the decline in ideological vigor could be seen in the period after the 1973 war, when a resurgence of the party's nationalist-religious ideology, led by the Tze'irim faction, was in evidence especially on two key issues, personal status (the who is a Jew question) and the administered territories (the public debate over the integral unity of Eretz Yisrael). The party joined the short-lived Meir government only after obtaining a one-year moratorium on the question of who is a Jew and a guarantee that a national referendum in the form of new elections would be held on the question of returning any part of the West Bank to Arab control. Until similar assurances were forthcoming from the new prime minister, Yitzhak Rabin, Mafdal, for the first time in its and Israel's history, refused to participate in the formation of a new government.

Furthermore, while Mafdal's dominant component, ha-Po'el ha-Mizrahi, has always been deeply involved with the pragmatic aspects of providing services to its members, even this activity is conceived in ideological terms. By the very scope of its activities Mafdal may be the source of employment, housing, or other material benefits for its members. At the same time, it provides a social milieu, protects and propagates values (particularly via its educational system), and offers other intangible, yet potent, satisfactions. Agudah, which provides little in the way of services and has little patronage to dispense, yields its members (or adherents) almost nothing but such intangible satisfactions. It remains a prime example of the survival of the ideological party in the Israeli political system.

The ideological differences between the religious parties are not limited to questions of internal structure, membership, leadership, and the like. As we have seen, they cover the spectrum of issues and policy preferences which constitute Mafdal's program of nationalization of religion and Agudah's program of institutionalized separatism. (Here, as on many other issues, PAY lacks a distinctive image and borrows aspects of the programs of the other two parties.) Similarly, they affect the size, scope, sources of strength, and style of the parties and are reflected in the socioeconomic characteristics of the voterships, memberships, and elites of the respective parties. Thus, as our analysis has indicated, Mafdal's support is not only much larger than either Agudah's or PAY's but far more evenly spread across the country; its voters live in urban and rural areas alike, in poor and in rich neighborhoods. Its truly national, heterogeneous character is limited only by its religious orientation. Agudah's appeal is narrow, and its support is confined to socioeconomically homogeneous urban neighborhoods.

Furthermore, the scope of Mafdal involvements and undertakings—political, social, economic—are far broader than those of Agudah or PAY. Indeed, they are second only to those of Mapai in size and complexity.[13] Mafdal's ideology expresses concern with the nature of the state and the community, which the Tze'irim faction seeks to apply more broadly to the political and economic spheres. The party is frequently drawn into controversy and conflict with other groups in the society, and its record of accomplishment is uneven. While Agudah would also prefer to organize life in the state according to its world view, it limits itself to attempting to assure that its adherents can live their lives according to their traditional customs. Within this more circumscribed framework, it has been notably successful. It generally does not, as a political party, attempt to impose its values on Israeli society at large. There may be some small comfort for some secularists in the knowledge that they have more to fear from the "moderate" Mafdal than from the "militant" Agudah.

Nowhere are the differences between the two world views more clearly demarcated than in the separate educational systems each party continues to guard zealously, despite claims and legal guarantees of "non-party education." The state religious and the independent systems are the keystones of the parties' respective socialization programs. Along with the parties' youth movements and machinery for absorbing immigrants, the education systems have thus far managed to maintain, if not to increase, the number and percentage of voters and hence to maintain the same level of political representation for their constituents in the state of Israel. Given the rapid modernization that that state has undergone and the small size, divided nature, and limited human and financial resources of the religious parties, which confront a dominant secular socialist party bent on *mamlakhtiyut,* this accomplishment is no mean feat. Whether it can be maintained depends largely on the continued effectiveness of the parties' systems of socialization. While there is evidence that religious party strength may have declined (the number of Mafdal Kneset members dropped from twelve to ten and of Agudah-PAY members from six to five in the admittedly unusual and probably exceptional circumstances of the elections right after the 1973 war), there is also evidence indicating that selective increases may be possible.

Impact on the System

While the religious parties have been fairly successful in representing and serving their constituents and protecting and promoting their interests, as defined by their respective ideologies—which is, after all, a chief function of political parties—their impact on the Israeli political system as a whole is much less clear and much more controversial. The parties have been subject to sometimes valid and often scathing criticism from various quarters.

Because they have brought such fundamental questions as the nature of the state and its legal and educational systems and the definition of who is a Jew into the political arena, even when the state was fighting for its survival, the religious parties have been viewed as a disruptive force in the system, a potential permanent "opposition of principle."[14] They have the dubious distinction of having caused more governments to fall than any other party or parties. Their insistence upon the maintenance of broad spheres of autonomy within the state—religious state education, independent education, the Ministry of Religions, the rabbinical courts, the religious councils, to name a few—has helped prevent the bureaucracy from becoming more rationalized, neutral, and efficient. In this respect, as in their implacable opposition to any change in the system of proportional representation which would dilute their power, they are profoundly conservative parties, acting as a brake on political development. Furthermore, the demands of the religious parties, a numerical minority, for religious strictures on public and private behavior in such vital areas as marriage and divorce, public transportation and entertainment on the Sabbath, dietary laws, recognition of non-orthodox variants of Judaism, and so on, have infringed upon civil liberties to the point, it has been argued, of endangering democracy in Israel.[15] Even in terms of their own values, the parties are often seen as prostituting religion by their politization of it and by their emphasis on its outward forms and institutional interests rather than on its spiritual and humanistic values.[16] A number of well-publicized scandals involving religious

party leaders in Israel and some of their leading supporters abroad
have further damaged the parties' images.

A variety of remedies have been proposed both within and
outside the religious community to satisfy these criticisms. In fact,
each is a variation on the theme of the separation of religion and
state. The critics range from radical secularists like Kneset member
Shulamit Aloni, head of the small Citizens' Rights Movement, and
former Kneset member Uri Avneri, both of whom advocate the
complete separation of religion and state, to radical religionists like
the Neturei Qarta, who advocate virtually identical solutions for
entirely opposite reasons. Representatives of the reform and conservative movements abroad and their small but growing membership in Israel urge that the orthodox rabbinate's official monopoly
be ended and that secular personal status laws be instituted or that
these movements receive legal parity with orthodoxy. Within the
orthodox community, individual thinkers such as Yeshayahu Leib-
owitz and Efrayim Urbach (the latter is the founder of the Movement for Torah Judaism) have urged the disestablishment and de-
politization of religion in Israel, opting for purely voluntaristic adherence to autonomous *kehilot,* a solution reminiscent of those of
the early Agudah ideologues like Isaac Breuer.

What all these critics share is their desire for the dissolution
of the religious parties. In this they have been joined by many
leading figures of the Labor party—Ben-Gurion and Meir among
others—who wish to reduce or eliminate the dependence of Labor
upon Mafdal for secure coalitions. Hence the religious parties have
been called upon to dissolve themselves or to allow themselves to
be eliminated by electoral engineering. Their adherents have been
advised to join the larger parties. Religious interests, the argument
runs, would still be cared for by the major parties (presumably
Labor and Likud), in response to pressure from religious interest
groups incorporated therein. Thus, it is argued, "The withdrawal,
or even the dissolution, of the religious parties does not necessarily
have to result in the abolition of the Ministry of Religious Affairs,
the Chief Rabbinate, the local Religious Councils, or the Religious
Courts. All these institutions could be safeguarded on a nonparty
basis, lifting them above political bargaining. Although the secular
majority may, by democratic procedures, curtail the work of any of
these institutions, religion stands to benefit less and lose more by

the continued functioning of the religious parties and by their high pressure, extortionist, and predatory activities.''[17]

Given the tone of such criticisms, the religious parties might well be wary of those who seek to eliminate them while assuring them of the continuity of their basic interests. Those who advocate such a change are either willfully and cynically inattentive to or blissfully unaware of the realities of politics, in Israel or elsewhere. Apart from its theological, spiritual, and personal aspects, religion, particularly a this-worldly one like Judaism, has, like other organized interests in society, certain institutional and communal concerns which seek political expression. In polities where group interests are channeled through large amorphous broker parties, like those in the United States, interest groups can be organized within or outside of the parties. In most multiparty systems, however, interests are aggregated only on the governmental or coalition level, and the major interests are themselves generally organized into parties.

As long as the Israeli political system remains substantially unchanged, the religious parties contend with some justification that they have as much right to organize politically as parties representing less comprehensive concerns and that they would sacrifice their religious interests—above and beyond their institutional self-interest—by disbanding at this time. Without the vehicle of a party (or parties) to represent their positions at the Kneset or coalitional governmental level, where national policy is made, their concerns, even if channeled through a larger party, would have to compete with those of entrenched groups there. For example, the Histadrut would have prior claim to Labor loyalties, and religious issues would be subordinated to internal factional squabbling rather than projected onto the broader scope of national politics. Furthermore, sizeable numbers of religious individuals have long voted for one or the other of the two major parties and these parties have long had religious sections, all without any palpable change in their essentially secularist policies. Disestablishment of religion, which the religious parties see as the aim of those who seek to dissolve them, would also put religious interests at a distinct disadvantage in a welfare state such as Israel, where all social services are supplied by the State and where high taxation leaves little capital in private hands for a voluntary religious community life to flourish, as it does in the United States.

The religious parties also resent their portrayal as a religious minority tyrannizing a secular majority. While it is true that their voting strength is only 15 percent at best, they contend that this reflects the salience of economic and security issues for many religious voters. A truer approximation of the social strength of the religious parties may be seen in the percentage of school-age pupils—twice the percentage of religious-party voters—whose parents voluntarily choose to educate them in one of the education-socialization systems of the religious parties. Apart from this group, there is evidence that a majority of the Israeli public, for whatever reasons of sentiment, historical, or nationalist consciousness, or cultural affinity, views the role of religion in both the public and private spheres in Israel as an important, legitimate, and legitimating factor in Israeli public life.[18]

The religious parties have also served to maintain the political system. New regimes everywhere need legitimacy and often seek it by attempting to appeal to the historical, and particularly the religious, sentiments of the population.[19] While this is important for regimes which merely represent a change in personnel or in policy over their predecessors, it is essential for those which must create a constituency out of immigrants in a situation of great political, economic, and military pressure.

In Israel, the religious parties, especially during the first four years of the state's existence, when they were joined in the United Religious Front and the basic compromises and provisions of the status quo on religion were being worked out, served just such a function. To Israeli citizens, to many Jews abroad, and to non-Jews as well, their presence and participation attested to the link between the new Jewish state and Jewish history. This "automatic" legitimation precluded recourse to other far less democratic methods that other newly independent and rapidly modernizing and mobilizing states have been known to adapt, under far less trying circumstances. It is this concern for preserving the legitimacy and authenticity of the Jewish state, the parties contend, rather than any mischievous meddling on their part that compels them to raise basic issues of principle.

More recently, and particularly since the 1967 war, some thoughtful voices in non-orthodox circles have been raised in defense of the voluntary acceptance of private and public observance of religious law because of its importance for national unity and despite the possible incidental infringement upon individual civil liberties that may ensue:

> It is fitting for those in the nonreligious group, though they have no tie to religion for its own sake, to accept cheerfully the burden of many regulations which create the conditions for national unity and continued existence. These would include the marriage laws, observance of the dietary laws in public institutions, and the like. Furthermore, such consent from the nonreligious community should properly be given voluntarily, on the basis of its own interests and views. It should not have to come as a result of political pressure. . . . tradition is not the sole interest of the religious group. . . . The nonreligious groups have an interest in fostering the observance of tradition.[20]

In the absence of such voluntary acceptance, the religious parties claim that national unity mandates that they enforce certain behavior by law.

Furthermore, the religious parties, and particularly Mafdal, far from being disruptive, have served another most vital system maintenance function. Mafdal has brought down more governments than any other party, but it has also, like Mapai, participated in every government from the establishment of the state up to the present. The much-vaunted stability of the Israeli multi-party system, which is generally attributed solely to Mapai, has been in fact almost as much the result of Mafdal's continuing presence. As for allegations of corruption, the religious parties claim they have no monopoly on this phenomenon, as evidenced by the present scandal-ridden Rabin government. And as for their being a threat to democracy by insisting on the maintenance of autonomous spheres and of proportional representation, the religious parties respond, on an operational level, that they are not alone in these demands and that the true nature of pluralist democracy allows for such diversity, though they have been reluctant to accord such democratic rights to non-orthodox variants of Judaism. If pressed to the ideological wall, they would probably insist that the Torah, not abstract democratic principles, is the final authority.

The Experience of Other Systems

An examination of religious parties in other systems, while uncovering differences in detail, reveals some interesting parallels that belie Sartori's assertion that Israel "defies any generalization."[21] Indeed, religious parties in other multiparty systems tend, on the whole, to be important elements in maintaining the system.

The Dutch case is particularly instructive, as its basic structural characteristics resemble those of Israel.[22] There are three religious parties in the Netherlands, though they represent two different religions, Protestantism and Catholicism. The Protestants are divided between two parties, each of which claims to be orthodox, much as in Israel. One of the two is less fundamentalist and more closely identified with the established church, like Mafdal. The other "prefer[s] the subcultural isolation of true believers . . . to what they fear . . . would at most be an empty official theology" and therefore "consciously opted for the lesser evil of a permanent minority position"[23]—an accurate description of Agudat Yisrael as well.

The Dutch religious parties were created in the nineteenth century in reaction to the modernist, secularist trends which had overtaken religion and society in the wake of the social and economic modernization sparked by the French Revolution: indeed, one of the parties is called the "anti-revolutionary" party. It was the school issue—control over the means of socialization—that was the catalyst in the formation of the Dutch religious parties, as it was for those of Israel. Beginning with state recognition of and subsidies to separate religious elementary school systems, the parties have expanded to secondary, technical, and higher education, like the Israeli case.

As in Israel, the proportional representation system enables the Dutch religious parties to flourish. Though they together constitute a majority, their expedient and temporary cooperation with each other recalls the activities of the URF in the early 1950s. Each party prefers to maintain its separate identity. There even are extremist splinter parties that serve as "gadflies, forcing the larger parties not to stray too far from their ideological position lest they lose votes,"[24] reminiscent of the Neturei Qarta, PAGI, la-Mifneh, and the like.

The formation of coalition governments and their composition also resembles the Israeli case. Prolonged pre-agreement wrangling is followed by fairly stable governments. Central to the stability of the governments in both cases are one or more of the religious parties. In Holland the Catholic party, for instance, has regularly participated in every government coalition (like Mafdal in Israel), whether allied with the Socialists or the Liberals.

Despite their common interest in religion and tradition, it is inaccurate and simplistic to lump the religious parties of Holland together. There is little or no competition between them for votes, since each has its own constituency. The phenomenon of *Verzuiling* (pillarization or vertical cross-class compartmentalization of society), whereby, very much as we described in Israel, each religious party has its own system of socialization from cradle to grave, extends from educational and recreational groups to business and labor organizations. The latter in particular have tended to democratize the religious parties in ways reminiscent of the relationship between ha-Po'el ha-Mizrahi and Mafdal in Israel.

Because of *Verzuiling,* the three religious parties in Holland have a much more heterogeneous social following than the Liberals and Socialists. This has tended to draw the religious parties toward a centrist position and to make them natural brokers between conflicting interests, first within their own orbit, but indirectly also in society at large.[25] Such heterogeneity, moderation, and brokerage is characteristic of Mafdal. And, as in the case of Mapai, the Dutch Socialist (as well as the Liberal) party has abandoned its anti-clericalist stance and has begun to appeal to the natural constituency of the religious parties by establishing religious groups in its own structure.

Daalder might well have been speaking of Israel when he summarizes the role and nature of the Dutch religious parties:

> It should be stressed that the religious subcultures hardly answer to Gabriel Almond's description of "significant survivals, 'outcroppings' of older cultures and their political manifestations," remnants that are attributable only to "uneven patterns of development" and "failure on the part of the middle classes in the nineteenth century to carry through a thorough-going secularization of the political culture." On the contrary, far from being traditionalist remnants, they themselves pioneered modern political techniques and have on the

whole adjusted well to the processes of modern industrial development. The thrust of secularization has been countered by a large
number of burgeoning social organizations *within* each subculture that
seek to cope with the complex social problems of the modern industrial era and do so successfully on an explicitly religious basis.[26]

While the Netherlands example most closely resembles the
Israeli case, further suggestive comparisons of stable multiparty
systems based in large part on religious parties are possible. In
Belgium Catholics hold the balance of power between Liberals and
Socialists, and the society is similarly fragmented into "spiritual
families" criss-crossed by linguistic-ethnic cleavages.[27] Even more
central to the multiparty system is the Christian Democratic party
of Italy, the dominant postwar party and the only one which has
broad inter-class strength.[28] Its recruitment ability, much like that
of Mafdal, is limited only by its religious character.[29] While basically a two-party system, Austria's twenty-year experience of permanent coalition of Catholics and Socialists, each based on a
Verzuiling-like "layer" and sharing the government and bureaucracy on the basis of a fixed "*proporz*" (like the "party key" in
Israel),[30] strongly resembles that of the stable multiparty systems.[31] In Germany's multiparty system also, a religious party, the
Christian Democrats, though substantially de-ideologized,[32] has
provided stability both in leadership and in opposition. Even in
Lebanon, which was never more than a "precarious republic" at
best,[33] it was the delicate internal balance of religious parties and
communities (legally based, not unlike Israel's, on the old Ottoman
millet system) that rendered the system closer to democracy than
any other state in the Middle East (except Israel). Only when that
balance was upset by forces essentially external to the political
system, albeit linked to internal groups, did the country undergo
the major political upheaval of the long civil war which only now
seems to be abating.

These examples put into serious question the unidirectional
model of modernization. To explain these traditionalist phenomena,
that model must allow for numerous exceptions that cast its validity
as a heuristic tool in doubt. A more modest, realistic, and balanced
interpretation of the modernization phenomenon, based on the cases
of Israel and other systems, including some very recent and exotic

ones,[34] is in order. One might argue that the multifaceted forces of modernization set in motion a series of political, economic, and social forces which, while fairly universal in their external manifestations, take very different shape even within a particular cultural setting. Reactions to them range from total rejection, as in the case of Agudah, to total acceptance, as in the case of some secularist groups, to an attempt at accommodation between modern and traditional forces which may produce a new synthesis of values and forms which is neither wholly holy nor wholly profane—the position actually taken, if not proclaimed, by Mafdal.

None of these reactions need be permanent or irreversible. Secularists may suddenly find that without some of the traditional principles which they may have flippantly dismissed, the fundamental legitimacy of their society may be open to the most damning attack and subversion. Such, for instance, appears to be at the crux of some of the recent decisions of the Israeli Supreme Court on the question of who is a Jew. Religionists may find the balancing act between fundamentalism and secularism too taxing, and may revert to one or the other extreme.

Some of the innovative ideas and structures devised by the religious parties as accommodations to modernity, as we have indicated in Israel and as Daalder suggests in the Netherlands, may be imitated and adopted by the non-religious parties, themselves seeking an accommodation with legitimating national traditions. Thus, in addition to the "contagion from the left" that Duverger saw overtaking all parties in the 1950s, and the "contagion from the right" which Epstein, Kirchheimer, and others saw in the 1960s, what may be called a "contagion from on high" may be discerned in the 1970s, an era of heightened religious and ethnic political awareness which is only incidentally related to material measurements. If anything, the consciousness of such phenomena will at least help restore a third dimension to political analysis, which has been on a two-dimensional, left-right plane since the days of Karl Marx. It is that same economic determinism which underlies and undermines the unidirectional modernization theory. The point, however, is that each reaction to the challenges of modernization is legitimate, perhaps durable and viable, and no doubt sincere. It is only through the recognition of the legitimacy of the diversity it entails that modernization will bring its manifold blessings upon humanity.

$\mathcal{N}otes$

Notes to Chapter 1

1. See, for example, Ervin Birnbaum, *The Politics of Compromise: State and Religion in Israel* (Rutherford, N.J.: Fairleigh Dickinson University Press, 1970); Norman L. Zucker, *The Coming Crisis in Israel: Private Faith and Public Policy* (Cambridge, Mass.: MIT Press, 1973).

2. Maurice Duverger, *Political Parties,* trans. B. and R. North, 2d rev. ed. (New York: John Wiley & Sons, 1959), p. xxiii.

3. Giovanni Sartori, "European Political Parties: The Case of Polarized Pluralism," in *Political Parties and Political Development,* ed. Joseph LaPalombara and Myron Weiner (Princeton: Princeton University Press, 1966), p. 160, n. 37.

4. Gabriel A. Almond and James S. Coleman, eds., Introduction, *The Politics of the Developing Areas* (Princeton: Princeton University Press, 1960), p. 63.

5. Gabriel A. Almond and G. Bingham Powell, Jr., *Comparative Politics: A Developmental Approach* (Boston: Little, Brown, 1966), ch. 11.

6. Daniel Lerner, *The Passing of Traditional Society* (New York: The Free Press, 1958), pp. 398–413.

7. Ben Halpern, *The Idea of the Jewish State,* 2d ed. (Cambridge, Mass.: Harvard University Press, 1969), p. 16.

8. See Walter Laqueur, ed., *The Israel-Arab Reader: A Documentary History of the Middle East Conflict,* (New York: Bantam Books, 1969), pp. 6–11.

9. *Ibid.,* pp. 11–12.

10. For a selection of their writings in English translation and a more complete bibliography on the subject of early Zionism, see Arthur Hertzberg, ed., *The Zionist Idea: A Historical Analysis and Reader* (Garden City, N.Y.: Doubleday and Herzl Press, 1959).

11. For a more detailed analysis of the pre-state period in relation to Palestine, see J.C. Hurewitz, *The Struggle for Palestine* (New York: W. W. Norton, 1950); and Christopher Sykes, *Cross Roads to Israel* (London: New English Library, 1965).

12. For a concise discussion of British motivations, see Nadav Safran, *The United States and Israel* (Cambridge, Mass.: Harvard University Press, 1963), pp.

24–26. For a more detailed consideration, see Leonard Stein, *The Balfour Declaration* (London: Vallentine & Mitchell, 1961), and Isaiah Friedman, *The Question of Palestine, 1914–1918: British-Jewish-Arab Relations* (New York: Schocken Books, 1973).

13. Cited in Laqueur, *Israel-Arab Reader,* pp. 134–42.

14. See Amitai Etzioni, "The Decline of Neo-Feudalism: The Case of Israel," in Moshe Lissak and Emanuel Gutmann, eds., *Political Institutions and Processes in Israel* (Jerusalem: Hebrew University, 1971), pp. 70–87.

15. For a more detailed analysis of the phenomenon, see Dan Horowitz and Moshe Lissak, *Mi-Yishuv li-Medinah* [From Yishuv to state] (Jerusalem: Hebrew University, 1972).

16. For a more detailed treatment of the Israeli political system as a whole, see Safran, *United States and Israel;* Leonard Fein, *Politics in Israel* (Boston: Little, Brown, 1967).

17. For an authoritative, if somewhat formalistic and minutely detailed, description of the structures and functions of the Kneset, see Asher Tzidon, *Beit ha-Nivharim* [The House of Representatives], 6th rev. ed. (Tel Aviv: Ahiasaf, 1971).

18. Statistics on 1969 election results are drawn from the Central Bureau of Statistics, *Results of the Elections to the Seventh Kneset and the Local Authorities* (Jerusalem: Central Bureau of Statistics, 1970); 1973 results are from CBS, *Results of Elections to the Eighth Kneset and the Local Authorities* (Jerusalem: CBS, 1974).

19. For an examination of this process at work, see Peter Y. Medding, *Mapai in Israel: Political Organization and Government in a New Society* (Cambridge: The University Press, 1972), pt. 1.

Notes to Chapter 2

1. Ben Halpern, *The Idea of the Jewish State,* 2d ed. (Cambridge, Mass.: Harvard University Press, 1969), pp. 16, 17.

2. Juda L. [Yehudah Leib] Fishman [Maimon], *The History of the Mizrachi Movement,* trans. Harry Karp (New York: Mizrachi Hatzair of America, 1928), p. 38.

3. Y[ehudah] L[eib] Fishman, "Toldot ha-Mizrahi ve-Hitpathuto" [History and development of Mizrahi], in *Sefer ha-Mizrahi* [The Mizrahi book], ed. Y. L. Fishman (Jerusalem: Mosad ha-Rav Kook, 1946), p. 29.

4. *Ibid.,* p. 38.

5. *Kol Koreh* (Vilna: Mizrahi, 1902), pp. 1–3.

6. Fishman, *History,* p. 54.

7. Yitzhak Gush-Zahav [Goldschlag], *Mi-Vilna 'ad Yerushalayim* [From Vilna to Jerusalem] (Jerusalem: Ha-Merkaz ha-'Olami shel ha-Mizrahi [World headquarters of Mizrahi], 1954), pp. 12–13; Fishman, "Toldot," pp. 36–40.

8. Fishman, *History,* pp. 69–70.

9. Yeshayahu Wolfsberg, "Ha-Mizrahi ve-'Emdato Legabei ha-Ortodoksyah ha-

Bilti Tziyonit" [Mizrahi and its stand on non-Zionist orthodoxy], in *Yovel ha-Mizrahi* [Mizrahi anniversary book], ed. Y. L. Fishman (Jerusalem: Irgun 'Ezrah-Nehemyah, 1952), p. 258.

10. Halpern, *Jewish State*, pp. 16–17.
11. Wolfsberg, "Mizrahi," pp. 259–64.
12. See Fishman, "Toldot," p. 59.
13. Meir Ostrovsky [Ha-Meiri], *Toldot ha-Mizrahi be-Eretz Yisrael* [History of Mizrahi in Palestine] (Jerusalem: Reuven Mas, 1944), pp. 9–12.
14. Quoted in *ibid.*, p. 185.
15. Shlomo Hornik, "Histadrut ha-Mizrahi be-Eretz Yisrael" [The Mizrahi organization in Palestine], in *Mitzpeh* [Viewpoint], ed. Y. Bernstein (Jerusalem: Ha-Merkaz ha-'Olami shel ha-Mizrahi, 1953), p. 532.
16. Ostrovsky, *Toldot*, p. 15.
17. *Ibid.*, p. 16.
18. *Din ve-Heshbon shel ha-Ve'idah ha-'Olamit shel ha-Mizrahi, Antverpen* [Report of the world convention of Mizrahi, Antwerp] (Jerusalem: Ha-Merkaz ha-'Olami shel ha-Mizrahi, 1926), pp. 21, 22 (hereafter cited as *Report of Antwerp Convention*).
19. See Ostrovsky, *Toldot*, pp. 79–80.
20. *Ibid.*, pp. 23–24.
21. Hornik, "Histadrut," p. 532.
22. Netanel Katzburg, "Ha-Mizrahi, ha-Tziyonut, veha-Yahadut ha-Datit" [Mizrahi, Zionism, and religious Jewry], in *Mitzpeh* [Viewpoint], ed. Y. Bernstein (Jerusalem: Ha-Merkaz ha-'Olami shel ha-Mizrahi, 1953), p. 109.
23. Ostrovsky, *Toldot*, p. 26.
24. Fishman, "Toldot," p. 136.
25. For two opposite views on this question, see Fishman, "Toldot," p. 150; S. H. Landau, in *Din ve-Heshbon Me'et ha-Merkaz ha-'Olami . . . Mugash el ha-Ve'idah ha-'Olamit shel ha-Mizrahi, Antverpen* [Report of the world headquarters . . . submitted to the world convention of Mizrahi, Antwerp] (Jerusalem: Ha-Merkaz ha-'Olami shel ha-Mizrahi, 1926), p. 59 (hereafter cited as *Report to Antwerp Convention*).
26. Bernard D. Weinryb, *The Yishuv in Palestine—Structure and Organization* (New York: National Education and Political Committees of Hadassah, n.d. [ca. 1946–47]), p. 28.
27. Quoted in *ibid.*
28. Shmuel Hayyim Landau, *Kitvei . . .* (Warsaw: 1935), cited in Arthur Hertzberg, ed., *The Zionist Idea: A Historical Analysis and Reader* (Garden City, N.Y.: Doubleday and Herzl Press, 1959), pp. 434–35.
29. *Ibid.*, pp. 435, 437, 439.
30. Yosef Salmon, ed., *'Eduyot 'al Reishito shel ha-Po'el ha-Mizrahi* [Testimony on the beginnings of ha-Po'el ha-Mizrahi] (Jerusalem: Hebrew University, 1968), Testimony 2, p. 25, 3, pp. 9–11.
31. *Din ve-Heshbon Me'et ha-Merkaz ha-'Olami . . . Mugash el ha-Ve'idah ha-'Olamit shel ha-Mizrahi, Dantzig* [Report of the world headquarters . . . submitted to the world convention of Mizrahi, Danzig] (Jerusalem: Ha-Merkaz

ha-'Olami shel ha-Mizrahi, 1928), p. 59 (hereafter cited as *Report to Danzig Convention*); Mordekhai Zahavi, *Darkeinu* [Our way] (Jerusalem: Ha-Po'el ha-Mizrahi, the second in a series of nineteen pamphlets, 1923–35), pp. 6–9; Salmon, *'Eduyot*, Testimony 2, p. 4, 3, p. 11.

32. Such tendencies were evident in the Mizrahi as early as the 1926 Antwerp convention, when Mizrahi's opposition to the idea of the establishment of Trans-Jordan within the "natural boundaries" of Eretz Yisrael, which Mizrahi demanded, was voiced. See *Report of Antwerp Convention*, p. 44.

33. Salmon, *'Eduyot*, pp. 22–23.

34. *Report to Danzig Convention*, p. 65.

35. Yosef Salmon, "Shiluv ha-Sotzyalism 'im ha-Dat" [Coalescence of socialism with religion], *De'ot*, No. 40 (Spring 1971), p. 299.

36. Giovanni Sartori, "European Political Parties: The Case of Polarized Pluralism," in *Political Parties and Political Development*, ed. Joseph LaPalombara and Myron Weiner (Princeton: Princeton University Press, 1966), pp. 140–65.

37. Salmon, "Shiluv," pp. 297, 300.

38. *Report of Antwerp Convention*, pp. 57–58, 66–67, 75.

39. *Hukat Histadrut ha-Mizrahi ha-'Olamit* [Constitution of the World Mizrahi Organization] (Jerusalem[?]: Ha-Merkaz ha-'Olami shel ha-Mizrahi, 1926).

40. Fishman, "Toldot," p. 154.

41. Ya'akov Edelstein, "Avnei Negef ba-Behirot la-Rabanut" [Obstacles in the elections for the rabbinate], *Ha-Tzofeh*, December 17, 1971, p. 7.

42. Fishman, "Toldot," pp. 261, 264, 152, 157; Edelstein, "Arvei," p. 7.

43. "Elections of Rabbinical Officers and Rabbis of Locals Communities," *Palestine Gazette* 9 (1936), suppl. 1, pp. 230–34.

44. Helen Miller Davis, ed., *Constitutions, Electoral Laws, Treaties and States in the Near and Middle East* (Durham, N.C.: Duke University Press, 1953), p. 350.

45. "Resolutions of the Fourth National Convention of Mizrahi in Eretz Yisrael," cited in Ostrovsky, *Toldot*, p. 199; "Memorandum to the Royal Commission, 1936," cited in *Din ve-Heshbon Me'et ha-Merkaz ha-'Olami . . . Mugash la-Ve'idah ha-'Olamit be-Tzirikh* [Report of the world headquarters . . . submitted to the world convention of Mizrahi, Zurich] (Jerusalem[?]: Ha-Merkaz ha-'Olami shel ha-Mizrahi, 1937), pp. 74–75 (hereafter cited as *Report to Zurich Convention*).

46. "Religious Communities Organization Ordinance of February 15, 1926," *Official Gazette of the Government of Palestine*, No. 157, p. 64.

47. Ostrovsky, *Toldot*, pp. 170, 187, 189, 190, 191, 192, 193, 194, 197, 199, 201, 202, 205, 206, 208, 209, 210.

48. *Din ve-Heshbon Me'et ha-Merkaz ha-'Olami . . . Mugash la-Ve'idah ha-'Olamit shel ha-Mizrahi, Krakov* [Report of the world headquarters . . . submitted to the world convention of Mizrahi, Krakow] (Jerusalem[?]: Ha-Merkaz ha-'Olami shel ha-Mizrahi, 1935), pp. 3–5 (hereafter cited as *Report to Krakow Convention*).

49. Ostrovsky, *Toldot*, pp. 132–33.

50. *Report to Krakow Convention*, p. 6; Ostrovsky, *Toldot*, p. 135.
51. For the agreements with ha-Mizrahi ha-Vatik, see Ostrovsky, *Toldot*, pp. 135–38; for the agreements with ha-Po'el ha-Mizrahi, see *Report to Krakow Convention*, pp. 12–13.
52. *Report of Antwerp Convention*, pp. 7–12, 52; also published separately as Moshe Avigdor Amiel, *He-Yesodot ha-Idiologiyyim shel ha-Mizrahi* [The ideological foundations of Mizrahi] (Warsaw: Mizrahi, 1934); see also Amiel, "Shuv 'al ha-Yesodot . . . " [More on the ideological . . .], *Ha-Tur* 14, nos. 32 (August 10, 1934), pp. 3–5, 33 (August 17, 1934), 34 (August 24, 1934), pp. 3–4.
53. Yehudah Leib Fishman, "Le-Heshbonah shel Histadruteinu" [Taking account of our organization], *Ha-Tur* 14, nos. 24 (June 5, 1934), pp. 3–5, 26 (June 22, 1934), pp. 3–4, 27 (July 6, 1934), pp. 3–5.
54. *Din ve-Heshbon shel ha-Merkaz ha-'Olami . . . Mugash la Ve'idah ha-'Olamit shel ha-Mizrahi, Zhenivah* [Report of the world headquarters . . . submitted to the world convention of the Mizrahi, Geneva] (Jerusalem: Ha-Merkaz ha-'Olami shel ha-Mizrahi, 1939), pp. 81–83, 89–90 (hereafter cited as *Report to Geneva Convention*).
55. *Ibid.*, pp. 16–18.
56. *Ibid.*
57. Remarks of Moshe Shapira in *Din ve-Heshbon Mugash le-Tzirei ha-Ve'idah ha-'Olamit ha-Yod Het shel ha-Mizrahi ve-ha-Po'el ha-Mizrahi* [Report presented to the delegates of the eighteenth world Mizrahi and ha-Po'el ha-Mizrahi convention] (Jerusalem: Ha-Merkaz ha-'Olami shel ha-Mizrahi, 1949), p. 30 (hereafter cited as *Report to Eighteenth World Convention*).
58. *Shalosh Shanim: Din ve-Heshbon Mugash le-Tzirei ha-Ve'idah ha-Yod Alef shel ha-Po'el ha-Mizrahi* [Three years: report presented to the delegates to the eleventh ha-Po'el ha-Mizrahi convention] (Tel Aviv[?]: Histadrut ha-Po'el ha-Mizrahi be-Yisrael, ha-Va'ad ha-Po'el, n.d.), p. 40 (hereafter cited as *Report to Eleventh ha-Po'el ha-Mizrahi Convention*).
59. Maurice Duverger, *Political Parties*, trans. B. and R. North, 2d rev. ed. (New York: John Wiley & Sons, 1959), pp. 63ff.
60. Ostrovsky, *Toldot*, pp. 76–77.
61. Moshe Shapira, in *Ha-Hitya'atzut ha-Penimit ha-'Olamit ha-Sheniyyah shel Netzigei ha-Mizrahi veha-Po'el ha-Mizrahi be-Yisrael uva-Tefutzot* [The second internal world consultation of Mizrahi and ha-Po'el ha-Mizrahi in Israel and the Diaspora] (Jerusalem: Ha-Merkaz ha-'Olami shel ha-Mizrahi, 1953), p. 15 (hereafter cited as *Second Consultation*).
62. Peter Y. Medding, *Mapai in Israel: Political Organization and Government in a New Society* (Cambridge: The University Press, 1972), p. 238.
63. *Ha-Ofek* 2, no. 2 (1952), p. 2.
64. Michael Hazani, *Histadrut, Miflagah, Tenu'ah* [Organization, party, movement] (Tel Aviv: La-Mifneh, 1952), p. 3.
65. See Reuven Gafni, in *Din ve-Heshbon Mefurat: ha-Ve'idah ha-Shevi'it shel ha-Po'el ha-Mizrahi* [Detailed report: the seventh ha-Po'el ha-Mizrahi convention] (Tel Aviv: Torah va-'Avodah Library, 1935), pp. 50, 53–55 (hereafter cited as *Report of Seventh ha-Po'el ha-Mizrahi Convention*).

66. *Ha-Ofek* 2, no. 5 (1953).

67. *Ha-Po'el ha-Mizrahi bi-Shenot 5702–5709: Sikumei Pe'ulah la-Ve'idah ha-'Asirit* [Ha-Po'el ha-Mizrahi in the years 1942–1949: summary of activity for the tenth convention] (Tel Aviv: Ha-Po'el ha-Mizrahi, 1950), p. 13 (hereafter cited as *Ha-Po'el ha-Mizrahi in 1942–1949*).

68. *Ha-Ofek* 1, nos. 1 (1952), pp. 1–2, 2 (1952), p. 3; 4, no. 2 (1955), p. 2.

69. Hazani, *Histadrut*, p. 4.

70. La-Mifneh Faction, *Matza' la-Ve'idah ha-'Asirit* [Platform for the tenth convention] (Tel Aviv: La-Mifneh, 1949), pp. 6–7; *Report of Seventh ha-Po'el ha-Mizrahi Convention*, p. 81; *Din ve-Heshbon la-Ve'idah ha-Sheminit* [Report to eighth convention] (Tel Aviv: Ha-Po'el ha-Mizrahi, 1942), pp. 21–23.

71. D. Intriglator in *Din ve-Heshbon shel ha-Ve'idah ha-'Asirit shel ha-Po'el ha-Mizrahi* [Report of tenth ha-Po'el ha-Mizrahi convention] (Jerusalem[?]: Ha-Po'el ha-Mizrahi, 1950[?]), pp. 162–70; and Hazani, *Histadrut*, p. 22.

72. Moshe Unna, *Hatza'ah le-Tokhnit ha-Miflagah* [Proposal for the party program] (Tel Aviv: La-Mifneh, 1952); letter from Moshe Unna to Gary S. Schiff, July 9, 1972.

73. *Report to Eleventh ha-Po'el ha-Mizrahi Convention*, p. 6.

74. Y. Refael and Y. Bernstein in *Quntresim le-Ba'ayot ha-Po'el ha-Mizrahi* [Pamphlets on ha-Po'el ha-Mizrahi problems], No. 2 (Jerusalem: Ha-Reshimah ha-Meuhedet, 1952), pp. 3, 11–13.

75. Otto Kirchheimer, "The Transformation of the Western European Party System," in Joseph LaPalombara and Myron Weiner, eds., *Political Parties and Political Development* (Princeton: Princeton University Press, 1966), especially p. 190.

76. *Ha-Hitya'atzut ha-Penimit ha-'Olamit shel Netzigei ha-Mizrahi veha-Po'el ha-Mizrahi be-Yisrael uva-Tefutzot* [The internal world consultation of Mizrahi and ha-Po'el ha-Mizrahi in Israel and the Diaspora] (Jerusalem: Ha-Merkaz ha-'Olami shel ha-Mizrahi, 1953), pp. 3–4 (hereafter cited as *First Consultation*).

77. *Ha-Hitya'atzut ha-Penimit ha-'Olamit ha-Shelishit shel Netzigei ha-Mizrahi veha-Po'el ha-Mizrahi be-Yisrael uva-Tefutzot* [The third internal world consultation of Mizrahi and ha-Po'el ha-Mizrahi in Israel and the Diaspora] (Jerusalem: Ha-Merkaz ha-'Olami shel ha-Mizrahi, 1954), pp. 6, 10 (hereafter cited as *Third Consultation*).

78. *Pirkei Pe'ulah: Din ve-Heshbon Mugash le-Tzirei ha-Ve'idah ha-Yod Bet shel ha-Po'el ha-Mizrahi* [Annals of activities: report presented to the delegates of the twelfth ha-Po'el ha-Mizrahi convention] (Tel Aviv[?]: Ha-Va'ad ha-Po'el shel ha-Po'el ha-Mizrahi be-Yisrael, n.d.), p. 73 (hereafter cited as *Report to Twelfth ha-Po'el ha-Mizrahi Convention*).

79. *First Consultation*, p. 20.

80. *Ha-Hitya'atzut ha-Penimit ha-'Olamit ha-Revi'it shel Netzigei ha-Mizrahi veha-Po'el ha-Mizrahi be-Yisrael uva-Tefutzot* [The fourth internal world consultation of Mizrahi and ha-Po'el ha-Mizrahi in Israel and the Diaspora] (Jerusa-

lem: Ha-Merkaz ha-'Olami shel ha-Mizrahi, 1955), p. 24 (hereafter cited as *Fourth Consultation*).

81. *Report to Twelfth ha-Po'el ha-Mizrahi Convention*, pp. 10–11, 13, 221–22.

82. *Din ve-Heshbon shel ha-Ve'idah ha-'Olamit ha-Yod Tet shel ha-Mizrahi veha-Po'el ha-Mizrahi* [Report of the nineteenth Mizrahi and ha-Po'el ha-Mizrahi world convention] (Jerusalem: Ha-Merkaz ha-'Olami shel ha-Mizrahi veha-Po'el ha-Mizrahi, 1956), p. 189 (hereafter cited as *Report of Nineteenth World Convention*).

83. *Din ve-Heshbon shel ha-Ve'idah ha-Sh'neim 'Esrei shel ha-Po'el ha-Mizrahi* [Report of the twelfth ha-Po'el ha-Mizrahi convention] (Tel Aviv: Ha-Po'el ha-Mizrahi, n.d.), pp. 87–88 (hereafter cited as *Report of Twelfth ha-Po'el ha-Mizrahi Convention*).

84. *Bein Ve'idah le-Ve'idah: Din ve-Heshbon Mugash la-Ve-'idah ha-Yod Gimel shel Histadrut ha-Po'el ha-Mizrahi veha-Ve'idah ha-Bet shel ha-Mafdal* [Between convention and convention: report presented to the delegates to the thirteenth ha-Po'el ha-Mizrahi convention and the second Mafdal convention] (Tel Aviv: Ha-Po'el ha-Mizrahi, 1963), p. 244 (hereafter cited as *Report to Thirteenth ha-Po'el ha-Mizrahi Convention*).

85. Tzvi Bernstein in *Din ve-Heshbon: ha-Ve'idah ha-Yod Gimel shel Histadrut ha-Po'el ha-Mizrahi veha-V̌e'idah ha-Bet shel ha-Miflagah ha-Datit-Leumit* [Report of the thirteenth ha-Po'el ha-Mizrahi convention and the second national religious party convention] (Tel Aviv: Ha-Va'ad ha-Po'el shel ha-Po'el ha-Mizrahi be-Yisrael, 1965), pp. 139, 244–45 (hereafter cited as *Report of Thirteenth ha-Po'el ha-Mizrahi Convention*).

86. *Din ve-Heshbon Mugash le-Tzirei ha-Ve'idah ha-'Olamit ha-Kaf shel ha-Mizrahi veha-Po'el ha-Mizrahi* [Report presented to the delegates to the twentieth world convention of Mizrahi and ha-Po'el ha-Mizrahi], Part I: *General* (Jerusalem: Ha-Merkaz ha-'Olami shel ha-Mizrahi veha-Po'el ha-Mizrahi, 1962), p. 12 (hereafter cited as *Report to Twentieth World Convention*).

87. *Report to Thirteenth World Convention*, appendix, p. 57; Tzvi Bernstein in *Report of Thirteenth World Convention*, p. 143.

88. Bernstein, *Report of Thirteenth World Convention*, pp. 244–45.

89. "Hukat Histadrut ha-Po'el ha-Mizrahi be-Eretz Yisrael" [Constitution of ha-Po'el ha-Mizrahi organization in Israel], in *Hukat ha-Tenu'ah* [Constitution of the movement] (Tel Aviv: Mafdal, 1965), pp. 7–9.

90. "Hukat ha-Miflagah ha-Datit-Leumit, ha-Mizrahi veha-Po'el ha-Mizrahi" [The constitution of the National Religious Party, Mizrahi, and ha-Po'el ha-Mizrahi], in *ibid.*, pp. 3–4.

91. *Le-Sikumah shel Tekufah: Din ve-Heshbon Mugash la-Ve'idah ha-Shelishit shel ha-Miflagah ha-Datit-Leumit veha-Arba' 'Esrei shel Histadrut ha-Po'el ha-Mizrahi be-Yisrael* [The summation of a period: Report presented to the third convention of the National Religious Party and the fourteenth convention of the ha-Po'el ha-Mizrahi organization in Israel] (Tel Aviv[?]: Ha-Va'ad ha-Po'el ha-Meuhad shel ha-Tenu'ah, n.d. [ca. 1969]), p. 248 (hereafter cited as *Report to Third Mafdal Convention*).

92. *Ibid.*, p. 255.

Notes to Chapter 3

1. See Ya'akov Rosenheim, *Kol Ya'akov* [The voice of Jacob] (Tel Aviv: Netzah, 1954), p. 626.

2. *Ibid.*, p. 55.

3. O. Asher Reichel, *Isaac Halevy: Spokesman and Historian of Jewish Tradition* (New York: Yeshiva University Press, 1969), p. 113.

4. Ya'akov Rosenheim, *Zikhronot* [Memoirs] (Tel Aviv: She'arim, 1955), p. 38.

5. *Ibid.*, p. 120.

6. *Ibid.*

7. Joseph Friedenson, *A History of Agudath Israel* (New York: Agudath Israel of America, 1970), p. 14; Rosenheim, *Zikhronot*, p. 178.

8. *Ha-Knesiyah ha-Gedolah ha-Sheniyah shel Agudat Yisrael* [The second world convention of Agudat Yisrael] (Vienna: Ha-Merkaz ha-'Olami shel Agudat Yisrael, 1929), p. 23 (hereafter cited as *Second World Convention of Agudat Yisrael*).

9. See Rosenheim, *Kol Ya'akov*, p. 48, and *Zikhronot*, p. 179.

10. Ya'akov Rosenheim, *Ktavim* [Writings] (Jerusalem: Agudath Israel World Organization, 1970), p. 202.

11. Isaac Lewin, "Religious Judaism in Independent Poland," in *Israel of Tomorrow*, ed. Leo Jung, 2d rev. ed. (New York: Herald Square Press, 1949), 2: 451.

12. Moshe Blau, *'Al Homotayikh Yerushalayim* [On thy walls, O Jerusalem] (Bnei Braq: Netzah, 1967), p. 74.

13. *Ibid.*, p. 77.

14. Isaac Breuer, *The Jewish National Home*, trans. Miriam Aumann (Frankfurt a.m.: J. Kauffmann, 1926), pp. 26, 27, 53, 34–35, 62, 61, 88, 87.

15. *Ibid.*, p. 95, par. 1; p. 96, par. 4; p. 97, par. 9; p. 74.

16. Moshe Blau, in *Dvar Agudat Yisrael be-Sha'ah Zu* [The word of Agudat Yisrael at this hour] (Jerusalem: Ha-Va'adah ha-Mekhinah shel ha-Ve'idah ha-Artzit, 1941), p. 4.

17. *Mi Sam Keitz la-Ma'arakhah?* [Who put an end to the battle?] (Jerusalem: Agudat Yisrael, 1964), p. 38.

18. Blau, *'Al Homotayikh Yerushalayim*, p. 85.

19. Breuer, *Jewish National Home*, p. 36.

20. Blau, *'Al Homotayikh Yerushalayim*, pp. 88–91.

21. Avraham ben-Moshe Shmuel [pseud.], *Kol Koreh le-Shalom ve-Ahdut bein Agudat Yisrael uvein ha-Va'ad ha-Leumi be-Eretz Yisrael* [Proclamation calling for peace and unity between Agudat Yisrael and the Va'ad Leumi in Palestine] (Jerusalem: n.p., 1930).

22. *Mi Sam Keitz la-Ma'arakhah?*, p. 26.

23. Nadav Safran, *The United States and Israel* (Cambridge, Mass.: Harvard University Press, 1963), p. 69.

24. H. Mishkovsky, in *Dvar Agudat Yisrael be-Sha'ah Zu*, p. 9; Lewin, in *ibid.*; Wolf Blattberg, "Polish Jewry: Yesterday, Today, and Tomorrow," in *Israel of Tomorrow*, p. 419.

25. *Album of the Palestine Central Society of the Agudath Israel* (Frankfurt a.m.: n.p., n.d.), p. 24.
26. *Ha-Po'el ha-Haredi* [The religious worker] (Tel Aviv: n.p., 1935), p. 1.
27. Isaac Breuer, *'Am ha-Torah ha-Meurgan* [The organized Torah nation] (Tel Aviv: Netzah, 1944), p. 3.
28. Isaac Breuer, "Memorandum on the Attitude of Agudat Yisrael to the Jewish State Sent to the President of the World Agudat Yisrael, Rabbi Ya'akov Rosenheim" and "Program for a United Religious Front on the Question of a Constitution for the Jewish State," in *Homer le-Shealat Hitkonenut ve-Sidur ha-Medinah ha-Yehudit 'al Pi ha-Torah* [Material on the question of the preparation and organization of the Jewish state according to the Torah], ed. Isaac Lewin (New York: Research Institute for Post-War Problems of Religious Jews, 1947), pp. 5–10, 11–16 (hereafter cited as Lewin, *Material*).
29. Friedenson, *History*, pp. 36, 37; *Mi-Knesiyah li-Knesiyah* [From convention to convention] (Jerusalem: Agudat Yisrael World Organization, 1954), p. 35; J. C. Hurewitz, *The Struggle for Palestine* (New York: W. W. Norton, 1950), p. 78.
30. Bernard D. Weinryb, *The Yishuv in Palestine: Structure and Organization* (New York: National Education and Political Committees of Hadassah, n.d., [ca. 1946–47]), p. 29.
31. Jacob Rosenheim, *Agudist World-Problems* (New York: Agudas Israel World Organization, 1941), pp. 4–5.
32. Hurewitz, *Struggle for Palestine*, p. 208; Weinryb, *Yishuv*, p. 29.
33. Isaac Breuer, in *Dvar Agudat Yisrael be-Sha'ah Zu*, p. 5.
34. Ya'akov Landau, *Lifnei ha-Hakhra'ah* [Before the decision] (Tel Aviv: She'arim, 1944), p. 26.
35. S. Luria, in *Dvar Agudat Yisrael be-Sha'ah Zu*, p. 12.
36. S. Lustig, in *ibid*.
37. *Mi Knesiyah li-Knesiyah*, p. 36.
38. Weinryb, *Yishuv*, p. 29.
39. *Bein Ve'idah le-Ve'idah* [Between convention and convention] (Tel Aviv: Po'alei Agudat Yisrael, 1940), pp. 63, 9.
40. *Ibid.*, pp. 64–65.
41. *Ibid.*, pp. 71–72.
42. *Yedi'ot ha-Merkaz ha-Artzi shel Agudat Yisrael be-Eretz Yisrael* [Information from the national headquarters of Agudat Yisrael in Israel], No. 3, 1948, p. 1 (hereafter cited as *Information*).
43. These demands were outlined in a speech by Yitzhak Meir Levin in the Kneset, 8 Iyyar 5708 (1948); see *Mi-Knesiyah li-Knesiyah*.
44. See Kalman Kahana, in *Bein Ve'idah le-Ve'idah*, pp. 12, 13.
45. *Mi-Knesiyah li-Knesiyah*, p. 49.
46. *Bein Ve'idah le-Ve'idah*, pp. 60, 54.
47. *Mi-Knesiyah li-Knesiyah*, p. 56.
48. *Ibid.*, p. 93; *Pe'ulot ha-Tenu'ah: Pirkei Din ve-Heshbon Mugashim la-Ve'idah ha-Shevi'it* [Activities of the movement: chapters of the report presented to

the seventh convention] (Tel Aviv[?]: Po'alei Agudat Yisrael, 1969), p. 18
(hereafter cited as *Report to Seventh PAY Convention*).
49. Yitzhak Meir Levin, *Madu'a Parashnu meha-Koalitziyah?* [Why have we left
the coalition?] (Jerusalem: Agudat Yisrael World Organization, 1953), p. 25.
50. *Ha-Tzofeh*, February 28, 1951.
51. *Mi-Knesiyah li-Knesiyah*, pp. 24, 88.
52. *Dapim ve-'Uvdot* [Pages and facts] (Jerusalem: Agudat Yisrael World Organization, Information Department, 1960), p. 14.
53. *Report to Seventh PAY Convention*, p. 19.

Notes to Chapter 4

1. See Peter Y. Medding, *Mapai in Israel: Political Organization and Government
in a New Society* (Cambridge: The University Press, 1972), pp. 237–41, 184.
2. "Hukat ha-Miflagah ha-Datit-Leumit, ha-Mizrahi veha-Po'el ha-Mizrahi" [The
constitution of the National Religious Party, Mizrahi and ha-Po'el ha-
Mizrahi], in *Hukat ha-Tenu'ah* [Constitution of the movement] (Tel Aviv:
Mafdal, 1965), p. 4.
3. Medding, *Mapai in Israel*, p. 184.
4. "Hukat Histadrut ha-Po'el ha-Mizrahi be-Eretz Yisrael" [Constitution of ha-
Po'el ha-Mizrahi organization in Israel], in *Hukat ha-Tenu'ah*, p. 7.
5. Medding, *Mapai in Israel*, p. 104.
6. *Le-Sikumah shel Tekufah: Din ve-Heshbon Mugash la-Ve'idah ha-Shelishit shel
ha-Miflagah ha-Datit-Leumit veha-Arba' 'Esrei shel Histadrut ha-Po'el ha-
Mizrahi be-Yisrael* [The summation of a period: report presented to the third
convention of the National Religious Party and the fourteenth convention of
the ha-Po'el ha-Mizrahi organization in Israel] (Tel Aviv[?]: Ha-Va'ad ha-
Po'el ha-Meuhad shel ha-Tenu'ah, n.d. [ca. 1969]), p. 5 (hereafter cited as
Report to Third Mafdal Convention).
7. Medding, *Mapai in Israel*, p. 104.
8. *Ibid.*, pp. 114, 69, 71.
9. Refael Toledano in *Bein Ve'idah le-Ve'idah: Din ve-Heshbon Mugash la-
Ve'idah ha-Yod Gimel shel Histadrut ha-Po'el ha-Mizrahi veha-Ve'idah ha-
Bet shel ha-Mafdal* [Between convention and convention: report presented to
the delegates to the thirteenth ha-Po'el ha-Mizrahi convention and the second
Mafdal convention] (Tel Aviv: Ha-Po'el ha-Mizrahi, 1963), pp. 195–96 (hereafter cited as *Report to Thirteenth ha-Po'el ha-Mizrahi Convention*).
10. Medding, *Mapai in Israel*, p. 105.
11. *Hahlatot, Reshimot Havrei ha-Mosdot ha-Nivharim, ha-Ve'idah ha-Meuhedet
shel ha-Tenu'ah ha-Gimel shel ha-Mafdal veha-Yod Daled shel ha-Po'el ha-
Mizrahi* [Decisions, and lists of members of elected institutions, of the joint
convention of the movement, the third of Mafdal and the fourteenth of ha-
Po'el ha-Mizrahi] (Jerusalem-Tel Aviv: Ha-Mazkirut ha-Meuhedet shel ha-
Mafdal veha-Po'el ha-Mizrahi, 1969), p. 2 (hereafter cited as *Decisions*).

12. "Hukat Histadrut ha-Po'el ha-Mizrahi," p. 8.
13. *Report to Third Mafdal Convention,* p. 6.
14. "Hukat Histadrut ha-Po'el ha-Mizrahi," p. 8.
15. Medding, *Mapai in Israel,* p. 110.
16. *Report to Third Mafdal Convention,* p. 7.
17. *Report to Thirteenth ha-Po'el ha-Mizrahi Convention,* p. 9.
18. *Decisions,* pp. 60–61.
19. *Report to Thirteenth ha-Po'el ha-Mizrahi Convention,* p. 11.
20. *Report to Third Mafdal Convention,* p. 7.
21. *Ibid.,* pp. 9–10.
22. For examples, see *Report to Thirteenth ha-Po'el ha-Mizrahi Convention,* pp. 9–29.
23. *Report to Third Mafdal Convention,* p. 10.
24. *Decisions,* p. 62.
25. *Report to Third Mafdal Convention,* pp. 12, 14.
26. *Ibid.,* pp. 30–44.
27. *Ibid.,* pp. 30, 45.
28. *Ibid.,* pp. 45–55.
29. Medding, *Mapai in Israel,* p. 178.
30. *Report to Third Mafdal Convention,* p. 62.
31. Medding, *Mapai in Israel,* pp. 122–33.
32. *Hahlatot ha-Knesiyah ha-Gedolah ha-Hamishit* [The decisions of the fifth Knesiyah Gedolah] (Jerusalem: Agudat Yisrael World Organization, Information Department, 1964), p. 26 (hereafter cited as *Decisions of Fifth Knesiyah*).
33. *Dapim ve'Uvdot* [Pages and facts] (Jerusalem: Agudat Yisrael World Organization, Information Department, 1960), p. 7.
34. *Din ve-Heshbon Mugash le-Tzirei ha-Knesiyah ha-Gedolah ha-'Olamit ha-Hamishit shel Agudat Yisrael* [Report presented to the delegates of the fifth world convention of Agudat Yisrael] (Jerusalem: Agudat Yisrael World Organization, Information Department, 1964), p. 71 (hereafter cited as *Report to Fifth Agudah World Convention*).
35. *Decisions of Fifth Knesiyah,* p. 27.
36. *Ibid.,* p. 25.
37. *Report to Fifth Agudah World Convention,* pp. 11, 12.
38. Personal interview with Avraham Werdiger, member of Kneset, January 8, 1973.
39. *Pe'ulot ha-Tenu'ah: Pirkei Din ve-Heshbon Mugashim la-Ve-idah ha-Shevi'it* [Activities of the movement: chapters of the report presented to the seventh convention] (Tel Aviv[?]: Po'alei Agudat Yisrael, 1969), p. 3.
40. Amnon Barzilai, "Milhemet ha-Si'ot ba-Mafdal" ("The war of factions in Mafdal"), *ha-Aretz,* September 28, 1976, p. 9.
41. *Ha-Mifkad ha-Irguni* [The organizational survey] (Tel Aviv: Ha-Po'el ha-Mizrahi, Organization Department, 1966).
42. See *Report to Third Mafdal Convention,* p. 91.
43. *Ibid.,* p. 85.
44. *Bein Ve'idah le-Ve'idah: Din ve-Heshbon Mugash la-Ve'idah ha-Revi'it shel*

ha-Mafdal veha-Hameish 'Esrei shel ha-Po'el ha-Mizrahi [Between convention and convention: report presented to the fourth Mafdal convention and
the fifteenth ha-Po'el ha-Mizrahi convention] (Tel Aviv: Ha-Po'el ha-Mizrahi,
1973), pp. 113, 198 (hereafter cited as *Report to Fourth Mafdal Convention*).

45. Alan Arian, *The Choosing People: Voting Behavior in Israel* (Cleveland: The
Press of Case Western Reserve University, 1973), ch. 4.

46. *Ibid.,* p. 13, Table 3.4.

47. *Report to Third Mafdal Convention,* p. 86.

48. Data on the religious parties' elite have been drawn from a series of personal
interviews with current elite members and from sources listed in Table 4.3.

49. Avraham Brichta, "The Social and Political Characteristics of Members of the
Seventh Kneset," in A. Arian, ed., *The Elections in Israel: 1969* (Jerusalem:
Jerusalem Academic Press, 1972), p. 127.

50. *Ibid.,* p. 125.

51. *Ibid.,* p. 123.

52. *Ibid.,* p. 120.

53. Moshe M. Czudnowski, "Legislative Recruitment under Proportional Representation in Israel: A Model and a Case Study," *Midwest Journal of Political
Science* 14 (May 1970).

54. Personal interview, January 8, 1973.

55. Personal interview with Menahem Porush, December 25, 1972.

56. Brichta, "Seventh Kneset," p. 125.

57. *Ibid.,* p. 127.

58. *Ibid.,* p. 120.

59. *Ibid.,* p. 128.

60. Leon D. Epstein, *Political Parties in Western Democracies* (New York: Frederick A. Praeger, 1967), pp. 257–60, 199–200.

Notes to Chapter 5

1. See, for example, Leon D. Epstein, *Political Parties in Western Democracies*
(New York: Frederick A. Praeger, 1967), p. 9.

2. Daniel J. Elazar, "Local Government as an Integrating Factor in Israeli Society,"
in Michael Curtis and Mordecai Chertoff, eds., *Israel: Social Structure and
Change* (New Brunswick, N.J.: Transaction Books, 1973), p. 16.

3. Central Bureau of Statistics, *Results of Elections to the Seventh Kneset and to
the Local Authorities* (Jerusalem: Central Bureau of Statistics, 1970), p. xxi.

4. Maurice Duverger, *Political Parties,* trans. B. and R. North (New York: John
Wiley & Sons, 1959), 2d rev. ed., pp. 90–116.

5. *Le-Sikumah shel Tekufah: Din ve-Heshbon Mugash la-Ve'idah ha-Shelishit shel
ha-Miflagah ha-Datit-Leumit veha-Arba' 'Esrei shel Histadrut ha-Po'el ha-
Mizrahi be-Yisrael* [The summation of a period: report presented to the third
convention of the National Religious Party and the fourteenth convention of
the ha-Po'el ha-Mizrahi organization in Israel] (Tel Aviv[?]: Ha-Va'ad ha-

Po'el ha-Meuhad shel ha-Tenu'ah, n.d. [ca. 1969]), pp. 111–34 (hereafter cited as *Report to Third Mafdal Convention*); *Pe'ulot ha-Tenu'ah: Pirkei Din ve-Heshbon Mugashim la-Ve'idah ha-Shevi'it* [Activities of the movement: chapters of the report presented to the seventh convention] (Tel Aviv[?]: Po'alei Agudat Yisrael, 1969), pp. 15–17, 83–89 (hereafter cited as *Report to Seventh PAY Convention*).

6. *Din ve-Heshbon Mugash le-Tzirei ha-Knesiyah ha-Gedolah la-'Olamit ha-Hamishit shel Agudat Yisrael* [Report presented to the delegates of the fifth world convention of Agudat Yisrael] (Jerusalem: Agudat Yisrael World Organization, Information Department, 1964), pp. 95–96 (hereafter cited as *Report to Fifth Agudah World Convention*).

7. All statistical material in this chapter, unless otherwise noted, is taken from the sources noted in Table 5.1.

8. *Report to Third Mafdal Convention*, p. 205.

9. *Ibid.*, p. 225.

10. *Ibid.*, p. 77.

11. For a discussion of the Gush Emunim phenomenon, see Moshe Kohn, *Who's Afraid of Gush Emunim?* (Jerusalem: Jerusalem Post, n.d. [ca. 1976]).

12. Jacob M. Landau, *The Arabs in Israel: A Political Study* (London: Oxford University Press, 1969), p. 177.

13. *Ibid.*, p. 143.

14. *Report to Third Mafdal Convention*, p. 167.

15. *Bein Ve'idah le-Ve'idah: Din ve-Heshbon Mugash la-Ve'idah ha-Revi'it shel ha-Mafdal veha-Hameish 'Esrei shel ha-Po'el ha-Mizrahi* [Between convention and convention: report presented to the fourth Mafdal convention and the fifteenth ha-Po'el ha-Mizrahi convention] (Tel Aviv: Ha-Po'el ha-Mizrahi, 1973), p. 120 (hereafter cited as *Report to Fourth Mafdal Convention*).

16. *Ibid.*, p. 122.

Notes to Chapter 6

1. Letter from Rabbi Meir Bar-Ilan to Ben-Gurion, cited in *Din ve-Heshbon Mugash le-Tzirei ha-Ve'idah ha-'Olamit ha-Yod Het shel ha-Mizrahi veha-Po'el ha-Mizrahi* [Report presented to the delegates to the eighteenth world Mizrahi and ha-Po'el ha-Mizrahi convention] (Jerusalem: Ha-Merkaz ha-'Olami shel ha-Mizrahi, 1949), pp. 79–80 (hereafter cited as *Report to Eighteenth World Convention*).

2. *Din ve-Heshbon 'al Pe'ulot Misrad ha-Datot li-Shenat ha-Kesafim 1971–72 Mugash la-Kneset 'al Yedei Sar ha-Datot, Dr. Zerah Warhaftig* [Report on the activities of the Ministry of Religions for the fiscal year 1971–72 presented to the Kneset by the minister of religions, Dr. Zerah Warhaftig] (Jerusalem: Ministry of Religions, 1972) (hereafter cited as *Pe'ulot Misrad ha-Datot*).

3. For its legal basis see *Official Gazette of the Government of Palestine*, no. 157,

p. 64; "Ha-Takanot ha-Qov'ot et Shitat ha-Behirot o Minuyim shel Mo'etzet ha-Rabanut ha-Rashit, Lishkot ha-Rabanut ve-Rabenei ha-Kehilot" [The regulations governing the method of election or appointment of the Chief Rabbinate Council, rabbinical offices, and community rabbis], *'Iton Rishmi* [Official gazette], no. 582, April 9, 1936, cited in *Be-Ma'arekhet ha-'Am veha-Medinah: Qovetz Mugash la-Ve'idah ha-Bet shel ha-Mafdal veha-Yod Gimel shel Histadrut ha-Po'el ha-Mizrahi* [In the battle for the nation and the state: an anthology presented to the second Mafdal convention and the thirteenth ha-Po'el ha-Mizrahi convention] (Tel Aviv: Ha-Hanhalah ha-Merkazit, 1963), p. 51 (hereafter cited as *Be-Ma'arekhet*).

4. Menahem Elon, *Hakikah Datit* [Religious legislation] (Tel Aviv: Ha-Kibbutz ha-Dati, 1968), p. 10.

5. *Be-Ma'arekhet*, p. 51.

6. *Din ve-Heshbon Mugash le-Tzirei ha-Ve'idah ha-'Olamit ha-Kaf shel ha-Mizrahi veha-Po'el ha Mizrahi* [Report presented to the twentieth world convention of Mizrahi and ha-Po'el ha-Mizrahi] (Jerusalem: Ha-Merkaz ha-'Olami shel ha-Mizrahi, 1962), p. 267 (hereafter cited as *Report to Twentieth World Convention*).

7. Cited in *Be-Ma'arekhet*, pp. 53–56.

8. "Hok ha-Behirot le-Mo'etzet ha-Rabanut ha-Rashit, 5732/1972 [Chief rabbinate elections law 5732/1972], *Sefer ha-Hukim* [The book of laws], no. 649, 1972, p. 42.

9. "Takanot bi-Devar Sidrei Behirot le-Mo'etzet ha-Rabanut ha-Rashit" [Regulations on the matter of the procedures of the elections for the Chief Rabbinate Council], *Qovetz Takanot* [Anthology of regulations], no. 2837, 1972, p. 1043; and the amendments thereto in *Qovetz Takanot*, no. 2887, p. 15.

10. Elon, *Hakikah Datit*, p. 159.

11. *Le-Sikumah shel Tekufah: Din ve-Heshbon Mugash la-Ve'idah ha-Shelishit shel ha-Miflagah ha-Datit-Leumit veha-Arba' 'Esrei shel Histadrut ha-Po'el ha-Mizrahi be-Yisrael* [The summation of a period: report presented to the third convention of the National Religious Party and the fourteenth convention of the ha-Po'el ha-Mizrahi organization in Israel] (Tel Aviv[?]: Ha-Va'ad ha-Po'el ha-Meuhad shel ha-Tenu'ah, n.d. [ca. 1969]), p. 67 (hereafter cited as *Report to Third Mafdal Convention*).

12. Elon, *Hakikah Datit*, p. 31.

13. Zerah Warhaftig, cited in *Pirkei Pe'ulah: Din ve-Heshbon Mugash le-Tzirei ha-Ve'idah ha-Yod Bet shel ha-Po'el ha-Mizrahi* [Annals of activities: report presented to the delegates of the twelfth ha-Po'el ha-Mizrahi convention] (Tel Aviv[?]: Ha-Va'ad ha-Po'el shel ha-Po'el ha-Mizrahi be Yisrael, n.d.), p. 230 (hereafter cited as *Report to Twelfth ha-Po'el ha-Mizrahi Convention*).

14. Elon, *Hakikah Datit*, p. 31.

15. Warhaftig, cited in *Report to Twelfth ha-Po'el ha-Mizrahi Convention*, p. 232.

16. *Pe'ulot Misrad ha-Datot*, pp. 12–13.

17. Elon, *Hakikah Datit*, pp. 49–51.

18. *Ibid.*, pp. 49–50, 59, 69; interview with Hayyim Heifetz, legal advisor of the Ministry of Religions, December 7, 1972.

19. Moshe Krone, cited in *Din ve-Heshbon shel ha-Ve'idah ha-'Olamit ha-'Esrim shel ha-Mizrahi veha-Po'el ha-Mizrahi* [Report of the twentieth world convention of Mizrahi and ha-Po'el ha-Mizrahi] (Jerusalem: Ha-Merkaz ha-'Olami shel ha-Mizrahi veha-Po'el ha-Mizrahi, 1964), p. 194 (hereafter cited as *Report of the Twentieth World Convention*).

20. Cited in Emanuel Gutmann, ed., *Mishtar Medinat Yisrael: Sefer Mekorot* [The government of the state of Israel: A book of sources] (Jerusalem: Hebrew University, 1971), pp. 458–59.

21. Cited in Elon, *Hakikah Datit,* pp. 190–91.

22. Peter Y. Medding, *Mapai in Israel: Political Organization and Government in a New Society* (Cambridge: The University Press, 1972), p. 77.

23. *Din ve-Heshbon Mugash le-Tzirei ha-Knesiyah ha-Gedolah ha-'Olamit ha-Hamishit shel Agudat Yisrael* [Report presented to the delegates of the fifth world convention of Agudat Yisrael] (Jerusalem: Agudat Yisrael World Organization, Information Department, 1964), p. 80 (hereafter cited as *Report to Fifth Agudah World Convention*); *Pe'ulot ha-Tenu'ah: Pirkei Din ve-Heshbon Mugashim la-Ve'idah ha-Shevi'it* [Activities of the movement: chapters of the report presented to the seventh convention] (Tel Aviv[?]: Po'alei Agudat Yisrael, 1969), p. 54 (hereafter cited as *Report to the Seventh PAY Convention*).

24. *Report to Third Mafdal Convention,* p. 154.

25. Cited in Elon, *Hakikah Datit,* p. 200.

26. *Report to Third Mafdal Convention,* p. 148; *Din ve-Heshbon Mugash le-Tzirei ha-Ve'idah ha-'Olamit ha-Kaf Alef shel ha-Mizrahi veha-Po'el ha-Mizrahi* [Report presented to the delegates of the twenty-first world Mizrahi–ha-Po'el ha-Mizrahi convention], pt. 3: *The Movement in Israel* (Jerusalem: Ha-Merkaz ha-'Olami shel ha-Mizrahi veha-Po'el ha-Mizrahi, 1968), p. 70 (herafter cited as *Report to the Twenty-First World Convention, Israel*).

27. Samuel P. Huntington, *Political Order in Changing Societies* (New Haven: Yale University Press, 1968), p. 461.

28. Elon, *Hakikah Datit,* p. 16.

29. The other three were the supply of kosher food to all citizens (this was a time of government rationing and control of food imports); the maintenance of marriage and divorce according to Torah law (accomplished in the Rabbinical Courts Law of 1953); and the supply of religious services to the public at the state's expense (achieved in large measure by the Religious Services Law of 1949). See *Ha-Po'el ha-Mizrahi bi-Shenot 5702-5709: Sikumei Pe'ulah la-Ve'idah ha'Asirit* [Ha-Po'el ha-Mizrahi in the years 1942–1949: summary of activity for the tenth convention] (Tel Aviv: Ha-Po'el ha-Mizrahi, 1950), p. 23 (hereafter cited as *Summary of Tenth Convention*).

30. Elon, *Hakikah Datit,* p. 14.

31. *Ibid.*

32. *Mi-Knesiyah li-Knesiyah* [From convention to convention] (Jerusalem: Agudat Yisrael World Organization, 1954), p. 73.

33. Michael Hazani, ed., *Mi-Duhan ha-Kneset* [From the podium of the Kneset] (Tel Aviv[?]: Mafdal[?], n.d. [ca. 1965]), p. 66.

34. Cited in Elon, *Hakikah Datit*, p. 192.
35. *Ibid.*, p. 16.
36. *Ibid.*, p. 195.
37. *Report to the Twentieth World Convention*, pp. 271–72.
38. *Ibid.*, p. 270.
39. Elon, *Hakikah Datit*, p. 198.
40. *Ibid.*, pp. 63–64; *Report to the Twenty-First World Convention, Israel*, pp. 17–19.
41. Elon, *Hakikah Datit*, pp. 199–201.
42. *Ibid.*, pp. 208–9; *Report to the Twenty-First World Convention, Israel*, pp. 22–23.
43. *Report to Third Mafdal Convention*, p. 70; see Gutmann, *Mishtar Medinat Yisrael*, pp. 434–35.
44. *Ibid.*, p. 433.
45. *Report to Fourth Mafdal Convention*, pp. 81, 84.

Notes to Chapter 7

1. Peter Y. Medding, *Mapai in Israel: Political Organization and Government in a New Society* (Cambridge: The University Press, 1972), p. 227.
2. Yehudah Kuperman, "Ha-Yeshivah ha-Tikhonit bi-Medinat Yisrael" ["The yeshivah high school in the state of Israel"], in *Ha-Yeshivah ha-Tikhonit* [The yeshivah high school] (Jerusalem: Ministry of Education and Culture, Religious Education Department, 1971), pp. 53–56.
3. Yosef Goldschmidt, *Mi-Yesodot ha-Hinukh ha-Mamlakhti-Dati* [The foundations of religious state education] (Jerusalem: Ministry of Education and Culture, Religious Education Department, 1972), p. 76.
4. Cited in Meir Ostrovsky (Ha-Meiri), *Toldot ha-Mizrahi be-Eretz Yisrael* [History of Mizrahi in Palestine] (Jerusalem: Reuven Mas, 1944), p. 120.
5. Aharon F. Kleinberger, *Society, Schools and Progress in Israel* (Oxford: Pergamon Press, 1969), pp. 35–36.
6. Ruth Stanner, *The Legal Basis of Education in Israel* (Jerusalem: Ministry of Education and Culture, 1963), pp. 13–14.
7. *Mi-Knesiyah li-Knesiyah* [From convention to convention] (Jerusalem: Agudat Yisrael World Organization, 1954), p. 49.
8. *Ibid.*
9. Stanner, *Legal Basis*, pp. 32–47, 150–62.
10. *Din ve-Heshbon Mugash le-Tzirei ha-Ve'idah ha-'Olamit ha-Yod Tet* [Report presented to the delegates to the nineteenth world convention] (Jerusalem: Ha-Merkaz ha-'Olami shel ha-Mizrahi, 1955), p. 67 (hereafter cited as *Report to Nineteenth World Convention*); *Shalosh Shanim: Din ve-Heshbon Mugash le-Tzirei ha-Ve'idah ha-Yod Alef shel ha-Po'el ha-Mizrahi* [Three years: report presented to the delegates to the eleventh ha-Po'el ha-Mizrahi convention] (Tel Aviv[?]: Histadrut ha-Po'el ha-Mizrahi be-Yisrael, Ha-Va'ad ha-Po'el, n.d.), p. 15 (hereafter cited as *Report to Eleventh ha-Po'el ha-Mizrahi Convention*).

11. *Report to Nineteenth World Convention,* p. 69; *Report to Eleventh ha-Po'el ha-Mizrahi Convention,* p. 14.
12. *Ha-Tzofeh,* January 10, January 12, 1950.
13. *Report to Nineteenth World Convention,* p. 68; *Report to Eleventh ha-Po'el ha-Mizrahi Convention,* p. 14.
14. *Ibid.*
15. *Report to Nineteenth World Convention,* p. 69; *Report to Eleventh ha-Po'el ha-Mizrahi Convention,* p. 14.
16. *Report to Nineteenth World Convention,* p. 69; *Report to Eleventh ha-Po'el ha-Mizrahi Convention,* p. 15.
17. *Report to Nineteenth World Convention,* p. 70.
18. Moshe Shapira, cited in *Report to Eleventh ha-Po'el ha-Mizrahi Convention,* p. 206.
19. *Report to Nineteenth World Convention,* p. 70; *Report to Eleventh ha-Po'el ha-Mizrahi Convention,* p. 19.
20. *Report to Nineteenth World Convention,* p. 76; *Report to Eleventh ha-Po'el ha-Mizrahi Convention,* p. 19.
21. Medding, *Mapai in Israel,* p. 228.
22. Dan Horowitz and Moshe Lissak, *Mi-Yishuv li-Medinah* [From Yishuv to state] (Jerusalem: Hebrew University, 1972), p. 11.
23. Kleinberger, *Society, Schools and Progress,* p. 120.
24. *Ibid.,* p. 122.
25. Moshe Unna, *Bi-Sedeh ha-Hinukh ha-Dati* (In the field of religious education] (Tel Aviv: Mazkirut ha-Kibbutz ha-Dati, 1970), p. 79.
26. *Mi-Knesiyah li-Knesiyah,* pp. 50–53.
27. *Ibid.,* p. 50.
28. *Divrei ha-Kneset* [Kneset proceedings], Second Kneset, Twelfth Session, 10 (October 7, 1951), p. 198.
29. Cited in Stanner, *Legal Basis,* pp. 168–79; see also Kleinberger, *Society, Schools and Progress,* pp. 123–33.
30. Cited in Stanner, *Legal Basis,* p. 47.
31. *Ibid.,* pp. 48–49.
32. *Ibid.,* p. 48.
33. *Report to Nineteenth World Convention,* p. 84.
34. Kleinberger, *Society, Schools and Progress,* p. 127.
35. Goldschmidt, *Mi-Yesodot,* pp. 44–46.
36. *Le-Sikumah shel Tekufah: Din ve-Heshbon Mugash la-Ve'idah ha-Shelishit shel ha-Miflagah ha-Datit-Leumit veha-Arba' 'Esrei shel Histadrut ha-Po'el ha-Mizrahi be-Yisrael* [The summation of a period: report presented to the third convention of the National Religious Party and the fourteenth convention of the ha-Po'el ha-Mizrahi organization in Israel] (Tel Aviv[?]: Ha-Va'ad ha-Po'el ha-Meuhad shel ha-Tenu'ah, n.d., [ca. 1969]), p. 153 (hereafter cited as *Report to Third Mafdal Convention*).
37. *Report to Nineteenth World Convention,* pp. 105–7; Goldschmidt, *Mi-Yesodot,* pp. 57–58.
38. Stanner, *Legal Basis,* pp. 52–54.

39. Kleinberger, *Society, Schools and Progress*, pp. 127–28.
40. Stanner, *Legal Basis*, p. 49; *Report to Nineteenth World Convention*, p. 84.
41. *Mi-Knesiyah li-Knesiyah*, p. 56.
42. Stanner, *Legal Basis*, p. 171.
43. *Din ve-Heshbon Mugash le-Tzirei ha-Knesiyah ha-Gedolah ha-'Olamit ha-Hamishit shel Agudat Yisrael* [Report presented to the delegates of the fifth world convention of Agudat Yisrael] (Jerusalem: Agudat Yisrael World Organization, Information Department, 1964), pp. 122–24 (hereafter cited as *Report to Fifth Agudah World Convention*).
44. *Ibid.*, p. 133.
45. Kleinberger, *Society, Schools and Progress*, pp. 131–32.
46. *Din ve-Heshbon Mugash le-Tzirei ha-Ve'idah ha-'Olamit ha-Kaf shel ha-Mizrahi veha-Po'el ha-Mizrahi* [Report presented to the delegates to the twentieth world convention of Mizrahi and ha-Po'el ha-Mizrahi], pt. 2: *Education* (Jerusalem: Ha-Merkaz ha-'Olami shel ha-Mizrahi veha-Po'el ha-Mizrahi, 1962), p. 35 (hereafter cited as *Report to Twentieth World Convention*).
47. *Report to Third Mafdal Convention*, p. 90.
48. *Report to Twentieth World Convention*, pp. 42–44.
49. *Ibid.*, p. 44; Kleinberger, *Society, Schools and Progress*, p. 141.
50. *Din ve-Heshbon Mugash le-Tzirei ha-Ve'idah ha-'Olamit ha-Kaf Alef shel ha-Mizrahi veha-Po'el ha-Mizrahi* [Report presented to the twenty-first Mizrahi and ha-Po'el ha-Mizrahi world convention], pt. 2: *Education* (Jerusalem: Ha-Merkaz ha-'Olami shel ha-Mizrahi veha-Po'el ha-Mizrahi, 1968), p. 87 (hereafter cited as *Report to Twenty-First World Convention*).
51. See sample school day in *Ha-Yeshivah ha-Tikhonit*, p. 79.
52. Kleinberger, *Society, Schools and Progress*, p. 170; *Hatza'ah le-Sidur Ma'arekhet ha-Sha'ot be-Vatei Sefer Mamlakhtiyim-Datiyim, Tashlag* [Proposal for the organization of the system of hours in religious state schools, 1973] (Jerusalem: Ministry of Education and Culture, Religious Education Department, 1972); *Hatza'ah le-Sidur Ma'arekhet ha-Sha'ot be-Vatei Sefer ha-Hinukh ha-'Atzmai* [Proposal for the organization of the system of hours in the Hinukh 'Atzmai schools] (Jerusalem: Hinukh 'Atzmai Center, 1972).
53. *Report to Twentieth World Convention*, p. 89.
54. Kleinberger, *Society, Schools and Progress*, p. 111.
55. Goldschmidt, *Mi-Yesodot*, p. 65.
56. *Ibid.*, pp. 66, 68.
57. Kleinberger, *Society, Schools and Progress*, p. 176.
58. Goldschmidt, *Mi-Yesodot*, p. 71.
59. *Ibid.*, p. 72.
60. *Ibid.*, p. 69.
61. Kleinberger, *Society, Schools and Progress*, pp. 184–85.
62. See, for example, Yesha'yahu Bernstein, in *Din ve-Heshbon: Ha-Ve'idah ha-Yod Gimel shel Histadrut ha-Po'el ha-Mizrahi veha-Ve'idah ha-Bet shel ha-Miflagah ha-Datit-Leumit* [Report of the thirteenth ha-Po'el ha-Mizrahi convention and the second National Religious Party convention] (Tel Aviv: Ha-Va'ad ha-Po'el shel ha-Po'el ha-Mizrahi be-Yisrael, 1965), pp. 113–14 (hereafter cited as *Report of Second Mafdal Convention*).

63. *Din ve-Heshbon Mugash le-Tzirei ha-Ve'idah ha-'Olamit ha-Kaf Bet shel ha-Mizrahi veha-Po'el ha-Mizrahi* [Report presented to the delegates to the twenty-second Mizrahi and ha-Po'el ha-Mizrahi world convention]; pt. 2: *Education* (Jerusalem: Ha-Merkaz ha-'Olami shel ha-Mizrahi veha-Po'el ha-Mizrahi, 1973), p. 5 (hereafter cited as *Report to Twenty-Second World Convention*); *Sekirah 'al Pe'ulot ha-Merkaz* [Report on the activities of the center] (Jerusalem: Ha-Merkaz le-Hinukh ha-Dati be-Yisrael, 1973), p. 10.

64. *Ma'akav Aharei Bogrei Batei Sefer Tikhoniyim Datiyim 1954–1960* [Survey of religious high school graduates 1954–1960] (Jerusalem: Ha-Merkaz le-Hinukh ha-Dati be-Yisrael, n.d.) (hereafter cited as *Ma'akav*); *Seker Ma'akav Bogrei ha-Hinukh ha-Mamlakhti-Dati be-Yisrael 1954–1967* [Survey of graduates of religious state education in Israel 1954–1967] (Tel Aviv: Ha-Merkaz le-Hinukh ha-Dati be-Yisrael, n.d.) (hereafter cited as *Seker*). Also appended to *Report to Twenty-Second World Convention*.

65. However, the party's two youth movements, B'nei 'Akivah and Religious Working Youth, as well as PAY's 'Ezrah and the religious scout movement, operate in the religious state schools and are state-subsidized therein, thus extending the colonization and nationalization of the system.

66. Yosef Goldschmidt, in *Report of Second Mafdal Convention,* p. 117; Tzvi Bernstein, *ibid.,* p. 140.

Notes to Chapter 8

1. *Din ve-Heshbon Mugash le-Tzirei ha-Ve'idah ha-'Olamit ha-Kaf shel ha-Mizrahi veha-Po'el ha-Mizrahi* [Report presented to the delegates to the twentieth world convention of Mizrahi and ha-Po'el ha-Mizrahi), pt. 1: *General* (Jerusalem: Ha-Merkaz ha-'Olami shel Mizrahi veha-Po'el ha-Mizrahi, 1962), p. 293 (hereafter cited as *Report to Twentieth World Convention*).

2. Zerah Warhaftig, *ibid.,* p. 293.

3. *Ibid.,* p. 299.

4. See Emanuel Gutmann, ed., *Mishtar Medinat Yisrael: Sefer Mekorot* [The government of the state of Israel: a book of sources] (Jerusalem: Hebrew University, 1971), pp. 399–401.

5. *Ibid.,* pp. 402–26.

6. *Jerusalem Post,* January 27, 1972.

7. *Jerusalem Post,* January 9, 1973.

8. *Jerusalem Post,* January 21, 25, 27, 1972.

9. Jewish Telegraphic Agency, *Daily News Bulletin,* May 1, 1973.

10. *Jerusalem Post,* November 26, 1972.

Notes to Chapter 9

1. Joseph LaPalombara and Myron Weiner, "The Origin and Development of Politi-

cal Parties,'' in *Political Parties and Political Development,* ed. J. LaPalombara and M. Weiner (Princeton: Princeton University Press, 1966), p. 7.

2. Alfred Grosser, ''France: Nothing But Opposition,'' in R. Dahl, ed., *Political Oppositions in Western Democracies* (New Haven: Yale University Press, 1966), pp. 7, 89–90.

3. Maurice Duverger, *Political Parties,* trans. B. and R. North (New York: John Wiley & Sons, 1959), p. xxix.

4. *Ibid.,* p. xxx.

5. *Ibid.,* p. xxxff.

6. *Ibid.,* p. xxxiv.

7. *Ibid.,* p. 64.

8. *Ibid.,* p. 91.

9. Otto Kirchheimer, ''The Transformation of the Western European Party Systems,'' in *Political Parties and Political Development,* ed. J. LaPalombara and M. Weiner (Princeton: Princeton University Press, 1966), p. 190.

10. Leon D. Epstein, *Political Parties in Western Democracies* (New York: Frederick A. Praeger, 1967), pp. 257–60.

11. The question of the end of ideology in relation to Israel as a whole is a much debated one. Lester Seligman, on the basis of a study of Kneset members, saw a fundamental de-ideologization of the system; Alan Arian pointed to the continued importance of ideology in the system (see Lester G. Seligman, *Leadership in a New Nation* [New York: Atheneum, 1964]; Alan Arian, *Ideological Change in Israel* [Cleveland: The Press of Case Western Reserve University, 1968]).

12. Giovanni Sartori, ''European Political Parties: The Case of Polarized Pluralism,'' in LaPalombara and Weiner, *Political Parties,* p. 159.

13. Dan Horowitz and Moshe Lissak, *Mi-Yishuv li-Medinah* [From Yishuv to state] (Jerusalem: Hebrew University, 1972), p. 34.

14. Otto Kirchheimer, ''Germany: The Vanishing Opposition,'' in Dahl, *Western Democracies,* p. 238.

15. Ervin Birnbaum, *The Politics of Compromise: State and Religion in Israel* (Rutherford, N.J.: Fairleigh Dickinson University Press, 1970), p. 303.

16. Norman L. Zucker, *The Coming Crisis in Israel: Private Faith and Public Policy* (Cambridge, Mass.: MIT Press, 1973), p. 218.

17. Birnbaum, *Politics of Compromise,* p. 285.

18. Simon N. Herman, *Israelis and Jews; The Continuity of an Identity* (New York: Random House, 1971), pp. 120–21.

19. Gary S. Schiff, ''Religion and Political Legitimacy: Islam in Egypt 1952–1954,'' M.A. thesis, Department of Political Science and Middle East Institute, Columbia University, 1970.

20. Eliezer Schweid, *Israel at the Crossroads,* trans. A. M. Winters (Philadelphia: Jewish Publication Society of America, 1973), pp. 64–65.

21. Sartori, ''European Political Parties,'' p. 160.

22. Hans Daalder, ''The Netherlands: Opposition in a Segmented Society,'' in Dahl, *Western Democracies,* pp. 188–236; Epstein, *Political Parties,* pp. 71, 339.

23. Daalder, ''The Netherlands,'' p. 203.

24. *Ibid.*, p. 226.

25. *Ibid.*, p. 220.

26. *Ibid.*, pp. 213–14.

27. Val R. Lorwin, "Belgium: Religion, Class, and Language in National Politics," in Dahl, *Western Democracies,* pp. 147–87.

28. Samuel H. Barnes, "Italy: Oppositions on Left, Right, and Center," in *ibid.,* pp. 312, 323.

29. Sartori, "European Political Parties," p. 143.

30. Frederick C. Engelmann, "Austria: The Pooling of Opposition," in Dahl, *Western Democracies,* pp. 260–83.

31. Epstein, *Political Parties,* pp. 72–73.

32. Kirchheimer, "Transformation."

33. Michael C. Hudson, *The Precarious Republic: Political Modernization in Lebanon* (New York: Random House, 1968).

34. C. S. Whitaker, *The Politics of Tradition: Continuity and Change in Northern Nigeria* (Princeton: Princeton University Press, 1970).

Bibliography

Books

Almond, Gabriel A., and Coleman, James S., eds. *The Politics of the Developing Areas*. Princeton: Princeton University Press, 1960.

Almond, Gabriel A., and Powell, G. Bingham, Jr. *Comparative Politics: A Developmental Approach*. Boston: Little, Brown & Co., 1966.

Arian, Alan. *Ideological Change in Israel*. Cleveland: The Press of Case Western Reserve University, 1968.

———. *The Choosing People: Voting Behavior in Israel*. Cleveland: The Press of Case Western Reserve University, 1973.

———, ed. *The Elections in Israel: 1969*. Jerusalem: Jerusalem Academic Press, 1972.

Bentwich, J. S. *Ha-Hinukh bi-Medinat Yisrael* [Education in the state of Israel]. Tel Aviv: Chachik Publishing House, 1960.

Bernstein, Y., ed. *Mitzpeh* [Viewpoint]. Jerusalem: Ha-Merkaz ha-'Olami shel ha-Mizrahi, 1953.

Birnbaum, Ervin. *The Politics of Compromise: State and Religion in Israel*. Rutherford, N.J.: Fairleigh Dickinson University Press, 1970.

Blau, Moshe. *'Al Homotayikh Yerushalayim* [On thy walls, O Jerusalem]. B'nei Braq: Netzah, 1967.

Breuer, Isaac. *The Jewish National Home*. Translated by Miriam Aumann. Frankfurt am Main: J. Kauffmann, 1926.

———. *'Am ha-Torah ha-Meurgan* [The organized Torah nation]. Tel Aviv: Netzah, 1944.

Curtis, Michael, and Chertoff, Mordecai, eds. *Israel: Social Structure and Change.* New Brunswick, N.J.: Transaction Books, 1973.

Davis, Helen Miller, ed. *Constitutions, Electoral Laws, Treaties and States in the Near and Middle East.* Durham, N.C.: Duke University Press, 1953.

Deutsch, Karl W. *Nationalism and Social Communication.* Cambridge, Mass.: M.I.T. Press, 1953.

Duverger, Maurice. *Political Parties.* Translated by B. and R. North. 2d rev. Eng. ed. New York: John Wiley & Sons, 1959.

Elon, Menahem. *Hakikah Datit* [Religious legislation]. Tel Aviv: Ha-Kibbutz ha-Dati, 1968.

Epstein, Leon D. *Political Parties in Western Democracies.* New York: Frederick A. Praeger, 1967.

Fein, Leonard. *Politics in Israel.* Boston: Little, Brown, 1967.

Fishman, Juda L. [Yehudah Leib Maimon]. *The History of the Mizrachi Movement.* Translated by Harry Karp. New York: Mizrachi Hatzair of America, 1928.

Friedenson, Joseph. *A History of Agudath Israel.* New York: Agudath Israel of America, 1970.

Friedman, Isaiah. *The Question of Palestine, 1914–1918: British-Jewish-Arab Relations.* New York: Schocken Books, 1973.

Goldman, Eliezer. *Religious Issues in Israel's Political Life.* Jerusalem: Mador Dati, Youth and Hechalutz Department, World Zionist Organization, 1964.

Gush-Zahav [Goldschlag], Yitzhak. *Mi-Vilna 'ad Yerushalayim* [From Vilna to Jerusalem]. Jerusalem: Ha-Merkaz ha-'Olami shel ha-Mizrahi, 1954.

Gutmann, Emanuel, ed. *Mishtar Medinat Yisrael: Sefer Mekorot* [The government of the state of Israel: a book of sources]. Jerusalem: Hebrew University, 1971.

Halpern, Ben. *The Idea of the Jewish State.* 2d ed. Cambridge, Mass.: Harvard University Press, 1969.

Herman, Simon N. *Israelis and Jews; The Continuity of an Identity.* New York: Random House, 1971.

Hertzberg, Arthur, ed. *The Zionist Idea: A Historical Analysis and Reader.* Garden City, N.Y.: Doubleday & Co. and Herzl Press, 1959.

Horowitz, Dan, and Lissak, Moshe. *Mi-Yishuv li-Medinah* [From yishuv to state]. Jerusalem: Hebrew University, 1972.

Hudson, Michael C. *The Precarious Republic: Political Modernization in Lebanon.* New York: Random House, 1968.

Huntington, Samuel P. *Political Order in Changing Societies.* New Haven: Yale University Press, 1968.

Hurewitz, J. C. *The Struggle for Palestine.* New York: W. W. Norton, 1950.

Kleinberger, Aharon F. *Society, Schools and Progress in Israel.* Oxford: Pergamon Press, 1969.

Kohn, Moshe. *Who's Afraid of Gush Emunim?* Jerusalem: Jerusalem Post, n.d. [ca. 1976].

Landau, Jacob M. *The Arabs in Israel: A Political Study.* London: Oxford University Press, 1969.

LaPalombara, Joseph, and Weiner, Myron, eds. *Political Parties and Political Development.* Princeton: Princeton University Press, 1966.

Laqueur, Walter, ed. *The Israel-Arab Reader: A Documentary History of the Middle East Conflict.* New York: Bantam Books, 1969.

Lerner, Daniel. *The Passing of Traditional Society.* New York: The Free Press, 1958.

Lewin, Isaac, ed. *Homer le-Shealat Hitkonenut ve-Sidur ha-Medinah ha-Yehudit 'al Pi ha-Torah* [Material on the question of the preparation and organization of the Jewish state according to the Torah]. New York: Research Institute for Post-War Problems of Religious Jews, 1947.

Lissak, Moshe, and Gutmann, Emanuel, eds. *Political Institutions and Processes in Israel.* Jerusalem: Hebrew University, 1971.

Maimon, Yehudah Leib [Juda L. Fishman]. *The History of the Mizrahi Movement.* Translated by Harry Karp. New York: Mizrachi Hatzair of America, 1928.

Medding, Peter Y. *Mapai in Israel: Political Organization and Government in a New Society.* Cambridge: The University Press, 1972.

Mi va-Mi be-Yisrael 1971–72 [Who's who in Israel 1971–72]. Tel Aviv: Bronfman and Cohen, 1972.

Ostrovsky, Meir [Ha-Meiri]. *Toldot ha-Mizrahi be-Eretz Yisrael* [History of Mizrahi in Palestine]. Jerusalem: Reuven Mas, 1944.

Refael, Yitzhak, ed. *Entziklopediyah shel ha-Tziyonut ha-Datit* [Encyclopedia of religious Zionism]. 4 vols. Jerusalem: Mosad ha-Rav Kook, 1958–71.

Reichel, O. Asher. *Isaac Halevy: Spokesman and Historian of Jewish Tradition*. New York: Yeshiva University Press, 1969.

Rosenheim, Ya'akov [Jacob]. *Agudist World-Problems*. New York: Agudas Israel World Organization, 1941.

————. *Kol Ya'akov* [The voice of Jacob]. Tel Aviv: Netzah, 1954.

————. *Zikhronot* [Memoirs]. Tel Aviv: She'arim, 1955.

————. *Ktavim* [Writings]. Jerusalem: Agudat Yisrael World Organization, 1970.

Safran, Nadav. *The United States and Israel*. Cambridge, Mass.: Harvard University Press, 1963.

Salmon, Yosef, ed. *'Eduyot 'al Reishito shel ha-Po'el ha-Mizrahi* [Testimony on the beginnings of ha-Po'el ha-Mizrahi]. Jerusalem: Hebrew University, 1968.

Schiff, Gary S. "Religion and Political Legitimacy: Islam in Egypt 1952–1954." Master's thesis, Department of Political Science and Middle East Institute, Columbia University, 1970.

Schweid, Eliezer. *Israel at the Crossroads*. Translated by A. M. Winters. Philadelphia: Jewish Publication Society of America, 1973.

Sefer ha-Yovel le-Ya'akov Rosenheim/Festschrift fur Jakob Rosenheim. Frankfurt am Main: J. Kauffmann, 1931.

Seligman, Lester G. *Leadership in a New Nation*. New York: Atheneum, 1964.

Stanner, Ruth. *The Legal Basis of Education in Israel*. Jerusalem: Ministry of Education and Culture, 1963.

Stein, Leonard. *The Balfour Declaration*. London: Vallentine and Mitchell, 1961.

Sykes, Christopher. *Cross Roads to Israel*. London: New English Library, 1965.

Tidhar, David, ed. *Entziklopediyah le-Halutzei ha-Yishuv u-Vonav* [Encyclopedia of the yishuv and its builders]. Vols. 2–4, 8. Tel Aviv: Sefarim Rishmim, 1947–57.

Tzidon, Asher. *Beit ha-Nivharim* [The House of Representatives]. 6th rev. ed. Tel Aviv: Ahiasaf, 1971.

Unna, Moshe. *Hatza'ah le-Tokhnit ha-Miflagah* [Proposal for the party program]. Tel Aviv: La-Mifneh, 1952.

————. *Bi-Sedeh ha-Hinukh ha-Dati* [In the field of religious education]. Tel Aviv: Mazkirut ha-Kibbutz ha-Dati, 1970.

Warhaftig, Z.; Heifetz, H.; and Gelis, D., eds. *Dat u-Medinah ba-Hakikah* [Religion and state in legislation]. Jerusalem: Ministry of Religions, 1973.

Weinryb, Bernard D. *The Yishuv in Palestine: Structure and Organization.* New York: National Education and Political Committees of Hadassah, n.d. [ca. 1946–47].

Whitaker, C. S. *The Politics of Tradition: Continuity and Change in Northern Nigeria.* Princeton: Princeton University Press, 1970.

Who's Who in Israel and in the Work for Israel Abroad 1969–70. Tel Aviv: Bronfman and Cohen, 1970.

Yovel ha-Mizrahi [Mizrahi anniversary book]. Edited by Y. L. Fishman. Jerusalem: Irgun Ezrah-Nehemyah, 1952.

Zucker, Norman L. *The Coming Crisis in Israel: Private Faith and Public Policy.* Cambridge, Mass.: MIT Press, 1973.

ARTICLES

Barnes, Samuel H. "Italy: Opposition on Left, Right, and Center." In *Political Oppositions in Western Democracies,* edited by R. Dahl, pp. 303–31. New Haven: Yale University Press, 1966.

Barzilai, Amnon. "Milhemet ha Si'ot ba-Mafdal" [The war of factions in Mafdal]. *ha-Aretz,* September 28, 1976, p. 9.

Blattberg, Wolf. "Polish Jewry: Yesterday, Today, and Tomorrow." In *Israel of Tomorrow,* edited by Leo Jung. 2d rev. ed. New York: Herald Square Press, 1949. Vol. 2, pp. 413–43.

Blau, Moshe. "Memorandum of Rabbi Moshe Blau on the Question of the Possibility of Participation in the Preparatory Committee's Work on a Constitution for the Jewish State" and "Program for the Demands of the Orthodox on the

Question of the Constitution for the Jewish State." In *Homer le-Shealat Hitkonenut ve-Sidur ha-Medinah ha-Yehudit 'al Pi ha-Torah* [Material on the question of the preparation and organization of the Jewish state according to the Torah], edited by Isaac Lewin. New York: Research Institute for Post-War Problems of Religious Jews, 1947.

Breuer, Isaac. "Memorandum on the Attitude of Agudat Yisrael to the Jewish State Sent to the President of the World Agudat Yisrael, Rabbi Ya'akov Rosenheim" and "Program for a United Religious Front on the Question of a Constitution for the Jewish State." In *Homer le-Shealat Hitkonenut ve-Sidur ha-Medinah ha-Yehudit 'al Pi ha-Torah* [Material on the question of the preparation and organization of the Jewish state according to the Torah], edited by Isaac Lewin. New York: Research Institute for Post-War Problems of Religious Jews, 1947.

Czudnowski, Moshe M. "Legislative Recruitment under Proportional Representation in Israel: A Model and a Case Study." *Midwest Journal of Political Science* 14 (1970).

Elazar, Daniel J. "Local Government as an Integrating Factor in Israeli Society." In *Israel: Social Structure and Change,* edited by M. Curtis and M. Chertoff. New Brunswick, N.J.: Transaction Books, 1973.

Fishman, Y. L. "Toldot ha-Mizrahi ve-Hitpathuto" [History and development of Mizrahi]. In *Sefer ha-Mizrahi* [The Mizrahi book], edited by Y. L. Fishman. Jerusalem: Mosad ha-Rav Kook, 1946.

Katzburg, Netanel. "Ha-Mizrahi, ha-Tziyonut, veha-Yahadut ha-Datit" [Mizrahi, Zionism, and religious Jewry]. In *Mitzpeh* [Viewpoint], edited by Y. Bernstein, pp. 105–13. Jerusalem: Ha-Merkaz ha-'Olami shel ha-Mizrahi, 1953.

Kirchheimer, Otto. "Germany: The Vanishing Opposition." In *Political Opposition in Western Democracies,* edited by R. Dahl, pp. 237–59. New Haven: Yale University Press, 1966.

———. "The Transformation of the Western European Party Systems." In *Political Parties and Political Development,* edited by J. LaPalombara and M. Wiener, pp. 177–200. Princeton: Princeton University Press, 1969.

Kuperman, Yehudah. "Ha-Yeshivah ha-Tikhonit bi-Medinat Yisrael" [The yeshivah high school in the state of Israel]. In *Ha-Yeshivah ha-Tikhonit* [The yeshivah high school]. Jerusalem: Ministry of Education and Culture, Religious Education Department, 1971.

Landau, David. "The Rabbinate Elections: Are They Necessary?" *Jerusalem Post Magazine,* August 25, 1972.

Lewin, Isaac. "Religious Judaism in Independent Poland." In *Israel of Tomorrow*, edited by Leo Jung. 2d rev. ed. New York: Herald Square Press, 1949. Vol. 2, pp. 445–55.

Lorwin, Val R. "Belgium: Religion, Class, and Language in National Politics." In *Political Oppositions in Western Democracies*, edited by R. Dahl, pp. 147–87. New Haven: Yale University Press, 1966.

Maimon, Yehudah Leib [Juda L. Fishman]. "Le-Heshbonah shel Histadruteinu" [Taking account of our organization]. *Ha-Tur*, June 8, 1934, June 22, 1934, July 6, 1934.

———. "Toldot ha-Mizrahi ve-Hitpathuto" [History and development of Mizrahi]. In *Sefer ha-Mizrahi* [The Mizrahi book], edited by Y. L. Fishman. Jerusalem: Mosad ha-Rav Kook, 1946.

Salmon, Yosef. "Shiluv ha-Sotzyalizm 'im ha-Dat" [Coalescence of Socialism with Religion]. *De'ot*, No. 40 (Spring 1971).

Sartori, Giovanni. "European Political Parties: The Case of Polarized Pluralism." In *Political Parties and Political Development*, edited by Joseph LaPalombara and Myron Weiner, pp. 137–76. Princeton: Princeton University Press, 1966.

Wolfsberg, Yeshayahu. "Ha-Mizrahi ve-'Emdato le-Gabei ha-Ortodoksyah ha-Bilti Tziyonit" [Mizrahi and its attitude toward non-Zionist orthodoxy]. In *Yovel ha-Mizrahi* [Mizrahi anniversary book], edited by Y. L. Fishman, pp. 256–67. Jerusalem: Irgun'Ezrah-Nehemyah, 1952.

PERIODICALS AND PRESS

Ha-Aretz.

Ha-Modi'a [Agudat Yisrael daily].

Ha-Ofek.

Ha-Tzofeh [Mafdal daily].

Ha-Tzofeh Supplement.

Jerusalem Post.

Jerusalem Post Magazine.

Jewish Telegraphic Agency, *Daily News Bulletin.*

She'arim [PAY daily].

PARTY PUBLICATIONS

MAFDAL

Amiel, Moshe Avigdor. *Ha-Yesodot ha-Idiologiyyim shel ha-Mizrahi* [The ideological foundations of Mizrahi]. Warsaw: Mizrahi, 1934.

Bein Ve'idah le-Ve'idah: Din ve-Heshbon Mugash la-Ve'idah ha-Revi'it shel ha-Mafdal veha-Hameish 'Esrei shel ha-Po'el ha-Mizrahi [Between convention and convention: report presented to the fourth Mafdal convention and the fifteenth ha-Po'el ha-Mizrahi convention]. Tel Aviv: Ha-Po'el ha-Mizrahi, 1973.

Bein Ve'idah le-Ve'idah: Din ve-Heshbon Mugash la-Ve'idah ha-Yod Gimel shel Histadrut ha-Po'el ha-Mizrahi veha-Ve'idah ha-Bet shel ha-Mafdal [Between convention and convention: report presented to the delegates to the thirteenth ha-Po'el ha-Mizrahi convention and the second Mafdal convention]. Tel Aviv: Ha-Po'el ha-Mizrahi, 1963.

Be-Ma'arekhet ha-'Am veha-Medinah: Kovetz Mugash la-Ve'idah ha-Bet shel ha-Mafdal veha-Yod Gimel shel Histadrut ha-Po'el ha-Mizrahi [In the battle for the nation and the state: an anthology presented to the second Mafdal convention and the thirteenth ha-Po'el ha-Mizrahi convention]. Tel Aviv: Ha-Hanhalah ha-Merkazit, 1963.

Din ve-Heshbon shel ha-Ve'idah ha-'Olamit ha-Yod Tet shel ha-Mizrahi veha-Po'el ha-Mizrahi [Report of the nineteenth Mizrahi and ha-Po'el ha-Mizrahi world convention]. Jerusalem: Ha-Merkaz ha-'Olami shel ha-Mizrahi veha-Po'el ha-Mizrahi, 1956.

Din ve-Heshbon: ha-Ve'idah ha-Yod Gimel shel Histadrut ha-Po'el ha-Mizrahi veha-Ve'idah ha-Bet shel ha-Miflagah ha-Datit-Leumit [Report of the thirteenth ha-Po'el ha-Mizrahi convention and the second National Religious Party convention]. Tel Aviv: Ha-Va'ad ha-Po'el shel ha-Po'el ha-Mizrahi be-Yisrael, 1965.

Din ve-Heshbon la-Ve'idah ha-Sheminit [Report to eighth convention]. Tel Aviv: Ha-Po'el ha-Mizrahi, 1942.

Din ve-Heshbon Me'et ha-Merkaz ha-'Olami . . . Mugash el ha-Ve'idah ha-'Olamit shel ha-Mizrahi, Antverpen [Report of the world headquarters . . . submitted to the world convention of Mizrahi, Antwerp]. Jerusalem: Ha-Merkaz ha-'Olami shel ha-Mizrahi, 1926.

Din ve-Heshbon Me'et ha-Merkaz ha-'Olami . . . Mugash el ha-Ve'idah ha-'Olamit shel ha-Mizrahi, Dantzig [Report of the world headquarters . . . submitted to the world convention of Mizrahi, Danzig]. Jerusalem: Ha-Merkaz ha-'Olami shel ha-Mizrahi, 1928.

Din ve-Heshbon Me'et ha-Merkaz ha-'Olami . . . Mugash la-Ve'idah ha-'Olamit be-Tzirikh [Report of the world headquarters . . . submitted to the world convention of Mizrahi, Zurich]. Jerusalem[?]: Ha-Merkaz ha-'Olami shel ha-Mizrahi, 1937.

Din ve-Heshbon Me'et ha-Merkaz ha-'Olami . . . Mugash la-Ve'idah ha-'Olamit shel ha-Mizrahi, Krakov [Report of the world headquarters . . . submitted to the world convention of Mizrahi, Krakow]. Jerusalem[?]: Ha-Merkaz ha-'Olami shel ha-Mizrahi, 1935.

Din ve-Heshbon Mefurat: ha-Ve'idah ha-Shevi'it shel ha-Po'el ha-Mizrahi [Detailed report: the seventh ha-Po'el ha-Mizrahi convention]. Tel Aviv: Torah va-'Avodah Library, 1935.

Din ve-Heshbon Mugash le-Tzirei ha-Ve'idah ha-'Olamit ha-Kaf Alef shel ha-Mizrahi veha-Po'el ha-Mizrahi [Report presented to the delegates to the twenty-first Mizrahi and ha-Po'el ha-Mizrahi world convention]. Jerusalem: Ha-Merkaz ha-'Olami shel ha-Mizrahi veha-Po'el ha-Mizrahi, 1968. Pt. 2: Education; Pt. 3: The movement in Israel.

Din ve-Heshbon Mugash le-Tzirei ha-Ve'idah ha-'Olamit ha-Kaf Bet shel ha-Mizrahi veha-Po'el ha-Mizrahi [Report presented to the delegates to the twenty-second Mizrahi and ha-Po'el ha-Mizrahi world convention]. Jerusalem: Ha-Merkaz ha-'Olami shel ha-Mizrahi veha-Po'el ha-Mizrahi, 1973. Pt. 2: Education.

Din ve-Heshbon Mugash le-Tzirei ha-Ve'idah ha-'Olamit ha-Kaf shel ha-Mizrahi veha-Po'el ha-Mizrahi [Report presented to the delegates to the twentieth world convention of Mizrahi and ha-Po'el ha-Mizrahi]. Jerusalem: Ha-Merkaz ha-'Olami shel ha-Mizrahi veha-Po'el ha-Mizrahi, 1962. Pt. 1: General; Pt. 2: Education.

Din ve-Heshbon Mugash le-Tzirei ha-Ve'idah ha-'Olamit ha-Yod Het shel ha-Mizrahi veha-Po'el ha-Mizrahi [Report presented to the delegates to the eighteenth world Mizrahi and ha-Po'el ha-Mizrahi convention]. Jerusalem: Ha-Merkaz ha-'Olami shel ha-Mizrahi, 1949.

Din ve-Heshbon Mugash le-Tzirei ha-Ve'idah ha-'Olamit ha-Yod Tet [Report presented to the delegates to the nineteenth world convention]. Jerusalem: Ha-Merkaz ha-'Olami shel ha-Mizrahi, 1955.

Din ve-Heshbon shel ha-Merkaz ha-'Olami . . . Mugash la-Ve'idah ha-'Olamit shel ha-Mizrahi, Zhenivah [Report of the world headquarters . . . submitted to the world convention of Mizrahi, Geneva]. Jerusalem: Ha-Merkaz ha-'Olami shel ha-Mizrahi, 1939.

Din ve-Heshbon shel ha-Ve'idah ha-'Asirit shel ha-Po'el ha-Mizrahi [Report of the tenth ha-Po'el ha-Mizrahi convention]. Jerusalem[?]: Ha-Po'el ha-Mizrahi, 1950[?].

Din ve-Heshbon shel ha-Ve'idah ha-'Olamit ha-'Esrim shel ha-Mizrahi veha-Po'el ha-Mizrahi [Report of the twentieth world convention of Mizrahi and ha-Po'el ha-Mizrahi]. Jerusalem: Ha-Merkaz ha-'Olami shel ha-Mizrahi veha-Po'el ha-Mizrahi, 1964.

Din ve-Heshbon shel ha-Ve'idah ha-'Olamit shel ha-Mizrahi, Antverpen [Report of the world convention of Mizrahi, Antwerp]. Jerusalem: Ha-Merkaz ha-'Olami shel ha-Mizrahi, 1926.

Din ve-Heshbon shel ha-Ve'idah ha-Shneim 'Esrei shel ha-Po'el ha-Mizrahi [Report of the twelfth ha-Po'el ha-Mizrahi convention]. Tel Aviv: Ha-Po'el ha-Mizrahi, n.d.

Hahlatot, Reshimot Havrei ha-Mosdot ha-Nivharim, ha-Ve'idah ha-Meuhedet shel ha-Tenu'ah ha-Gimel shel ha-Mafdal veha-Yod Daled shel ha-Po'el ha-Mizrahi [Decisions, and lists of members of elected institutions, of the joint convention of the movement, the third of Mafdal and fourteenth of ha-Po'el ha-Mizrahi]. Jerusalem and Tel Aviv: Ha-Mazkirut ha-Meuhedet shel ha-Mafdal veha-Po'el ha-Mizrahi, 1969.

Ha-Hitya'atzut ha-Penimit ha-'Olamit ha-Revi'it shel Netzigei ha-Mizrahi veha-Po'el ha-Mizrahi be-Yisrael uva-Tefutzot [The fourth internal world consultation of Mizrahi and ha-Po'el ha-Mizrahi in Israel and the Diaspora]. Jerusalem: Ha-Merkaz ha-'Olami shel ha-Mizrahi, 1955.

Ha-Hitya'atzut ha-Penimit ha-'Olamit ha-Shelishit shel Netzigei ha-Mizrahi veha-Po'el ha-Mizrahi be-Yisrael uva-Tefutzot [The third internal world consultation of Mizrahi and ha-Po'el ha-Mizrahi in Israel and the Diaspora]. Jerusalem: Ha-Merkaz ha-'Olami shel ha-Mizrahi, 1954.

Ha-Hitya'atzut ha-Penimit ha-'Olamit ha-Sheniyyah shel Netzigei ha-Mizrahi veha-Po'el ha-Mizrahi be-Yisrael uva-Tefutzot [The second internal world consultation of Mizrahi and ha-Po'el ha-Mizrahi in Israel and the Diaspora]. Jerusalem: Ha-Merkaz ha-'Olami shel ha-Mizrahi, 1953.

Ha-Hitya'atzut ha-Penimit ha-'Olamit shel Netzigei ha-Mizrahi veha-Po'el ha-Mizrahi be-Yisrael uva-Tefutzot [The internal world consultation of Mizrahi and ha-Po'el ha-Mizrahi in Israel and the Diaspora]. Jerusalem: Ha-Merkaz ha-'Olami shel ha-Mizrahi, 1953.

Ha-Mifkad ha-Irguni [The organizational survey]. Tel Aviv: Ha-Po'el ha-Mizrahi, Organization Department, 1966.

Ha-Po'el ha-Mizrahi bi-Shenot 5702-5709: Sikumei Pe'ulah la-Ve'idah ha-'Asirit [Ha-Po'el ha-Mizrahi in the years 1942–1949: summary of activity for the tenth convention]. Tel Aviv: Ha-Po'el ha-Mizrahi, 1950.

Hazani, Michael. *Histadrut, Miflagah, Tenu'ah* [Organization, party, movement]. Tel Aviv: La-Mifneh, 1952.

————, ed. *Mi-Duhan ha-Kneset* [From the podium of the Kneset]. Tel Aviv[?]: Mafdal?, n.d. [ca. 1965].

"Hukat ha-Miflagah ha-Datit-Leumit, ha-Mizrahi veha-Po'el ha-Mizrahi" [The constitution of the National Religious Party, Mizrahi and ha-Po'el ha-Mizrahi]. In *Hukat ha-Tenu'ah* [Constitution of the movement]. Tel Aviv: Mafdal, 1965.

Hukat ha-Tenu'ah [Constitution of the movement]. Tel Aviv: Mafdal, 1965.

"Hukat Histadrut ha-Po'el ha-Mizrahi be-Eretz Yisrael" [Constitution of ha-Po'el ha-Mizrahi organization in Israel]. In *Hukat ha-Tenu'ah* [Constitution of the movement]. Tel Aviv: Mafdal, 1965.

Hukat Histadrut ha-Mizrahi ha-'Olamit [Constitution of the world Mizrahi organization]. Jerusalem[?]: Ha-Merkaz ha-'Olami shel ha-Mizrahi, 1926.

Kol Koreh. Vilna: Mizrahi, 1902.

La-Mifneh Faction. *Matza' la-Ve'idah ha-'Asirit* [Platform for the tenth convention]. Tel Aviv: La-Mifneh, 1949.

Le-Sikumah shel Tekufah: Din ve-Heshbon Mugash la-Ve'idah ha-Shelishit shel ha-Miflagah ha-Datit-Leumit veha-Arba' 'Esrei shel Histadrut ha-Po'el ha-Mizrahi be-Yisrael [The summation of a period: report presented to the third convention of the National Religious Party and the fourteenth convention of the ha-Po'el ha-Mizrahi organization in Israel]. Tel Aviv[?]: Ha-Va'ad ha-Po'el ha-Meuhad shel ha-Tenu'ah, n.d. [ca. 1969].

Ma'akav Aharei Bogrei Batei Sefer Tikhoniyim Datiyim 1954–1960 [Survey of religious high school graduates 1954–1960]. Jerusalem: Ha-Merkaz le-Hinukh ha-Dati be-Yisrael, n.d.

Pirkei Pe'ulah: Din ve-Heshbon Mugash le-Tzirei ha-Ve'idah ha-Yod Bet shel ha-Po'el ha-Mizrahi [Annals of activities: report presented to the delegates of the twelfth ha-Po'el ha-Mizrahi convention]. Tel Aviv[?]: Ha-Va'ad ha-Po'el shel ha-Po'el ha-Mizrahi be-Yisrael, n.d.

Quntresim le-Ba'ayot ha-Po'el ha-Mizrahi [Pamphlets on ha-Po'el ha-Mizrahi problems]. Jerusalem: Ha-Reshimah ha-Meuhedet, 1952. Nos. 2–3.

Seker Ma-'akav Bogrei Batei Sefer Tikhoniyim Datiyim 1954–1967 [Survey of graduates of religious state education in Israel 1954–1967]. Tel Aviv: Ha-Merkaz le-Hinukh ha-Dati bi-Yisrael, n.d.

Sekirah 'al Pe'ulot ha-Merkaz [Report on activities of the center]. Jerusalem: ha-Merkaz ha-Hinukh ha-Dati be-Yisrael, 1973.

Shalosh Shanim: Din ve-Heshbon Mugash le-Tzirei ha-Ve'idah ha-Yod Alef shel ha-Po'el ha-Mizrahi [Three years: report presented to the delegates to the eleventh ha-Po'el ha-Mizrahi convention]. Tel Aviv[?]: Histadrut ha-Po'el ha-Mizrahi be-Yisrael, ha-Va'ad ha-Po'el, n.d.

Zahavi, Mordekhai. *Darkeinu* [Our way]. Jerusalem: Ha-Po'el ha-Mizrahi, 1923–35. No 2 of a series of 19 pamphlets.

AGUDAT YISRAEL

Album of the Palestine Central Society of the Agudath Israel. Frankfurt am Main: n.p., n.d.

Dapim ve-'Uvdot [Pages and facts]. Jerusalem: Agudat Yisrael World Organization, Information Department, 1960.

Din ve-Heshbon Mugash le-Tzirei ha-Knesiyah ha-Gedolah ha-'Olamit ha-Hamishit shel Agudat Yisrael [Report presented to the delegates of the fifth world convention of Agudat Yisrael]. Jerusalem: Agudat Yisrael World Organization, Information Department, 1964.

Dvar Agudat Yisrael be-Sha'ah Zu [The word of Agudat Yisrael at this hour]. Jerusalem: Ha-Va'adah ha-Mekhinah shel ha-Ve'idah ha-Artzit, 1941.

Hahlatot ha-Knesiyah ha-Gedolah ha-Hamishit [The decisions of the fifth Knesiyah Gedolah]. Jerusalem: Agudat Yisrael World Organization, Information Department, 1964.

Ha-Knesiyah ha-Gedolah ha-Sheniyyah shel Agudat Yisrael [The second world convention of Agudat Yisrael]. Vienna: Ha-Merkaz ha-'Olami shel Agudat Yisrael, 1929.

Hatza'ah le-Sidur Ma'arekhet ha-Sha'ot be-Vatei Sefer ha-Hinukh ha-'Atzmai [Proposal for the organization of the system of hours in the Hinukh 'Atzmai schools]. Jerusalem: Hinukh 'Atzmai Center, 1972.

Levin, Yitzhak Meir. *Madu'a Parashnu meha-Koalitzyah?* [Why have we left the coalition?]. Jerusalem: Agudat Yisrael World Organization, 1953.

―――. Speech in Kneset, 8 Iyyar 5708 (1948), cited in *Mi-Knesiyah li-Knesiyah* [From convention to convention]. Jerusalem: Agudat Yisrael World Organization, 1954.

―――. *Ha-Reka' shel ha-Mashbeir ha-Memshalti* [The background of the government crisis]. Jerusalem: Agudat Yisrael World Organization, Information and Propaganda Department, 1971.

Mi-Knesiyah li-Knesiyah [From convention to convention]. Jerusalem: Agudat Yisrael World Organization, 1954.

Mi Sam Keitz la-Ma'arakhah? [Who put an end to the battle?]. Jerusalem: Agudat Yisrael, 1964.

Shmuel, Avraham ben-Moshe [pseud.]. *Kol Koreh le-Shalom ve-Ahdut bein Agudat Yisrael uvein ha-Va'ad ha-Leumi be-Eretz Yisrael* [Proclamation calling for peace and unity between Agudat Yisrael and the Va'ad Leumi in Palestine]. Jerusalem: n.p., 1930.

Yedi'ot ha-Merkaz ha-Artzi shel Agudat Yisrael be-Eretz Yisrael [Information from the national headquarters of Agudat Yisrael in Israel], 1948. No. 3.

Yireh ha-Kahal ve-Yishpot. Jerusalem: Ha-Modi'ah, 1952.

PO'ALEI AGUDAT YISRAEL

Bein Ve'idah le-Ve'idah [Between convention and convention]. Tel Aviv: Po'alei Agudat Yisrael, 1940.

Ha-Po'el ha-Haredi [The religious worker]. Tel Aviv: 1935.

Landau, Ya'akov. *Lifnei ha-Hakhra'ah* [Before the decision]. Tel Aviv: She'arim, 1944.

Le-Heshbon 'Olameinu [Summing up our world]. Jerusalem: Va'ad Yedidei PAGI, 1944.

Pe'ulot ha-Tenu'ah: Pirkei Din ve-Heshbon Mugashim la-Ve'idah ha-Shevi'it [Activities of the movement: chapters of the report presented to the seventh convention]. Tel Aviv[?]: Po'alei Agudat Yisrael, 1969.

GOVERNMENT PUBLICATIONS

Central Bureau of Statistics. *Israel Government Yearbook.* 1957, 1958, 1960–61, 1965, 1966, 1967, 1968, 1970, 1971, 1972.

————. *Results of the Elections to the Third Kneset and the Local Authorities.* Jerusalem: Central Bureau of Statistics, 1956.

————. *Results of the Elections to the Fourth Kneset and the Local Authorities.* Jerusalem: Central Bureau of Statistics, 1961.

————. *Results of the Elections to the Fifth Kneset and the Local Authorities.* Jerusalem: Central Bureau of Statistics, 1964.

————. *Results of the Elections to the Sixth Kneset and the Local Authorities.* 2 vols. Jerusalem: Central Bureau of Statistics, 1967.

————. *Results of the Elections to the Seventh Kneset and the Local Authorities.* Jerusalem: Central Bureau of Statistics, 1970.

————. *Statistical Abstract of Israel.* No. 10, 1958–59; No. 13, 1962; No. 14, 1963; No. 15, 1964; No. 18, 1967; No. 19, 1968; No. 20, 1969; No. 21, 1970; No. 22, 1971; No. 25, 1974; No. 26, 1975.

————. *Results of the Elections to the Eighth Kneset and the Local Authorities.* Jerusalem: Central Bureau of Statistics, 1974.

Din ve-Heshbon 'al Pe'ulot Misrad ha-Datot li-Shenat ha-Kesafim 1971–72 Mugash la-Kneset 'al Yedei Sar ha-Datot, Dr. Zerah Warhaftig [Report on the activities of the Ministry of Religions for the fiscal year 1971–72 presented to the Kneset by the minister of religions, Dr. Zerah Warhaftig]. Jerusalem: Ministry of Religions, 1972.

Divrei ha-Kneset [Kneset proceedings]. Second Kneset, 12th sess., 10 (October 7, 1951).

"Elections of Rabbinical Officers and Rabbis of Local Communities." *Palestine Gazette 9,* April 9, 1936, suppl. 1.

Goldschmidt, Yosef. *Mi-yesodot ha-Hinukh ha-Mamlakhti-Dati* [The foundations of religious state education]. Jerusalem: Ministry of Education and Culture, Religious Education Department, 1972.

"Ha-Takanot ha-Qov'ot et Shitat ha-Behirot o Minuyim shel Mo'etzet ha-Rabanut ha-Rashit, Lishkot ha-Rabanut ve-Rabanei ha-Kehilot" [The regulations governing the method of election of appointment of the chief rabbinate council, rabbinical offices, and community rabbis]. *'Iton Rishmi,* Mispar 582 mi-Yom 9 April 1936 [Official Gazette, No. 582, April 9, 1936].

Hatza'ah le-Sidur Ma-arekhet ha-Sha'ot be-Vatei Sefer Mamlakhti-Datiyim, Tashlag [Proposal for the organization of the system of hours in religious state schools, 1973]. Jerusalem: Ministry of Education and Culture, Religious Education Department, 1972.

Ha-Yeshivah ha-Tikhonit [The yeshivah high school]. Jerusalem: Ministry of Education and Culture, Religious Education Department, 1971.

"Hok ha-Behirot le-Mo'etzet ha-Rabanut ha-Rashit, 5732/1972" [Chief rabbinate elections law 5732/1972]. In *Sefer ha-Hukim* [The book of laws]. 649, 5732/1972.

Official Gazette of the Government of Palestine, No. 157.

Qovetz Takanot [Anthology of regulations]. 2837, 2887, 5732/1972.

Sefer ha-Hukim [The book of laws]. 649, 5732/1972.

State of Israel. *Government Yearbook.* 5711 (1950) to 5732 (1971–72). Jerusalem: Government Printer, 1950–1972.

"Takanot bi-Devar Behirot le-Mo'etzet ha-Rabanut ha-Rashit" [Regulations on the matter of the procedures of the elections for the chief rabbinate council]. In *Qovetz Takanot* [Anthology of regulations]. 2837, 2887, 5732/1972.

Index

MODERN MIDDLE EAST SERIES
Middle East Institute,
Columbia University

1. Allworth, Edward. *Nationalities of the Soviet East*. New York: Columbia University Press, 1971.

2. Hirsch, Eva. *Poverty and Plenty on the Turkish Farm, a Study of Income Distribution in Turkish Agriculture*. New York: Middle East Institute of Columbia University, 1970.

3. Waterbury, John. *The Commander of the Faithful: The Moroccan Political Elite—A Study in Segmented Politics*. New York: Columbia University Press, 1970.

4. Yar-Shater, Ehsan, ed. *Iran Faces the Seventies*. New York: Praeger, 1971.

5. Greenwald, Carol Schwartz. *Recession as a Policy Instrument. Israel, 1965–1969*. London: C. Hurst and Company, 1973.

6. Smolansky, Oles M. *The Soviet Union and the Arab East under Khrushchev*. Lewisburg, Pa.: Bucknell University Press, 1974.

7. Crosbie, Sylvia Kowitt. *A Tacit Alliance. France and Israel from Suez to the Six Day War*. Princeton: Princeton University Press, 1974.

8. Katakura, Motoko. *Bedouin Village*. Tokyo: University of Tokyo Press, 1976.

9. Schiff, Gary S. *Tradition and Politics: The Religious Parties of Israel*. Detroit: Wayne State University Press, 1977.

*Gary S. Schiff is currently Director of Middle East Affairs,
National Jewish Community Relations Advisory Council,
and visiting assistant professor of political science at Yeshiva University. He received the Ph.D. in political science
from Columbia University in 1973 and has been assistant
professor of Jewish studies and political science at the City
College, City University of New York.*

*The manuscript was edited by Jean Owen. The book was
designed by Mary Primeau. The typeface for the text is
Times Roman designed under the supervision of Stanley
Morison about 1931. The display face is Legend designed by
F.H.E. Schneidler about 1937.*

*The text is printed on International Paper Company's Book-
mark paper, and the book is bound in Columbia Mills' Fic-
tionette cloth over binder's boards. Manufactured in the
United States of America.*